Building Web Applications
with UML

The Addison-Wesley Object Technology Series

Grady Booch, Ivar Jacobson, and James Rumbaugh, Series Editors

For more information check out the series web site [http://www.awl.com /cseng/otseries/] as well as the pages on each book [http://www.awl.com/cseng/I-S-B-N/] (I-S-B-N represents the actual ISBN, including dashes).

David Bellin and Susan Suchman Simone, *The CRC Card Book*, ISBN 0-201-89535-8

Robert V. Binder, *Testing Object-Oriented Systems: Models, Patterns, and Tools*, ISBN 0-201-80938-9

Bob Blakley, *CORBA Security: An Introduction to Safe Computing with Objects*, ISBN 0-201-32565-9

Grady Booch, *Object Solutions: Managing the Object-Oriented Project*, ISBN 0-8053-0594-7

Grady Booch, *Object-Oriented Analysis and Design with Applications, Second Edition*, ISBN 0-8053-5340-2

Grady Booch, James Rumbaugh, and Ivar Jacobson, *The Unified Modeling Language User Guide*, ISBN 0-201-57168-4

Don Box, *Essential COM*, ISBN 0-201-63446-5

Don Box, Keith Brown, Tim Ewald, and Chris Sells, *Effective COM: 50 Ways to Improve Your COM and MTS-based Applications*, ISBN 0-201-37968-6

Alistair Cockburn, *Surviving Object-Oriented Projects: A Manager's Guide*, ISBN 0-201-49834-0

Dave Collins, *Designing Object-Oriented User Interfaces*, ISBN 0-8053-5350-X

Jim Conallen, *Building Web Applications with UML*, ISBN 0-201-61577-0

Bruce Powel Douglass, *Doing Hard Time: Designing and Implementing Embedded Systems with UML*, ISBN 0-201-49837-5

Bruce Powel Douglass, *Real-Time UML, Second Edition: Developing Efficient Objects for Embedded Systems*, ISBN 0-201-65784-8

Desmond F. D'Souza and Alan Cameron Wills, *Objects, Components, and Frameworks with UML: The Catalysis Approach*, ISBN 0-201-31012-0

Martin Fowler, *Analysis Patterns: Reusable Object Models*, ISBN 0-201-89542-0

Martin Fowler, *Refactoring: Improving the Design of Existing Code*, ISBN 0-201-48567-2

Martin Fowler with Kendall Scott, *UML Distilled, Second Edition: Applying the Standard Object Modeling Language*, ISBN 0-201-65783-X

Ian Gorton, *Enterprise Transaction Processing Systems: Putting the CORBA OTS, Encina++ and OrbixOTM to Work*, ISBN 0-201-39859-1

Peter Heinckiens, *Building Scalable Database Applications: Object-Oriented Design, Architectures, and Implementations*, ISBN 0-201-31013-9

Christine Hofmeister, Robert Nord, Soni Dilip, *Applied Software Architecture*, ISBN 0-201-32571-3

Ivar Jacobson, Grady Booch, and James Rumbaugh, *The Unified Software Development Process*, ISBN 0-201-57169-2

Ivar Jacobson, Magnus Christerson, Patrik Jonsson, and Gunnar Overgaard, *Object-Oriented Software Engineering: A Use Case Driven Approach*, ISBN 0-201-54435-0

Ivar Jacobson, Maria Ericsson, and Agneta Jacobson, *The Object Advantage: Business Process Reengineering with Object Technology*, ISBN 0-201-42289-1

Ivar Jacobson, Martin Griss, and Patrik Jonsson, *Software Reuse: Architecture, Process and Organization for Business Success*, ISBN 0-201-92476-5

David Jordan, *C++ Object Databases: Programming with the ODMG Standard*, ISBN 0-201-63488-0

Philippe Kruchten, *The Rational Unified Process: An Introduction*, ISBN 0-201-60459-0

Wilf LaLonde, *Discovering Smalltalk*, ISBN 0-8053-2720-7

Dean Leffingwell and Don Widrig, *Managing Software Requirements: A Unified Approach*, ISBN 0-201-61593-2

Chris Marshall, *Enterprise Modeling with UML: Designing Successful Software through Business Analysis*, ISBN 0-201-43313-3

Lockheed Martin Advanced Concepts Center and Rational Software Corporation, *Succeeding with the Booch and OMT Methods: A Practical Approach*, ISBN 0-8053-2279-5

Thomas Mowbray and William Ruh, *Inside CORBA: Distributed Object Standards and Applications*, ISBN 0-201-89540-4

Bernd Oestereich, *Developing Software with UML: Object-Oriented Analysis and Design in Practice*, ISBN 0-201-39826-5

Meilir Page-Jones, *Fundamentals of Object-Oriented Design in UML*, ISBN 0-201-69946-X

Ira Pohl, *Object-Oriented Programming Using C++, Second Edition*, ISBN 0-201-89550-1

Rob Pooley and Perdita Stevens, *Using UML: Software Engineering with Objects and Components*, ISBN 0-201-36067-5

Terry Quatrani, *Visual Modeling with Rational Rose 2000 and UML*, ISBN 0-201-69961-3

Brent E. Rector and Chris Sells, *ATL Internals*, ISBN 0-201-69589-8

Paul R. Reed, Jr., *Developing Applications with Visual Basic and UML*, ISBN 0-201-61579-7

Doug Rosenberg with Kendall Scott, *Use Case Driven Object Modeling with UML: A Practical Approach*, ISBN 0-201-43289-7

Walker Royce, *Software Project Management: A Unified Framework*, ISBN 0-201-30958-0

William Ruh, Thomas Herron, and Paul Klinker, *IIOP Complete: Middleware Interoperability and Distributed Object Standards*, ISBN 0-201-37925-2

James Rumbaugh, Ivar Jacobson, and Grady Booch, *The Unified Modeling Language Reference Manual*, ISBN 0-201-30998-X

Geri Schneider and Jason P. Winters, *Applying Use Cases: A Practical Guide*, ISBN 0-201-30981-5

Yen-Ping Shan and Ralph H. Earle, *Enterprise Computing with Objects: From Client/Server Environments to the Internet*, ISBN 0-201-32566-7

David N. Smith, *IBM Smalltalk: The Language*, ISBN 0-8053-0908-X

Daniel Tkach, Walter Fang, and Andrew So, *Visual Modeling Technique: Object Technology Using Visual Programming*, ISBN 0-8053-2574-3

Daniel Tkach and Richard Puttick, *Object Technology in Application Development, Second Edition*, ISBN 0-201-49833-2

Jos Warmer and Anneke Kleppe, *The Object Constraint Language: Precise Modeling with UML*, ISBN 0-201-37940-6

Building Web Applications with UML

Jim Conallen

ADDISON–WESLEY

An imprint of Addison Wesley Longman, Inc.

Reading, Massachusetts • Harlow, England • Menlo Park, California
Berkeley, California • Don Mills, Ontario • Sydney
Bonn • Amsterdam • Tokyo • Mexico City

Many of the designations used by manufacturers and sellers to distinguish their products are claimed as trademarks. Where those designations appear in this book, and Addison Wesley Longman, Inc. was aware of a trademark claim, the designations have been printed with initial capital letters or in all capitals.

The author and publisher have taken care in the preparation of this book, but make no expressed or implied warranty of any kind and assume no responsibility for errors or omissions. No liability is assumed for incidental or consequential damages in connection with or arising out of the use of the information or programs contained herein.

The publisher offers discounts on this book when ordered in quantity for special sales. For more information, please contact:

Pearson Education Corporate Sales Division
One Lake Street
Upper Saddle River, NJ 07458
(800) 382-3419

Visit AW on the Web: www.awl.com/cseng/

Library of Congress Cataloging-in-Publication Data
Conallen, Jim.
    Building web applications with UML / Jim Conallen.
      p. cm. -- (Addison-Wesley object technology series)
    Includes bibliographical references and index.
    ISBN 0-201-61577-0 (alk. paper)
    1. Web site development. 2. Application software--Development. 3. UML (Computer
science I. Title. II. Series

TK5015.888.C654 1999
005.7'2--dc21   99-049970

Executive Editor: J. Carter Shanklin
Editor: Krysia Bebick
Production Coordinator: Sarah Weaver
Project Management: Diane Freed
Cover Design: Simone Payment
Compositor: Rob Mauhar

ISBN 0-201-61577-0
Text printed on recycled and acid-free paper.
1 2 3 4 5 6 7 8 9 10-MA-0302010099
First printing, December 1999

For mom and dad, who gave me life;
for Brenda, who makes it worthwhile;
and for Eion and Sean, whom I live it for.

Contents

Preface

Late in 1996, I downloaded the preview edition of Microsoft's Active Server Pages. It was my first taste of what could be done on the Web. Even then I could see the potential for sophisticated Web applications. I began to investigate alternative architectures: CGI (Common Gateway Interface) and Allaire's Cold Fusion. Even before then, I had started tinkering with the Java beta and later bought Symantec's Café to experiment with this new language.

At that time, I was an independent consultant working for AT&T in New Jersey. The project had nothing to do with the Web, so my only opportunity to experiment with this technology was during the evenings and whatever spare time I could find. In the end, it was all worth it. I learned a lot and was prepared for the coming onslaught and frenzy of Web application development.

My first opportunity to build a real Web application came at the request of a friend whose father owned a live cut rose wholesale and retail company, Hortico Nurseries Inc. Hortico was interested opening up a retail sales front on the newly emerging Internet. Together with a mutual friend, Jeff Wilkinson, we built our first production e-commerce site. The site was simple. It allowed customers to browse and to search a database of more than 1,400 varieties of roses and even to place orders. At first, the site didn't generate as many orders as we had hoped, but it did expose Hortico to a new market and certainly helped its sales grow in other ways. To the best of our knowledge, Hortico was the first Web site to make a comprehensive catalog of rose varieties and pictures available to the Internet community. Jeff has pretty much taken over the management of the site, and I help when I can. He has gone on to win awards for Web site design for some of his other projects, and I moved on to other contracts.

My first professional contract dealing with Web applications was with a small start-up company in the healthcare business. This experience got me even more involved with the subtleties of building Active Server Pages (ASP) applications, especially with the issues of managing server-side resources and transaction management in a Web application environment. I learned a lot about the use of client-side scripting, applets, and ActiveX controls. I also learned a valuable lesson about testing applications: Client machines with different operating systems can behave differently with the exact same HTML, Java, and browser code. All of these experiences have driven me even more to a belief that Web applications need to be modeled and built just like any other complex software system. In the years that followed, I continued to experiment with the latest Web technologies and consulted with other companies with Web-related issues.

All throughout my Web application experiences, I tried to practice my object-oriented skills in the area of Web application development. I had little problem applying use case analysis, and it wasn't until I started creating analysis and design models that I realized that things were going to get difficult. When creating a Web application, my conceptual focus was always on the Web page. My idea of a model kept revolving around the concept of a site map. I knew that the navigation paths throughout the system were incredibly important to the understanding of the application and that any model of the system would have to include them.

My earliest attempts at modeling Web applications started with Rumbaugh's OMT (Object Modeling Technique); later, when UML version 0.8 was publicly released, I began to apply it. I knew that for any modeling technique to be useful, it needed to both capture the relevant semantics of Web-specific elements, such as Web pages and hyperlinks and their relations to the back-end elements of the system—middle tier objects and databases. At the time, I found both OMT and UML inadequate to express the things I thought were important in a Web application.

Being a somewhat successful object practitioner and engineer, I jumped to the conclusion that a whole new development methodology and notation were needed. After all, if the existing methods and notation didn't have what I needed, the obvious solution was to invent new ones. This, of course, is a trap that many of us in the software industry fall into. In my free time, I started to draft new graphical and semantic ways to represent Web application architectures. Proud of my work, I began showing it to two of my colleagues: Joe Befumo and Gerald Ruldolph, both experienced object practitioners. Their immediate reaction was: *Why?* I tried to explain the issues involved with Web application development and the need for visually expressing their designs. Yet everyone I spoke with continued to think that developing a new method and notation was a little overkill.

I started to rethink what I was doing. I wasn't so arrogant to think that I was still right and everyone else wrong. I had more homework to do. I reexamined my original needs: to express Web application designs at the appropriate level of abstraction and detail, and most important, as a part of the rest of the system's design. Since UML was taking the industry by storm, I realized that anything I did would have to work with UML.

So I went back to the UML. By now, it was in version 0.91, and a new concept was included: stereotypes. At first, I was clueless to what a stereotype was. The UML specification is not the easiest reading, after all. It was long and difficult, but I knew that any success in the area of modeling Web applications had to come from this direction. Eventually, I started to understand what was meant by stereotyping and the other extension mechanisms: tagged values and constraints. I was finally starting to see light at the end of the tunnel.

I now had a mechanism with which I could introduce new semantics into the UML grammar without disturbing the existing semantics. I always knew that the key was to provide a consistent and coherent way to model Web-specific elements at the right level of abstraction with the models of the rest of the system. The UML extension mechanism provided me with the framework to do so.

The next step was to start defining the extension by creating stereotypes, tagged values, and constraints. For me, the ability to use custom icons in diagrams with stereotyped elements went a long way to ease my concern for intuitive diagrams; also, Rational Rose, my visual modeling tool of choice,[1] had just introduced a way to use one's own stereotypes in Rose models. I quickly created a set of icons for Web page abstractions. I tried to make them consistent, mostly rectangular with the stereotype indication in the upper-left corner. I used filled-in dog ears[2] to represent pages and unfilled dog ears to denote components. Icons without any dog ears typically represented contained classes, which cannot be requested directly by a Web browser. The icon for Web page components is similar to the icon used by the three amigos—Grady Booch, James Rumbaugh, and Ivar Jacobson— in their book, *The Unified Modeling Language User Guide* (Addison Wesley Longman, 1999).

Looking back, I remember spending less than a day to draw up the icons. I didn't spend much time on it then, since I always believed that eventually someone with a little more experience would design some meaningful ones. In the almost two years since then, they have remained essentially the same. I am surprised that I have received absolutely no comments on the style of the icons from the hundred or more people who have been using them. I think that for this version of the extension, the style of icons is going to stick.

As the extension evolved and a lot of the details and inconsistencies were getting corrected, I always kept an eye out for code-generation possibilities. In my mind, the modeling technique could be validated if it were possible, in theory only, to unambiguously generate and reverse engineer code. Since most of my experience was with Microsoft Active Server Pages, I began creating Rational Rose scripts to forward engineer ASP code. I've tailored the scripts to create Java Server Pages code also; from a code structure point of view the two are very similar.

From that point, things proceeded at a tremendous rate. I published a white paper on the Internet and presented the topic at the 1998 Rational User's Conference in Orlando, Florida. Grady Booch took an interest in the work and encouraged me. Addison Wesley Longman asked whether I was interested in expanding the topic into a book. If I had only known how difficult was going to be to write, I'm not sure that I would have agreed. I followed the original white paper with a stream of other articles for both online and print publications and started to get a regular stream of e-mail comments on the extension.

---

1. All of the sample models used in this effort were developed with Rational Rose. I had worked with the Rose tools for many years prior to this and have recently given up independent consulting to join the Rational team. (My praise of the Rose tool, however, would have been made even if I were not a current Rational employee.)

2. A *dog ear* is the slang term for a bent or folded corner of paper.

By the time this book hits the streets, I will have introduced the topic at five professional conferences and written at least a dozen articles and white papers on the topic. Ideally, this book will continue to propel the recognition that Web application development is a serious topic and one from which we can learn and adopt the successful practices of the past.

Jim Conallen
August 1999

Acknowledgments

Authoring a book has always been a dream of mine, and like most realized dreams, they are never done alone. This book is more than an essay of my experiences with object-oriented web application development; rather, it is the joined effort of a number of individuals and the sacrifices of many close to me.

As a software engineer I never needed to understand the publishing industry. Publishing a book is certainly more than just writing words, as I found out. The team at Addison Wesley Longman—J. Carter Shanklin, Krysia Bebick, and Kristin Erickson—helped me through this process, and I thank them dearly for all their work, encouragement, and gentle reminders of impending deadlines.

This book has been reviewed by a number of people, all of whom I graciously thank for their time, effort, and honesty. Going through those reviews was a humbling experience, yet it was essential in ensuring that this book would be readable and interesting. My thanks go to Ron Lusk, Compaq Computer Corporation, Craig Olague, Grady Booch, Ben P. Ansell, Neil Williams, and Jeffrey Hammond, Rational Software.

I must give extra thanks to Ben Ansell who early on found some of my initial material and worked with me to improve it. Extra thanks also goes to Grady Booch who, after finding my obscure white paper, was kind enough to send a short e-mail message to me saying it was a "great paper." That little note of encouragement helped me put aside nagging fears that what I was doing was wrong and inappropriate.

The writing of this book took much more time that I had originally thought. During the first few weeks of writing, my wife and I welcomed our second child into this world. I can remember many hours writing and working the material in this book when I really just wanted to be cuddling and playing with my two children. There were moments when things got difficult and frustrations high, but through it all I had constant support from Brenda, my wife, without which I would have ever been able to complete this book.

Part One

Introduction and Summary of Web-Related Technologies

Chapter 1
Introduction

What Is This Book?

This is a book about Web application development. It is not a cookbook for building Web applications; nor does it present a new methodology. It is just a guide for the project manager, architect, analyst/designer, and implementer of Web applications—anyone who wants to build robust, scalable, and feature-rich Web applications using the proven object-oriented techniques that traditional client/server applications have been built with for years now. This book builds on the techniques of object-oriented application development rather than defining its own.

Most of the ideas expressed in this book are not original, and for good reason. Many of the concepts and methods described in this book have developed and evolved over years of practice in multiple domains. These object-oriented practices have enabled projects to be delivered on time and on budget and, most important, have made them predictable. For the most part the object-oriented principles described in this book are based on the collective works of Grady Booch, Jim Rumbaugh, and Ivar Jacobson, who are also known as the "three amigos."

The amigos are the principal creators of the Unified Modeling Language (UML). The UML is a notation for visually expressing the models of software-intensive systems. For many, the UML also represents a method, although technically this is incorrect. UML is just a language, but like any language, it expresses things with certain biases. In particular, UML expresses system models and designs in an object-oriented fashion, even though it is being used to express system types as varied as generic business organizational structures and processes to real-time embedded system designs.

The term UML is included in this book's title because it is at the heart of the discussions of building Web applications. Most of the original work in this text is in the Web

Application Extension for UML (WAE), which extends the UML notation with additional semantics and constraints to permit the modeling of Web-specific architectural elements as a part of the rest of the system's model. A major theme in this book is that it is critical to model all of a system's business logic, regardless of where or how it is being implemented in the system. For Web applications, this means that in our UML models, we need to capture the execution of business logic in Web pages in client-side scripts and components. By having a single, central model of all of the business logic in a system, we are better able to understand it and eventually to elaborate on it in future releases of the system.

Many object-oriented software development methodologies are in use today. When viewed from a very high level, they all are pretty much the same, although not many people might admit this. The "object-oriented way of things" begins with requirements definition, usually in the form of use cases (see Chapter 8), and, through a series of translations, defines a detailed design model (see Chapter 10) that is used to directly drive the code-writing stage. The process discussed in this book most closely resembles the Rational Unified Process (RUP) and the ICONIX Unified Process (see Chapter 6). However, the ideas and concepts can be equally applied to many other methods that use the UML as their notation.

Even though this book describes in some detail the process of creating Web applications, it is not meant to be a complete process handbook. The process of developing software is such a large topic that the vast majority of the material in it would have very little "Web application"–specific material in it. Instead of creating a complete process manual for Web application development, I have decided instead to create a book that introduces some of the basics of the process, just enough to set the context for the Web application–specific discussions. In this way, the reader can identify and understand the important aspects of Web application development without its being tied too closely to a specific software development process. With this separation of Web application development material from the process, it is easier for those with specialized and customized development processes to use the material in this book.

Who Should Read This Book?

This book introduces architects and designers of client/server systems to the issues and techniques of developing for the Web. The book will give the project manager an understanding of the technologies and issues related to developing Web applications. Since this book builds on existing object-oriented methodologies and techniques, it does not attempt to introduce them. It is expected that the reader has some familiarity with object-oriented principles and concepts and with UML in particular. It is also expected that the reader is familiar with at least one Web application architecture or environment.

For the client/server architect, this book serves as a guide to the technologies and issues of Web applications. The system architect needs to make decisions about which technologies are appropriate to serve the business needs as expressed by the requirements and use cases. Chapter 7 defines three major architectural patterns that can describe a Web application's architecture. By examining these patterns and their advantages and disadvantages, the architect can make decisions that will define the technological bounds of the application. As with any engineering discipline, the architect must consider the tradeoffs for each technology to be used in the application architecture. With a solid understanding of the technologies available and their consequences, the architect can put together an appropriate combination that best meets the needs of the business problem.

For the analyst and designer, this book introduces a UML extension suitable for expressing Web application design. The key goals of this extension are to

- Model the appropriate artifacts, such as Web pages, page relationships, navigation routes, client-side scripts, and server-side page generation
- Model at the appropriate level of abstraction and detail
- Enable the Web-specific elements of the model to interact with the rest of the system's elements

The analyst/designer will be able to express the execution of the system's business logic in terms of UML models. The idea is to have one unified model of a system's business logic. In the model, some of the business logic is executed by traditional server-side objects and components—middle-tier components, transaction-processing monitors, databases, and so on—and some of it by Web elements, such as browsers and client-side scripts.

For the project manager, this book discusses the potential problems and issues of developing Web applications. It also serves as a guide to the responsibilities and activities of the roles of development team members. The book also discusses other roles in the development process. The project manager, being responsible for the overall health of a project, needs a clear understanding of all of the roles and responsibilities of people involved with the process.

Book Organization

This book is divided into 11 chapters, including this introductory one. Conceptually, the book is also divided into two major parts. In Part One, Chapters 2 through 5 are essentially an introduction to Web application technologies and concepts, which provide the foundation on which the second part of the book is based. The first chapters can be skipped by readers intimately familiar with Web application architectures; however, at least a cursory reading is still suggested.

Chapter 2, Web Application Basics, is an introduction to the very basic Web application architecture. We define the term Web application, thereby defining its scope and focus. The chapter continues with a definition of the principal communication mechanisms and languages. Web application–enabling technologies are discussed. These are the infrastructures that transform simple Web sites, or Web systems, into business logic execution systems.

Most of the complexities of designing Web applications are encountered when the client performs some of the business logic in the system. The technologies for allowing this are described in Chapter 3, Dynamic Clients. Common Web technologies, such JavaScript, applets, and ActiveX controls, are discussed. The Document Object Model (DOM) is introduced as the main object interface to client-side resources.

The basic Web application architecture as described by the technologies in Chapters 2 and 3 is capable of delivering very useful Web applications and is especially useful for public Internet applications, such as retail store fronts. For some applications, these basic ingredients are insufficient to deliver the sophisticated level of functionality that some applications require. The limiting factors are often the fundamental technologies of HTTP and HTML themselves. Web applications can be extended to encompass and use other communication and formatting technologies in addition to HTTP and HTML. The most common of these technologies are reviewed and discussed in Chapter 4, Beyond HTTP and HTML.

The final chapter of the first part is Chapter 5, Security. No matter how nonthreatening or uninteresting an application may be, if it is on the Internet, security is a concern. Even for intranet applications, security should be a concern. Securing a Web application is in many ways much harder than a traditional client/server application. By their very nature Web servers are open to requests to any node on the network. The trick to making an application secure is in understanding the nature of security risks. Unfortunately, no one product or service that you buy can guarantee a secure application. Security needs to be designed into an application, and needs to be continually maintained in that application. New security holes in off-the-shelf software are being discovered all the time. Eventually, one of them will represent a risk to your application. By designing your system with this in mind, managing the next security risk to pop up will be one step easier.

The second half of this book, Chapters 6–11, is devoted to the process of building Web applications. In Chapter 6, The Process, the entire process of developing object-oriented systems is reviewed. This chapter outlines the Rational Unified Process and the ICONIX Unified Process with enough detail to justify the activities discussed in the remainder of the book. If you are not using one of these processes, don't worry. There is a very good chance that the rest of the material in this book can be applied to your own software development process, provided that it uses UML as its standard notation.

Chapter 7 discusses the activities of defining the architecture of a Web application. Even though this activity usually follows a nearly complete examination of the requirements and use cases of the system, it is discussed earlier to help create the mindset of developing Web applications. Since the process used here is an iterative and incremental one, the use case specifiers[1] will have in the backs of their minds a Web system architecture when defining and elaborating the system's use cases. In theory, this shouldn't be the case; in practice, however, and in an incremental and iterative process, it is not necessarily wrong to place use cases in the context of a specific architecture.

Chapter 8, Requirements and Use Cases, reviews the process of gathering a system's requirements and defining the system's use cases. All sorts of requirements can be gathered to help specify a particular system. One of the most useful techniques for gathering functional requirements is with use cases, which provide a structured way of gathering and expressing the functional requirements of a system. Use cases describe the interaction between a user, or actor, of the system and the system. Use cases are textual documents that describe, in the language of the domain, *what* the system should do without specifying *how* it should. The "hows" are expressed in the following two chapters.

---

1. The individuals who write the detailed specifications of a use case. A use case is a textual description of the interaction of a system's user (actor) and the system.

The next step in the process is to analyze the use cases of the system and to express them in terms of classes and relationships. This is the topic of Chapter 9, Analysis. Analysis is the activity of transforming the requirements of a system into a design that can be realized in software. An analysis model is created that contains classes, as well as class collaborations that exhibit the behavior of the system as defined by the use cases.

Chapter 10, Design, discusses how to transform the analysis model into something that maps directly into components of the system: delivered modules. This is the first chapter to use the Web Application Extension (WAE) for UML; this is the first step in the process whereby the architecture formally meets the requirements of the system. Chapter 10 discusses the detailed design of Web pages and client-side scripts. Additional Web-specific elements and relationships are also discussed. The majority of the original work of this book is in Chapters 10 and 11.

Once the design model is completed, it can be directly mapped into executable code. Chapter 11, Implementation, discusses the creation of code from the UML model. The examples in this chapter use Microsoft's Active Server Pages base applications. ASP was chosen as the sample target environment for two reasons. First and foremost, it is the Web application environment that I am most familiar with; second, the native language of ASP is VBScript. VBScript, for all its advantages and disadvantages, is a very readable language. Given the alternatives of Java, C/C++, Cold Fusion, and others, it is most likely that readers will be able to follow without too much difficulty the structure and algorithms expressed in the sample code.

Chapter 2

Web Application Basics

Web applications evolved from Web sites or Web systems. The first Web sites, created by Tim Berners-Lee while at CERN (the European Laboratory for Particle Physics), formed a distributed hypermedia system that enabled researchers to have access directly from their computers to documents and information published by fellow researchers. Documents were accessed and viewed with a piece of software called a browser, a software application that runs on a client computer. With it, the user can request Web documents from other computers on the network and render the documents on the user's display. To view a document, the user must start the browser and enter the name of the document and the name of the host computer on which it can be found. The browser sends a request for the document to the host computer. The request is handled by a software application called a Web server, an application usually run as a service, or daemon,[1] that monitors network activity on a special port (usually port 80). The browser sends a specially formatted request for a document (Web page) to the Web server through this network port. The Web server receives the request, locates the document on its local file system, and sends the document back to the browser (see Figure 2-1).

This Web system is a hypermedia system because the resources in the system are linked to one another. The term Web comes from looking at the system as a set of nodes with interconnecting links. From one viewpoint, it looks like a spider's web. The links provide a means to navigate the resources of the system. Most of the links are to textual documents, but the system can also be used to distribute audio, video, and custom data. Links make navigation to other documents easy. The user simply clicks on a link in the document, and the browser interprets that as a request to load the referenced document or resource in its place.

---

1. A service, or daemon, is a software program that runs continuously on the computer, usually in the background, and doesn't send information to the console display.

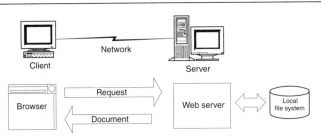

FIGURE 2-1　Basic web system

A Web application builds on, or extends, a Web system to add business functionality. In its simplest terms, a Web application is a Web system that allows its users to execute business logic with a Web browser. This is not a very precise definition, but then most people's conception of what a Web application is not either. There is a subtle distinction between a Web application and a Web site. For the purpose of this book, a Web application is a Web site where user input (navigation through the site and data entry) affects the state of the business (beyond, of course, access logs and hit counters). In essence, a Web application uses a Web site as the front end to a more typical application.

HTTP

Browsers and Web servers use a special protocol, the HyperText Transfer Protocol, which defines exactly how a browser should format and send a request to a Web server. The client browser sends a document request consisting of a line of ASCII characters terminated by a carriage return, line-feed pair. A well-behaved server will not require the carriage return character. This request consists of the word GET, a space, and the location of the document relative to the root of the Web server's file system. When a Web server/site is configured, it is usually set up to use a particular directory on the host machine's local file system as the Web site's root directory. Documents are found relative to this directory.

A full specification for the document is called a uniform resource locator (URL). It identifies the protocol (HTTP), host machine name, optional port number, and the document name/location. A URL is a single word (no spaces). If any further words are found on the request line, they are either ignored or treated according to the full HTTP spec.[2]

A URL is a way to specify an object (resource) on the network. It is like the network equivalent for specifying a file name on a file system. A URL can be used to request many different types of objects with different protocols. In addition to HTTP, commonly used Internet protocols include news, ftp, gopher, and file. Each protocol is specific to the type of information or resource it represents.

---

2. The complete specification for HTTP version 1.1 can be found on the World Wide Web Consortium (W3C) Web site: www.w3c.org.

When HTTP is specified, the object is a Web page. The following URL requests a Web page from a host machine called romana.

```
http://romana/specs/wd/cav43.html
```

The document name is cav43.html and is located in the directory /specs/wd/. This directory is relative to the Web site's root directory on the Web server. A more explicit reference to this page could include the port number

```
http://romana:80/specs/wd/cav43.html
```

However, the default port number, 80, is usually assumed for all HTTP requests.

It is possible to configure the Web server to listen to a port other than 80. This is often done to create a "private" Web site. Some Web servers monitor an additional port and use it for Web configuration. This allows Web masters—those responsible for managing a Web server and site—to remotely manage a Web server's configuration with just a browser. This type of configuration tool is an example of a small Web application.

One of the important design goals of Web systems in general is that it be robust and fault tolerant. In the first Web systems at CERN, Web documents, computers, and network configurations were often subject to change. This meant that it was very possible for Web pages to contain links to documents or host computers not existing anymore. It is even possible for the HTML specification itself to change, by adding new elements, or tags. The browsers and Web servers of the system have to gracefully deal with these conditions.

This desire for a high degree of fault tolerance led in part to the decision to use a *connectionless* protocol like HTTP as the principal protocol for managing document requests. HTTP is considered *connectionless* because as soon as the request is made and fulfilled, the connection between the client and the server is terminated. The connection is broken by the server when the whole document has been transferred. The client may abort the transfer by breaking the connection before the transfer completes, in which case the server doesn't record any error condition. The server doesn't need to store any information about the request after disconnection. This enables hosts and clients to act more independently and is more resistant to temporary network outages.

HTTP runs over TCP (Transmission Control Protocol) but could run over any connection-oriented service. TCP, a lower-level network protocol used by the Internet and many company networks, enables computers to make connections and to exchange information with one another. TCP (usually combined with IP, or Internet Protocol) is an implementation of layers in the OSI (Open Systems Interconnection) Reference Model for network communications.[3]

A related protocol, HTTPS, or HTTP with Secure Sockets Layer (SSL), is similar to straight HTTP; however, it uses encryption to help "secure" the communication. This protocol is

---

3. OSI (Open Systems Interconnection) was officially adopted as an international standard by the International Organization of Standards (ISO). Currently, it is Recommendation X.200 of the International Telecommunications Union.

used on the Internet for handling sensitive data, such as personal and financial information. Security and encryption are discussed in more detail in Chapter 5, Security.

Like everything related to technology, HTTP is evolving. At the time of this writing, HTTP version 1.1 is the operating version on the Internet. A new version, HTTP-NG, is being defined by the W3C. The purpose of the HTTP-NG Project is to tackle the current deficiencies by using sound engineering practices: modularity, simplicity and layering. The goal of this redesign is much higher evolvability, flexibility, and performance than what we have in the current Web.[4]

HTTP-NG is concerned principally with making Internet communications more efficient but with an eye toward more sophisticated functionality. It is hoped that HTTP-NG will extend the concept "objects" on the Internet, making it easier to enable distributed object communications.

HTML

In addition to establishing the network connections and protocols for document interchanges, browsers also need to render the document on a display. TCP/IP and HTTP don't address this at all. The rendering of content is managed by the browser. This is where the HyperText Markup Language (HTML) fits in. HTML, used to express the content and visual formatting of a Web page, is a *tag language* based on the Standard Generalized Markup Language (SGML), a much broader language used to define markup languages for particular purposes. HTML is just one specific application of SGML, suited to the presentation of textual documents. HTML contains tags that define how text is to be formatted on the display: font, size, color, and so on. Some tags point to images to include in the display, as well as define links to other Web pages. Like HTTP, HTML is an evolving standard managed by the World Wide Web Consortium (W3C) standards body.[5] At the time of this writing, HTML 4.0 is the current W3C recommendation and is based on the earlier HTML 3.2 and HTML 2.0 specifications.

One important thing to note is that HTML specifies how documents should be displayed on a computer display. This raises several problems when the Web system needs to enable users to print formatted documents. Many documents, especially forms, have strict printing requirements. If a Web application needs to allow users to print forms or documents in which the typesetting is important—such as page breaks, font sizes, and margins— additional elements will have to be added to the system. HTML does not address printing directly (yet), so Web applications that need this capability must include additional components in their architecture.

HTML defines a set of tags that can be used either to tell the browser how to render something or to define a link to another Web page. All tags are enclosed by angled brackets

---

4. HTTP-NG statement of purpose www.w3c.org/Protocols/HTTP-NG/.

5. The W3C is a vendor-neutral organization that manages many of the Internet standards, such as HTTP and HTML.

(< and >). Tags are usually used in pairs, with beginning and ending tags. For example, the emphasis tag: <em> italicizes a word. A sample sentence and the HTML to render it follow:

This is really *neat.*

```
This is really <em>neat</em>.
```

Some tags accept parameters, which are placed inside the brackets and are usually a parameter name, followed by an equal sign and then the value, enclosed by double quotation marks. The following HTML for a hyperlink to another Web document uses the anchor tag, <a>:

```
The HTML 4.0 spec can be found at the
<a href="http://www.w3c.org">W3C Web site</a>.
```

Most browsers render the hyperlink with an underscore:

The HTML 4.0 spec can be found at the W3C Web site.

The anchor tag uses the parameter href to define the location and the type of the link.

HTML pages are usually text files on the Web server's file system. The language was originally intended to be easy to learn, so that people interested in publishing content could easily specify how the content should be rendered. The key points here are "easy to learn" and "any display terminal. " Since a Web system is, potentially, made up of many different types of computers, there needed to be a device-independent way to specify basic formatting commands. For example, specifying a specific font by name would be a problem if the browser's computer didn't recognize the font name or didn't have the ability to render that particular font.

This was not a problem for early Web page writers, who were more interested in the content than in the presentation. The language was therefore simple enough to express only the basic formatting capabilities expected for the scientific community. The first generation of Web pages were all written manually, without the aid of WYSIWYG editors.

When the Internet and the Web became commercial, this simple language and its limitations did become a problem. Exact formatting of pages is very important to companies, especially e-commerce companies on the Internet. As with print advertisement, the look of a page is very important to potential customers and clients. HTML evolved to meet these needs, enabling more precise formatting of content by introducing new tags and parameters to the language.

What didn't change, though, was the fact that the document content and the presentation information are still coupled. The content of an HTML-formatted Web page is a mix of document content (the text or pictures that are displayed by the browser) and rendering instructions (bold, indent, font size, and so on). For example, the following HTML fragment produces a bulleted list:

```
<p>The <em>new</em> <strong>HTML
4.0</strong> specification includes
additional support for</p>
<ul>
 <li>Style sheets </li>
 <li>Internationalization </li>
 <li>Accessibility </li>
 <li>Tables and Forms </li>
 <li>Scripting and multimedia </li>
</ul>
```

The *new* **HTML 4.0** specification includes additional support for

- Style sheets
- Internationalization
- Accessibility
- Tables and Forms
- Scripting and multimedia

All of the formatting commands are embedded with the content of the document. It is possible to separate some of the formatting specifics from the content with style sheets, but even with their use, complete separation is not possible.

Style sheets are a specification that allows Web page authors to define a separate layout—color, font, margins, and so on—document that could be used by many other content documents. This helps maintain a consistent look and feel across a Web site.

It should be noted that some browsers, especially older ones, do not support the use of style sheets. Even so, the W3C recommends their use, and is continuing to refine HTML so that in the future, there is an even further separation of content and presentation. The emergence of XML, discussed in Chapter 4, plays a key role in this separation.

One mechanism for separating the content of an HTML page from its presentation is server-side includes (SSI). The government organization NCSA (National Center for Supercomputing Applications) has defined a simple tag that can be used to include HTML fragments that need to be shared across a number of response pages. Typically, these are standard prologs, epilogs, or legal disclaimers and copyright notices. By separating the content over several shared pages, it is possible to manage a single point of update. The tag simply specifies the name of a file in the Web site's file system:

```
<!--#include file="filename"-->
```

HTML has special tags that allow the Web page author to use multimedia information, such as images, sound, and video, in addition to textual information. Instead of embedding the multimedia data in the page with the text, the tags specify separate URLs for each item. This means that the browser will make an additional request and connection to the server for each image or multimedia item mentioned in the original Web page. To the Web application architect and designer, this means that certain exception situations need to be taken into account when designing the application. These situations usually are invalid URLs or missing files. It also implies that Web applications with lots of images and multimedia types may pay significant network performance penalties when establishing so many discrete connections. Remember, the choice of a connectionless protocol benefits the robustness of the system, not its performance.

A full discussion of HTML and its tags will not be discussed here, since it is beyond the scope of this book and has been done very well in countless other books. What needs to be discussed here, however, is the architecturally significant elements of the language, especially as they relate to Web applications. Like separating content from presentation, the architecturally significant elements of a Web page need to be brought out and modeled as such. For example, a design model of a Web application is not very interested in the font size or color of the text used in a display, but it is very interested in the sets of Web pages that can be navigated to. The following sections discuss these important elements of HTML.

Anchors

A hyperlink to another Web page is created with the HTML anchor tag <a>. The tag uses several parameters, the most important of which is the href parameter. This parameter specifies the linked document's URL and may contain a Relative URL, not specifying the Web server or directory. These would be inherited by the current page's values. For example, the following anchor tag is perfectly acceptable:

```
We have a full line of <a href="prod.html">products</a> to choose from.
```

In this example, the link is to a page on the same machine and in the same directory as the current page.

In addition to the location and name of the Web page, an anchor can pass along parameters with the page request. When parameters are specified in a page request, it usually means that the requested page is executable. The requested Web page is capable of accessing the parameter information and using it when building the returned page. Parameters are passed with the request as name/value pairs separated by the ampersand symbol (&). The parameters are separated from the Web page by a question mark symbol (?).

The following page request passes along two parameters: ProductID and RateCode. The ProductID is assigned the value 452, and the RateCode is given a value of B.

```
http://www.mystore.com/catalog/products.jsp?ProductID=452&RateCode=B
```

The requested page is products.jsp. The extension of the Web page gives a clue that the enabling technology used by the executable page is Java Server Pages.

In addition to href, the other significant parameter is target. When a hyperlink is selected, it typically loads the new document in the same browser window as the original document. This is not always the case. When frames are used to divide up a browser's display area, each frame displays a separate Web page in it. Frames are discussed in detail later.

When frames or multiple browsers are used, it is possible for a hyperlink to specify a specific frame or browser instance to load in. Frames and browser instances can be assigned any name, although there are a few reserved target names.

_blank	This target makes the link load into a new blank browser window. The new window is not assigned a name.
_parent	This target makes the link load in the immediate frameset parent of the document. It defaults to _self if the document has no parent.

_self   This target makes the link load in the same window the anchor was
            clicked in. This is the default behavior of an anchor.

_top   This target makes the link load in the full body of the window. It is a
            way to "break out" of a frameset.

In the following example, the anchor tag specifies a named target called maindoc.

```
<a href="chapt1.html" target="maindoc" >
 Chapter 2, Web Application Basics.
</a>
```

Forms

HTML form elements distinguish a Web site from a Web application. An HTML form is a
Web page part that can accept user input. This collection of fields allows users to enter text
or to select from a list. In addition to text boxes, form fields can be rendered by buttons,
check boxes, and radio buttons. If a Web page has a form in it, the browser will render that
page with the appropriate user interface controls and will allow the user to enter and to
change its values. Most forms contain a special button that, when clicked by the user, submits the form and its contents to the Web server as part of another Web page request. The
Web server receives a request for a special Web page, or executable module, that is capable of reading the form field's values and processing them on the server. The ultimate
result is a new HTML page[6] that is sent back to the requesting browser. See Figure 2-2.

More detailed discussions of form-processing *enabling technologies* are made later in
this chapter. The general concept, however, is that the executable page is used by the Web
server to process the form's values and to produce a new HTML page to send back to the

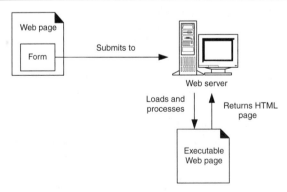

FIGURE 2-2   An executable Web page processing a form's data

---

6. Depending on the specific systems architecture, the output might be an XML document or
another document stream that the browser expects.

browser. Most often, the processing involves communicating with objects on the server or with databases. Forms are a key mechanism in the interaction of Web application users but by no means the only one. More sophisticated mechanisms for getting user input are discussed in Chapter 3, Dynamic Clients.

A form is defined by the `<form>` tag. The two principal parameters are `method` and `action`. The `action` parameter is the URL of the executable Web page that processes the form. The `method` parameter specifies how the data will be sent to the server. There are two valid values: `GET` and `POST`. When `GET` is used, the values of all of the fields in the form are appended to the URL as parameters. The Web server sees the form submission as a typical `GET` request, as if it were from a standard anchor tag. The W3C does not recommend using `GET`, since it has some internationalization problems and will not work for large forms. Instead, the value `POST` is preferred. The `POST` method tells the browser to package up the field values in a special section of the request, the data body.

Plain-vanilla HTML has only a few core form elements: `<input>`, `<select>`, and `<textarea>`. The `select` tag specifies either a list box or a drop-down list that the user can select something from. The `text area` tag is a multiline text input control and allows users to enter in large blocks of text. The `input` tag is really an overloaded tag that could be configured to act like a push button, a check box, a radio button, or a single-line text entry field.

The input tag's `name` parameter identifies the field's name, used by the executable Web page when processing the form's data. The input tag's `type` parameter determines what type of user interface control should be used and what type of data to accept. The most common values are:

Checkbox	Displays a check box. If the user checks the box, the field's value will be assigned the value specified by the input tag's `value` parameter.
Hidden	Does not display a user interface control. Values are usually set here by either the executable page that created it or by client-side scripting and dynamic HTML.
Password	Displays a password-style entry field. Characters entered here are not displayed to the user.
Radio	Displays a radio button. The tag's `name` value defines the radio button group. When selected, the field associated with the radio button group is assigned the value specified by the `value` parameter.
Submit	Displays a push button. When the user clicks this button, the form and all its values are submitted to the server.
Text	Displays a single-line text entry box.

Other types exist, but these define the core set of input types that are used and available in most browser implementations. The key point here is that simple forms collect textual information from the user—either directly or by translating a check box, button, or list box selection into one—and define the mechanism by which it gets submitted to the server.

The following HTML fragment defines a simple form for collecting log-on information.

```
<form method="POST" action="cgi-bin/logon.pl">
<p>Username:
```

```
<input type="text" name="username" size="10"></p>
<p>Password:
<input type="password" name="password" size="10"></p>
<p>Logon as:</p>
<p>
<input type="radio" name="Role" value="Supervisor">Supervisor<br>
<input type="radio" name="Role" value="Clerk">Clerk<br>
<input type="radio" name="Role" value="Guest">Guest
</p>
<p><input type="submit" value="Logon" name="LogonBtn"></p>
</form>
```

The browser's rendering of the form is shown in Figure 2-3.

Frames

A controversial element in the HTML arsenal is the frameset. A frameset divides the browser's display area into rectangular regions, each rendering its own HTML document. The frameset tag defines the number of frames the display should be broken into and their sizes or proportions. Separate `<frame>` tags identify each of the frames with a target name and tell the browser which Web pages to request for each frame when initializing the page. Once a frameset page is loaded, with all of its individual frames loaded as well, the user can work with the page. The user can select a hyperlink in any of the displayed pages. The link might specify a new document for the frame that it is in or a page to be loaded in another named frame.

The most common use of frames is to define a table of contents and a main document frame. The Web page in the table of contents frame is typically a long list of entries, each a hyperlink to an area of the Web site. Each of the links specifies that the "main document" frame, or target, is where the linked Web page should be rendered.

The parameters `cols` and `rows` of the frameset tag define the initial size and number of frames in the set. For example, the value "20%, 50%, *" specifies three frames to be defined.

FIGURE 2-3   Rendered HTML form

The first occupies 20 percent of the screen, the second 50 percent, and the third the remaining space, 30 percent. Instead of percentages, explicit widths can be defined, and that's where the * value becomes useful. Of course, it is entirely possible for a frame to contain another frameset. This allows designers a little more freedom from a simple matrix frame design and can be used to produce any combination of rectangular regions in the browser's display.

The following HTML fragment defines a simple table of contents–like page. The table of contents appears in the leftmost frame and occupies 20 percent of the display.

```
<frameset cols="20%,80%">
 <frame name="toc" src="toc.html">
 <frame name="maindoc" src="intro.html">
</frameset>
```

Names are specified for each frame. A link in the table of contents frame would specify `maindoc` as the target for the link. For example, clicking on the following HTML link would display the Chapter 1 page in the main document frame. The table of contents frame would remain the same.

```
<a target="maindoc" href="chapter1.html">
Chapter 1. Web Application Basics</a>
```

The frameset Web page itself typically doesn't contain content. Most other Web pages do contain enough content to tell the user that a frames-capable browser is needed to view the page and provide a link to a page that doesn't require one. This is sometimes necessary on the Internet, since not all browsers support frames.

The controversy over frames centers on user interface preferences and complexity. Some people just don't like frames. Frames do, however, raise the level of complexity a bit, since now there are multiple Web pages interacting with the user at the same time. This is what make frames an architecturally significant element.

Web Applications

Web applications use enabling technologies to make their content dynamic and to allow users of the system to affect business logic on the server. The distinction between Web sites and Web applications is subtle and relies on the ability of a user to affect the state of the business logic on the server. If no business logic exists on a server, the system certainly should not be termed a Web application. For those systems on which the Web server—or an application server that uses a Web server for user input—allows business logic to be affected via Web browsers, the system is considered a Web application. For all but the simplest Web applications, the user needs to impart more than just navigational request information; typically, Web application users enter varied input data, which might be simple text, check box selections, or even binary and file information.

The distinction becomes even more subtle in the case of search engines, on which users do enter in relatively sophisticated search criteria. Search engines that are Web sites simply accept this information, use it in a form of database SELECT statement, and return the results. When the user finishes using the system, there is no noticeable change in the state of the search engine, except, of course, in the usage logs and hit counters. This is contrasted with Web applications that, for example, accept online registration information. A Web site that accepts course registration information from a user has a different state when the user finishes using the application.

The architecture for a Web site is rather straightforward. It contains the same principal components of a Web site: a Web server, a network connection, and client browsers. Web applications also include an application server, the addition of which enables the system to manage business logic and state. A more detailed discussion of Web application architectures can be found in Chapter 7, Defining the Architecture.

Session Management

One of the most common challenges of Web applications is managing client state on the server. Due to the connectionless nature of client and server communications, a server doesn't have an easy way to keep track of the state of each client using the system.

A session represents a single coherent use of the system. A session usually involves the use of many executable Web pages and lots of interaction with the business logic on the application server. Since achieving a use case goal often requires the successful execution of a number of executable Web pages, it is often useful to keep track of a client's progress throughout the session.

The most common example of keeping client state on the server can be found on the Internet at any e-commerce site. The use of virtual shopping carts is a nice feature of an online store. A shopping cart contains all of the items an online customer has selected from the store's catalog. In most sites, the shopper can check the contents of the cart at any time during the session. This feature requires that the server keep track of what the client has selected to add to the cart while browsing the store's catalog.

There are several ways to do this, the most common being the use of cookies. Cookies, a feature of browsers, allow a Web server to place a short string of characters—a cookie—in the browser. Cookies are persistent and can even last beyond the lifetime of a browser's execution. Many Internet Web sites use persistent cookies to "customize" their site for frequent users. The string can get quite large (about 4K), but most of the time, it's a short key that is used to identify a specific client session.

Session management mechanisms use cookies to index into a dictionary on the server that contains each client's state. A shopping cart site, for example, will place a cookie on the browser when the first site is first accessed. This cookie is a unique string that is used as a key into a dictionary of all of the site's current users' states. Each value in the dictionary is usually another dictionary whose values represent the state of a particular current user of the system. In the shopping cart site, the values would represent the items selected for purchase from the catalog.

Keeping a dictionary in memory for every user of the system could be very expensive if it never expired. For practical reasons, most session dictionaries are removed when the

Web application user either finishes the process or stops using the system for a set period of time. A session timeout value of 15 minutes is typical.

There are other ways to manage client state, but they involve the dynamic creation of every page in the scenario. If the scenario that requires the management of client state on the server is short and consists mainly of executable pages, it is possible to append, to every hyperlink used in the scenario, a parameter whose value is the index into state dictionary. No matter what technique is used, the management of client state on the server is almost always an issue in Web applications. Fortunately, many of the enabling technologies of Web applications provide these services for you.

Enabling Technologies

The enabling technologies for Web applications are varied, differentiated principally by the vendors. Enabling technologies are, in part, the mechanism by which Web pages become dynamic and respond to user input. There are several approaches to enabling a Web application. The earliest ones involved the execution of a separate module by the Web server. Instead of requesting an HTML-formatted page from the file system, the browser would request the module, which the Web server interpreted as a request to load and run the module. The module's output is usually a properly formatted HTML page but could be image, audio, video, or other data.

The original mechanism for processing user input in a Web system, the Common Gateway Interface (CGI),[7] is a standard way to allow Web users to execute applications on the server. Since letting users run applications on your Web server might not be the safest thing in the world, most CGI-enabled Web servers require CGI modules to reside in a special directory. Typically, the directory is named cgi-bin. CGI modules can be written in any language and can even be scripted. In fact, the most common language for small-scale CGI modules is PERL,[8] which is interpreted each time it is executed.

Even though HTML documents are the most common output of CGI modules, they can return any number of document types. They can send back to the client an image, plaintext (an ASCII document with no special formatting), audio, or even a video clip or references to other documents. In order for the browser to interpret the information properly, it must know what kind of document it is receiving. In order for the browser to know this, the CGI module must tell the server what type of document it is returning.

In order to tell the server whether a full document or a reference to one is being sent back, CGI requires a short header on the output. This header is ASCII text, consisting of separate lines followed by a single blank line. For HTML documents, the line would be

```
Content-type: text/html
```

---

7. The official specification can be found at http://hoohoo.ncsa.uiuc.edu/cgi/.

8. PERL (practical extraction and reporting language) is a scripting language created by Larry Wall and is known in UNIX circles as the software equivalent of duct tape.

If the CGI module does not build the returning HTML Web page, it can instead redirect the Web server to another Web page on the server or even another CGI module. To accomplish this, the CGI module simply outputs a header similar to

```
Location: /responses/default.html
```

In this example, the Web server is told to return the page `default.html` from the `responses` directory.

The two biggest problems with CGI are that it doesn't automatically provide session management services and that each and every execution of the CGI module requires a new and separate process on the application/Web server. Creating a lot of processes can be expensive on the server.

All of the available solutions overcome the multiprocess problems of CGI by adding plug-ins to the Web server. The plug-ins allow the Web server to concentrate on the servicing of standard HTTP requests and deferring executable pages to another, already running process. Some solutions, such as Microsoft's Active Server Pages, can even be configured to run in the same process and address space as the Web server itself, although this is not recommended.

Two major approaches to Web application–enabling technologies are used today: compiled modules and interpreted scripts. Compiled module solutions are CGI-like modules that are compiled loadable binaries executed by the Web server. These modules have access to APIs (application programming interfaces) that provide the information submitted by the request, including the values and names of all of the fields in the form and the parameters on the URL. The modules produce HTML output that is then sent back to the requesting browser. Some of the most popular implementations of this approach are Microsoft's Internet Server API (ISAPI), Netscape Server API (NSAPI), and Java servlets.

ISAPI and NSAPI server extensions can also be used to manage user authentication, authorization, and error logging. These extensions to the Web server are essentially a filter placed in front of the normal Web server's processing.

Compiled modules are a very efficient, suitable solution for high-volume applications. Their biggest drawbacks are related to development and maintenance. These modules usually combine business logic with HTML-page construction. The modules often contain many print lines of HTML tags and values, which can be confusing and difficult for a programmer to read.

The other problem is that each time the module needs to be updated (fixed), the Web application has to be shut down and the module unloaded before it can be updated. For most mission-critical applications, this is not much of a problem, since the rate of change in the application should be small. Also, it's likely that a significant effort would have been made by the QA/test team to ensure that the delivered application was free of bugs. For smaller, internal intranet applications, however, the rate of change might be significant. For example, the application might provide sets of financial or administrative reports. The logic in these reports might change over time, or additional reports might be requested.

Scripted pages are the other category of solutions. Whereas the compiled-module solution looks like a business logic program that happens to output HTML, the scripted page solution looks like an HTML page that happens to process business logic. A scripted page, a file in the Web server's file system, contains scripts to be interpreted by the server; the scripts interact with objects on the server and ultimately produce HTML output. The page is centered on a standard HTML Web page but includes special tags, or tokens, that are interpreted by an application server. Typically, the file name's extension tells the Web server which application server or filter should be used to preprocess the page. Some of the most popular vendor offerings in this category are Allaire's Cold Fusion, Microsoft's Active Server Pages, and Java Server Pages.

Figure 2-4 shows the relationship between components of the enabling technology and the Web server. The database in the figure, of course, could be any server-side resource, including external systems and other applications. This figure shows how the compiled module solution almost intercepts the Web page requests from the Web server and, in a sense, acts as its own Web server. In reality, the compiled module must be registered with the Web server before it can function. Even so, the Web server plays a very small role in the fulfillment of these requests.

The scripted-page solution, however, is invoked by the Web server only after it determines that the page does indeed have scripts to interpret. Typically, this is indicated by the file name extension (`.asp`, `.jsp`, `.cfm`). When the Web server receives a request for one of these pages, it first locates the page in the specified directory and then hands that page over to the appropriate application server engine or filter. The application server preprocesses the page, interpreting any server-side scripts in the page, and interacting with server-side resources, if necessary. The results are a properly formatted HTML page that is sent back to the requesting client browser.

Java Server Pages, even though they are scripted pages, get compiled and loaded as a servlet the first time they are invoked. As long as the server page doesn't change, the Web server will continue to use the already compiled server page/servlet. This gives Java Server Pages some performance benefits over the other scripted-page offerings.

The real appeal of scripted pages, however, is not their speed of execution but rather their ease of development and deployment. Typically, scripted pages don't contain most of

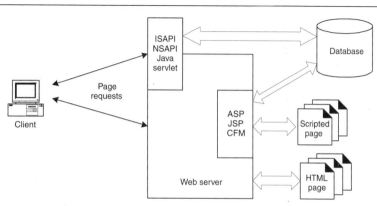

FIGURE 2-4   Web server–enabling technologies

the application's business logic; rather, the business logic is often found in compiled business objects that are accessed by the pages. Scripted pages are used mostly as the glue that connects the HTML user interface aspects of the system with the business logic components.

In any Web application, the choice of technologies depends on the nature of the application, the organization, and even the development team. On the server are a wealth of technologies and approaches that may be used. Many of these can be used together. Regardless of the choices made, they need to be expressed in the larger model of the system. The central theme in this book is: All of the architecturally significant components of a Web application need to be present in the system's models. Servers, browsers, Web pages, and enabling technologies are architecturally significant elements and need to be part of the model.

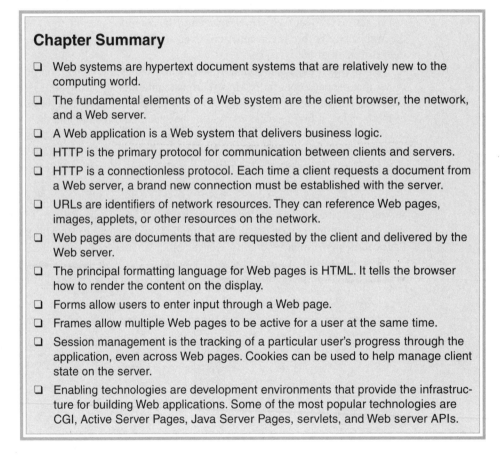

Chapter Summary

- ❏ Web systems are hypertext document systems that are relatively new to the computing world.
- ❏ The fundamental elements of a Web system are the client browser, the network, and a Web server.
- ❏ A Web application is a Web system that delivers business logic.
- ❏ HTTP is the primary protocol for communication between clients and servers.
- ❏ HTTP is a connectionless protocol. Each time a client requests a document from a Web server, a brand new connection must be established with the server.
- ❏ URLs are identifiers of network resources. They can reference Web pages, images, applets, or other resources on the network.
- ❏ Web pages are documents that are requested by the client and delivered by the Web server.
- ❏ The principal formatting language for Web pages is HTML. It tells the browser how to render the content on the display.
- ❏ Forms allow users to enter input through a Web page.
- ❏ Frames allow multiple Web pages to be active for a user at the same time.
- ❏ Session management is the tracking of a particular user's progress through the application, even across Web pages. Cookies can be used to help manage client state on the server.
- ❏ Enabling technologies are development environments that provide the infrastructure for building Web applications. Some of the most popular technologies are CGI, Active Server Pages, Java Server Pages, servlets, and Web server APIs.

Chapter 3
Dynamic Clients

The great distinction between Web sites and Web applications lies in the use of business logic. In Chapter 2, the discussions of Web applications and their enabling technologies all centered on implementing business logic only on the server. The client browser was just a simple, generalized user interface device that played no role in the execution of business logic. In the history of Web applications, that model didn't last long. When system designers, in particular client/server system designers, recognized the potential of the Web as a serious system architecture, they realized that it might be beneficial for client computers to share in the execution of some of the business logic. The idea was simple, but there were some problems to be solved, including issues of deployment and platform independence.

The simplest examples of business logic on the client are field and form validations. For example, a date entry field should never accept the date February 30, even though it is entirely possible to enter such a date in an ordinary text box. Without client-side validation, this value would be submitted with the form to the server and only there be identified as an invalid value. When this happens, the entire form is usually sent back to the user for correction. This number of server trips is expensive, since the time it takes for a form to submit itself to the server, receive processing, and get a response is on the order of seconds, not milliseconds.

In a traditional client/server system, the date value would probably be checked as it was entered, when it lost focus, or when the form was completed. Validation of the field would be done by the client machine, possibly by the user interface, since this action does not require server resources. Another option for traditional client/server designers is to use a specialized date input control, one that doesn't accept invalid dates.

An important concept needs to be made clear when discussing dynamic clients and business logic. Business logic is a rule, or process, that affects the business state of the system. For example, the computation of shipping charges is covered by business logic, since it involves the rules of the business and those of the postal service. Business logic is not concerned with presentation, however. The use of a date-picker control—a user interface widget that pops up a minicalendar for the user to select a date from—does not constitute business logic. It is just a device to capture user input; the device itself doesn't affect the business state of the system, just the data it collects. The use of the date in computing an age or expiration period, however, *is* business logic.

It is not surprising that the movement to enable dynamic clients was not originally driven by the need to execute business logic on the client. It, like many other aspects of Web development, was driven by the need to enhance the user interface rendered by Web pages. Many Web users, already familiar with computers, sought some of the same features found in their client applications, most significantly a responsive, dynamic user interface. Plain-vanilla Web pages aren't very dynamic and were never intended to be. Therefore, to give Web surfers new reasons to visit sites and to lay the groundwork for serious use of the Web as an application platform, HTML became dynamic.

For most Web applications, the key to the use of business logic on the client, particularly in the context of HTML pages, is that it has access only to the resources on the client. On the client, implementing a business rule that requires access to server resources doesn't make much sense, since the only way the rule can be implemented is by making additional page requests to the server.[1] The business logic that is implemented on the client needs to focus on the manipulation of the data present in Web page itself.

The manipulation of the content of a Web page is the central focus of client-side scripting and dynamic activity. To truly enable business logic or even user interface enhancements to be useful, they need access to virtually every aspect of the page they work within. The key to enabling dynamic clients lies in the ability to make Web page content accessible to scripts and modules that can be executed on the client and delivered by the Web page. As for the enabling technologies for the server, adding dynamic capabilities to the client comes in two major flavors: compiled and scripted. And as on the server, some blur these lines.

Document Object Model

Regardless of the underlying philosophy for enabling the client, both rely on the Document Object Model (DOM), a platform-neutral interface to the browser and the HTML documents it's rendering. The specification has been defined by the W3C,[2] and most of the browser manufacturers have implemented it in their latest versions. The idea is to have a common API that Web page developers[3] can use to manipulate the content in the HTML (and XML) document, as well as the resources of the browser itself.

With the DOM, programs and scripts can dynamically access and update document content, structure, and style. The document can be further processed by the browser and

---

1. It is possible for client-side components to have persistent and asynchronous communications with server-side objects, however; this type of Web architecture is covered in detail in Chapter 7, Defining the Architecture, and doesn't relate to HTML-page business logic.

2. The World Wide Web Consortium (W3C) of technology vendors and institutions is responsible for HTTP, HTML, XML, XSL, DOM, and other important Web and Internet standards.

3. Notice that I use the term "developer" instead of "author," since we are discussing client-side execution of code, not just content.

the results incorporated back into the presented page. The browser is now responsible for both the rendering of the HTML in the document, which could change after being received from the server, and the execution of scripts in the document, as well as compiled programs specified by the document.

Figure 3-1 shows the relationship among the browser, HTML document, scripts, compiled modules, and the DOM. The browser contains an HTML document. Contained in the document are scripts, or lines of interpretable code, that use the DOM interface. The HTML document also contains references to compiled modules, which also use the DOM interface. The browser is responsible for both rendering the dynamic HTML document and implementing the DOM interface for scripts and programs to modify the HTML document.

The name Document Object Model was chosen because it provides an object interface to HTML (and XML) documents. The documents are manipulated as objects, possessing both data and behavior. The collaboration of these objects represents the structure of the document. Because a document is a collaboration of objects, it can be represented by an object model. Take as an example the following HTML fragment:

```
<body>
<p>The new HTML 4.0 specification
includes additional support for</p>
<ul>
    <li>Style sheets </li>
    <li>Internationalization </li>
    <li>Accessibility </li>
    <li>Tables and Forms </li>
    <li>Scripting and multimedia </li>
</ul>
</body>
```

In this example, the HTML expresses a simple itemized list. A simplified[4] class diagram, shown in Figure 3-2, represents the structure of this document. An object diagram, shown in Figure 3-3, shows the relationships among the instances of the "objects" in the document.

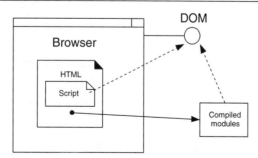

FIGURE 3-1   The Document Object Model interface

---

4. The class and instance diagram are simplified, since the diagram contains a large number of other elements that might confuse the main point of the diagram.

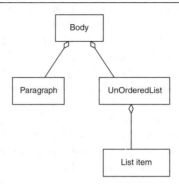

FIGURE 3-2   Class diagram of HTML document

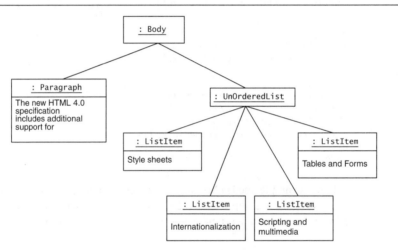

FIGURE 3-3   Object (instance) diagram of HTML document

The key point here is that the DOM specification gives all of these elements an object interface that is accessible by scripts or modules executing in the browser. The three principal goals of the DOM are to specify the

- Interfaces and objects used to represent and manipulate a document
- Semantics of these interfaces and objects, including both behavior and attributes
- Relationships and collaborations among these interfaces and objects

Another key aspect of the DOM is that it is vendor and platform neutral. Even though the specification comes with bindings for the Java language, it is language independent. All of the major browser manufacturers have implemented the DOM in their latest browser versions. Even though the DOM is a huge step in the direction of making client-side business logic a reality in a heterogeneous environment, it is far from complete. DOM Level 1 is just the first step.

The DOM Level 1 specification, current at the time of this writing, provides a good interface specification suitable for many uses of dynamic behavior on the client, but it is missing a few key elements, most notably events. The DOM Level 1 specification does not define an event mechanism; however, events, style sheets, iterators, and filters are being discussed in the Level 2 proposal.[5] To fill this gap, individual vendors have created similar, yet not completely compatible, implementations into their latest browser releases. The two major browser manufacturers, Microsoft and Netscape, have provided with their DOM implementation their own implementations of events and style sheet integration that can be used by client-side scripts and modules: dynamic HTML.

Dynamic HTML (DHTML) describes the combination of HTML, style sheets, and scripts that allows documents to be manipulated in a Web browser. DHTML is not a W3C specification or recommendation, so caution should be observed when designing systems that make use of incompatible elements of DHTML. It will probably be a few years before browser implementations and the Level 2 specification catch up with each other and become dominant on the public Internet.

Scripting

The most common scripting technology available in browsers today is JavaScript.[6] JavaScript, one part of the whole Java technology revolution, is an implementation of a scripting language that has its roots in the Java programming language. JavaScript was intended to be easier to learn and use than Java, since the first users of JavaScript would be interested mainly in enhancing user interfaces and would have more of an authoring background than a programming one.

The JavaScript language resembles Java but does not have Java's static typing and strong type checking. JavaScript's runtime environment is also smaller and has fewer data types than Java does. JavaScript is object based, not objected oriented, meaning that it uses built-in extensible objects but does not support user-defined classes or inheritance. Since JavaScript is not compiled, it uses dynamic binding, and all object references are checked at runtime. JavaScript supports functions without any special declarative requirements. This makes it easier for those new to programming to use.

Since JavaScript comes embedded in HTML pages, it needs to coexist in the document, just like any other element of the document. The `<script>` tag is used to define regions of JavaScript. The `<script>` tag, an extension to HTML, can enclose any number of JavaScript statements. The `<script>` tag marks the beginning of a JavaScript region, and the end tag `</script>` is required to mark the end of the region. Since the `<script>` tag can be used to denote scripts in other languages, a `language` parameter is usually added;

---

5. The DOM Level 2 Specification draft can be found on the W3C Web site: www.w3.org/DOM/.

6. Microsoft's Internet Explorer also allows the use of VBScript as a client-side scripting language; however, the vast majority of client scripts continue to be written with JavaScript.

otherwise, the default scripting would be at the mercy of the browser. Anything in between these tags is considered, from the DOM's point of view, written in the JavaScript language. The information between these tags is parsed by the JavaScript interpreter, not the DOM. In the following example, the HTML <script> tag identifies a simple JavaScript function call that displays a dialog box to the user:

```
<SCRIPT LANGUAGE="JavaScript">
    alert('Hello World.')
</SCRIPT>
```

Unfortunately, defining scripts is not as simple as that. Not all browsers are JavaScript capable, and even though a browser is built to be robust and fault tolerant, the earliest browsers do not gracefully handle JavaScript that they can't interpret. The problem stems from the fact that if a browser doesn't understand a tag, it just ignores it. For the most part, this works well. For example, if a browser doesn't understand the <font> tag it just ignores it and continues to use the default font. A problem occurs when an older browser ignores the <script> tag. The tag and its ending tag are ignored, but the content in between them, the JavaScript, is not. The browser attempts to parse this information like any other part of the document. Since JavaScript doesn't follow the same formatting or structuring rules as HTML, it is probable that an older browser will react badly and report a large number of warnings or errors. To guard against this situation, HTML and JavaScript comments are used to protect regions where an error might be generated by a non-JavaScript browser. In the following example, the <script> tag defines a function called isPositiveNum(). This function is probably called by the form-validation function prior to submitting it to the server. The very first line inside the script block is an HTML comment token (<!--).

```
<SCRIPT LANGUAGE="JavaScript">
<!-- Hide script from old browsers.
function isPositiveNum(s) {
    return (parseInt(s) > 0)
}
// End the hiding here. -->
</SCRIPT>
```

The last line in the script block is a JavaScript comment and is there only so that the HTML comment end token (-->) is ignored by the JavaScript interpreter. Like polyglot programs that compile error free under multiple languages, this code needs to behave well for both HTML and JavaScript.

JavaScript Objects

The Document Object Model, the main source of objects for JavaScript, puts an object interface on not only the HTML document but also the browser as well. JavaScript can interact with the browser to load a new page, examine the browser's history (previously loaded Web pages), or interact with other pages in neighboring frames.

The principal object to use when working with document content is the document object. A reference to it can be obtained through the document property of the window object, which is a globally available object in any JavaScript function. JavaScript uses "dot notation" to navigate through the properties and references associated with the document. For example, the following JavaScript function initializes a text field in a form with the current day of the week:

```
today = new Date();
weekdays = new Array("Sun", "Mon", "Tue", "Wed", "Thu", "Fri", "Sat");
dow = weekdays[today.getDay()];
window.document.forms["demo"].elements["inday"].value = dow;
```

In this script fragment, the variable today is set to the current date. An array of all of the possible weekdays is defined in the variable weekdays. The current day of the week is obtained by calling the getDay() method of the Date object, which returns an integer indicating the day of the week. This value is used to index into the weekdays array to obtain the current day of the week as a string and to assign it to the dow variable. The last line sets the value of a field in a form. The form is named "demo", and the field is an input text control named "inday".

To access the field and to set its value property, the object hierarchy is navigated by beginning with the window object, a browser-supplied global object that more or less represents the browser itself. This object has a property, called the document, that represents the HTML Web page. The document object has a forms collection, since it is possible to define multiple forms in a page. This collection of forms is indexed by the name of the form: "demo". Forms contain form elements, or input fields, that can be accessed by indexing the elements collection of the form object. Once a reference to the field is obtained, its value property is set with the current day of the week.

Most JavaScript interactions behave in this way, first performing the business logic calculations and then accessing the appropriate DOM interfaces to update the document. The trick to using JavaScript is gaining an understanding of the objects and interfaces you have to work with. The Document Object Model standard is a good place to start. It defines the object hierarchy that page scripts use to access the information in the document and even the browser itself. Figure 3-4 shows the object hierarchy available to scripts in a page.

Custom JavaScript Objects

Even though JavaScript is not a pure object-oriented language, it does provide a mechanism for encapsulation. Encapsulation is the ability to package and to hide data in an object. In JavaScript, you can create an instance of a generic object and assign it properties and even methods. For example, in the following JavaScript a generic object instance called cartLineItem is created. The dot operator is used to define and to assign values to four custom properties:

```
cartLineItem = new Object();
cartLineItem.productID = 'MG1234';
```

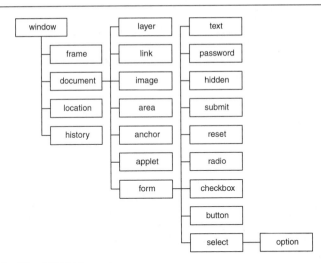

FIGURE 3-4 The DOM hierarchy

```
cartLineItem.productName = 'MGB Roadster (1935)';
cartLineItem.qty = 1;
cartLineItem.unitPrice = 36000;
```

The cartLineItem instance can be used later by any JavaScript with a reference to it. For example, the following statement displays to the user a message with the shopping cart line item's name and current quantity:

```
alert( 'You have ' + cartLineItem.qty + ' ' + cartLineItem.productName +
  ' in your shopping cart' );
```

Like properties, custom methods can be associated with objects. As long as the function has been defined earlier in the document, it can be assigned to an object. For example, the following function total() can be used as a member function of the cartLineItem instance. This function has access to its owning object through the operator this. In this function, the total() function computes the total amount for this line item (quantity times the price).

```
function total () {
  return (this.qty * this.unitPrice);
}
```

A function is assigned to an object, just like a property:

```
cartLineItem.total = total;
```

Once assigned to the object, the function can be called directly from the object cartLineItem.

```
cartLineItem = new Object();
cartLineItem.productID = 'MG1234';
cartLineItem.productName = 'MGB Mk I Roadster';
cartLineItem.qty = 2;
cartLineItem.unitPrice = 12500;
cartLineItem.total = total;
document.write( '<p>' + cartLineItem.qty + ' ' + cartLineItem.productName +
   ' will cost you $' + cartLineItem.total() + '</p>' );
```

That JavaScript code produces the following output on the browser screen:

```
2 MGB Mk I Roadster will cost you $25000
```

To make things a little easier, a prototype can be defined. This is similar to a C++ constructor. The prototype is a function that creates a custom object and, optionally, initializes the object's properties. In the case of a JavaScript object, the prototype must also include the object's functions. The prototype for a LineItem[7] object would be

```
function LineItem( id, name, qty, price ) {
  this.productID = id;
  this.productName = name;
  this.qty = qty;
  this.unitPrice = price;
  this.total = total;
}
```

With a prototype defined, an array of LineItem instances could be created with the following JavaScript:

```
var cartLineItem = new Array();
cartLineItem[0] = new LineItem ('MG123', 'MGB Mk I Roadster', 1, 36000 );
cartLineItem[1] = new LineItem ('AH736', 'Austin-Healey Sprite', 1, 9560 );
cartLineItem[2] = new LineItem ('TS225', 'Triumph Spitfire Mk I', 1, 11000 );
```

Events

As was mentioned before, JavaScript is not an objected-oriented language, and in a strict sense, neither is an HTML page. The DOM puts an object interface on an HTML page, but it is inherently still a document. JavaScript embedded in an HTML page inherently suffers from some of these same problems. Like the document itself, JavaScript is read and interpreted in the order it appears in the document. Any script blocks that contain executable JavaScript statements outside of a function definition are interpreted in the order they are read. Writing in-line scripts that initialize the page before the user starts to interact with it might be OK to write this way, although I still wouldn't encourage it.

---

7. Call it an old Smalltalk habit, but I like to capitalize the name of "class"-like objects and to use lowercase names for instances. In this example, the LineItem function is behaving like a constructor and hence is "class"-like.

A more structured way to organize JavaScript in an HTML page is to define functions that encapsulate very discrete behaviors and then have them executed as needed. A function would respond to an event; if the code needed to be executed when the document was first loaded, the event would be the onLoad event of the <body> element in the HTML page.

The concept and use of events in client-side activity is critical for most applications. An HTML or browser event is something that triggers a script or module into action. Typically, some user interaction with the browser or document triggers an event, although in some situations, the browser itself might be the source for the event. The event handler parameter defines the name of the function that will handle the event when it is fired. Not all elements in an HTML document receive all events. A summary of common events and handler function names, taken from the Netscape JavaScript Guide,[8] is given in Table 3-1.

Client-side programming is event driven. Except in the case of in-line JavaScripts (discouraged), all JavaScript functions are executed in response to an event. The <body> tag

TABLE 3-1   Summary of HTML Document Events

Event	Applies to	Occurs when	Event Handler
Abort	Images	User aborts the loading of an image (for example, by clicking a link or the Stop button).	onAbort
Blur	Windows, frames, and all form elements	User removes input focus from window, frame, or form element.	onBlur
Click	Buttons, radio buttons, check boxes, Submit buttons, Reset buttons, links	User clicks form element or link.	onClick
Change	Text fields, text areas, select lists	User changes value of element.	onChange
Error	Images, windows	The loading of a document or image causes an error.	onError
Focus	Windows, frames, and all form elements	User gives input focus to window, frame, or form element.	onFocus
Load	Document body	User loads the page in the Navigator.	onLoad
Mouseout	Areas, links	User moves mouse pointer out of an area (client-side image map) or link.	onMouseout
Mouseover	Links	User moves mouse pointer over a link.	onMouseOver
Reset	Forms	User resets a form (clicks a Reset button).	onReset
Select	Text fields, text areas	User selects form element's input field.	onSelect
Submit	Submit button	User submits a form.	onSubmit
Unload	Document body	User exits the page.	onUnload

8. Available at http://home.netscape.com/eng/mozilla/3.0/handbook/javascript/index.html.

of an HTML document defines the main textual content of the document and can generate the following events:

- onLoad
- onUnload
- onBlur
- onFocus

Generally, these events are fired when the content is created and destroyed and when it receives and loses user focus. The main controller function would probably handle the Load event of the <body> tag. In the following HTML example, the onLoad event handler is assigned to the main() function. When the event is fired, the main() function is executed. This function overwrites the original content of the page. The result is a Web page that displays the text "I am in control now, ha ha ha!" instead of "This is the normal content."

```
<script>
function main() {
  document.write( 'I am in control now, ha ha ha!' );
}
</script>

<html>

<head>
<title>test page</title>
</head>

<body onLoad="main()">

<p>This is the normal content. </p>

</body>
</html>
```

One of the most popular ways of using JavaScript over the Internet today is to animate menu items or buttons in a Web page. JavaScript functions handle the click, or mouseOver events, of Web page elements and alter the display to show nested menus, or new images. This type of JavaScript use, although important to the overall application, is not necessarily something that is considered architecturally significant. When modeling JavaScript in an application's analysis or design model, it is important to separate what constitutes business logic from what is presentation. JavaScript is very useful for both. When JavaScript is used to execute business logic—to enforce validation rules, perform calculations, and so on—the scripts belong in the design and, possibly, analysis models. When the scripts are used to enhance the presentation, they belong in the user interface models and prototypes.

Java Applets and Beans

Java technology has invaded nearly every aspect of Web development. JavaScript and Java applets are used to make the client dynamic. Java Server Pages and servlets are used on the server. JavaBeans, small reusable components that can be used to build larger Java programs and applets, have brought Java into the component world. The Java revolution has even extended into application server arena, with Enterprise JavaBeans (transactional objects) and Java Database Connectivity (JDBC). A full discussion of Java technologies is, of course, beyond the scope of this book, and, indeed any book, as a complete discussion would take a library of books! This section discusses an overview of Java applets and JavaBeans and some interesting architectural elements as related to making clients dynamic.

Using JavaScript in an HTML page is a simple way to make the client dynamic, but it does have its limitations. In addition to JavaScript compatibility problems, the use of scripts in Web pages can work only with the tools and information available in the page. Additionally, as the code becomes complex, the nice JavaScript features that make it easy to use and deploy become a problem. It is not difficult to have JavaScript code evolve into spaghetti code. This is where Java comes in.

Java is much better suited for solving the large problems that scripting is just not suitable for. In addition to being able to access the DOM, Java also has the ability to define its own user interface, something that even JavaScript can't do. Being a true object-oriented language, Java classes can be defined and inheritance used. Perhaps the most important feature of Java, though, is that it is platform neutral. This is particularly important to Web application developers, since Web applications often exist in heterogeneous environments. The Java enthusiast's mantra is "Write once, run everywhere."

The use of Java on the client is usually in the form of an applet, which is more or less a user interface control that is placed in a Web page. An applet is made up of both system and custom classes. A custom applet extends (inherits) from the Java applet class. Additional user interface capabilities are available with the Abstract Windowing Toolkit (AWT). The AWT is a Java class library that contains most of the user interface primitives and tools. More advanced user interface functions can be obtained from the Java Foundation Classes (JFC) and Swing components.[9]

Because applets are referenced by a Web page, they need to be identified by a tag. The <object> tag[10] is used to identify an applet and, most important, where it can be obtained. In addition to being platform neutral, Java applets are a good fit for the Web because their deployment is almost automatic. An <object> tag's parameters define the type of object (Java), the name of the class file to load and run, and, optionally, the location (URL) of the file or files on the network. In the HTML example that follows, an applet called Bubbles is displayed to the user. The text between the <object> begin and end tags is displayed in place of the applet for non-Java-enabled browsers.

---

9. In addition to basic user interface tools, 3-D user interface libraries and specifications also are available for the Java platform.

10. Previous versions of HTML had a separate <applet> tag. This tag, however, has been deprecated and the more general <object> tag is recommended instead.

```
<OBJECT codetype="application/java"
        classid="java:Bubbles.class"
        codebase="http://romana/javaclasses/">
Java applet that draws animated bubbles.
</OBJECT>
```

In this example, the `codetype` parameter indicates that the object is a Java applet. The `classid` parameter identifies the class name of the applet (the object that inherited the applet interface). The codebase indicates that the Java applet class file can be obtained from the server romana in the `javaclasses` directory and with HTTP. This means that the browser can get the applet by making another GET request to the Web server romana.

Parameters can be supplied to an applet within the context of the `<object>` tag. Separate `<param>` tags can be placed in between the `<object>` begin and end tags. The browser allows the applet to access these parameters. In the following example, two parameters are defined for the applet:

```
<OBJECT codetype="application/java"
        classid="java:DatePicker.class"
        codebase="http://romana/javaclasses/">
<PARAM name="format" value="mm-dd-yyyy"type="data">
<PARAM name="style" value="DropDown" type="data">
</OBJECT>
```

One of the nice things about Java applets is that, once they are downloaded to the client, they don't have to be downloaded again the next time they are invoked. Let's face it: The Internet is slow, and downloading large Java applets can be time consuming, especially over a slow modem. Caching applets on the client can save a lot of time. Each time the Web page is revisited, the browser checks to see whether the applet has already been downloaded and makes sure that it has the correct version. If the version has changed or if the cached applet no longer exists on the client, it is downloaded.

JavaBeans define a complete component model for the Java platform. They support the standard component architecture features of properties, events, methods, and persistence. Despite the early hype about object-oriented programming languages and their ability to reuse off-the-shelf classes to build bigger and more complex applications, the reuse of discrete classes never came to be. Instead, reuse came to be in the form of components. A component is built with classes and, like a class, has a singular purpose. The great distinction of a component is, however, its ability to integrate with other components and code that it never knew existed. The JavaBean component model gives Beans the following properties:

- *Introspection* enables an external component or tool to analyze how a JavaBean works. It is able to expose the details of its interface.
- *Events* allow JavaBeans to communicate and connect with one another.
- *Properties* allow developers to customize JavaBeans.
- *Persistence* allows customized JavaBeans to retain their customization.

When a Java applet or JavaBean is created, many class files usually make up the application. To help manage this, a Java Archive (JAR) file can be created to package up all of the class files into a single archive file. A JAR file is, essentially, a ZIP file that contains all of the class and auxiliary files necessary to execute an applet. A JAR file compresses the files, making them quicker to transmit over slow network connections.

In addition to easier management of Java files, one advantage of using JAR files is security. JAR files can be digitally signed. When a user accepts a digitally signed JAR file, the applet could be granted security privileges on the client machine that it might not otherwise have. Java applet, Bean, and JavaScript security issues are discussed in Chapter 5, Security.

ActiveX/COM

ActiveX is Microsoft's answer to reusable components. ActiveX is built on Microsoft's Component Object Model (COM). COM is an infrastructure in which developers can build components, each in the language of their own choice, and share these objects with one another to build bigger and more complex systems. ActiveX is just the brand name associated with a subset of these technologies. One of the key features of COM is that ActiveX/COM components are reusable by any program in the system, not just Web-related ones. COM is very much a part of the operating system. In fact, each release of the Windows operating system is increasingly coupled with the COM technology. When thinking about the Web, people generally have in mind the brand name ActiveX, not COM.[11]

An ActiveX object is very much like a JavaBean in that it can expose its interface at runtime and allow other objects to invoke methods on this interface with this new-found knowledge. In addition to runtime (late) binding, COM objects can be bound at compile time, since a COM object is pretty much just a dynamic link library (DLL). These two types of interfaces are called the *v-table interface* and the *dispatch interface*. The v-table interface derives its name from the C++ mechanism for implementing virtual functions; it's short for virtual function table. This interface is most useful when the code that is using the object is C++, although other languages can also use this style of interface. The v-table interface is bound at compile time and is fastest during execution time.

The dispatch interface (or disp-interface for short) is a late-binding interface. It was originally created for use by simpler languages, such as Visual Basic. Programs that use COM objects through the dispatch do not need to bind to the COM DLL; instead, they can create the object at runtime and query it for its interface programmatically. Dispatch interfaces are slower at runtime, since a certain amount of negotiation needs to take place for each function call. The great advantage of using dispatch, however, is the ability to upgrade components, adding new functions and properties, without having to recompile programs that depend on it.

In order to use an ActiveX object, especially when late binding to one, it must be installed on the computer that it is to run on. Installing an ActiveX object typically means

---

11. For the most part, the terms ActiveX and COM can be used interchangeably. I tend to use the term ActiveX when talking about specific components in use in a Web application and to use COM when speaking in general.

copying the DLL, EXE, or OCX[12] file to the local hard drive and adding a few entries to the registry. Since ActiveX objects often have dependencies on other ActiveX objects or DLLs, these too need to be installed on the computer.

ActiveX is used to extend client-side functionality in much the same way as Java applets do. ActiveX controls are placed with the `<object>` tag into an HTML page. ActiveX does have some pretty significant advantages over Java applets. For one, its security model allows ActiveX controls full rein over client operating system resources. In an Internet environment, this might be a problem, but for secure intranets, they offer increased capabilities over Java applets.[13]

ActiveX components can be made aware of the DOM. When included in a Web page and invoked by a browser, they can access the object model of the HTML page, as well as the browser itself. This means that an ActiveX component can control the content of the Web page it originally came in with, just as the JavaScript examples did earlier.

In Web applications, ActiveX components can be used to do two things: enhance the user interface and implement business logic. One of the most common uses of ActiveX on the Internet is, not surprisingly, as a user interface control. ActiveX components or controls can capture user input that is difficult to do in standard text boxes and selection lists. One of the most useful ActiveX controls is the `DatePicker` control. These types of controls allow a user to select a date from a pop-up calendar.

One of the key features that make ActiveX suitable for the Web is that the components can be automatically downloaded when needed. Typically when using ActiveX on the client, the control is packaged in a cabinet (`.cab`) file. This is similar to Java JAR files and like them, they can be digitally signed. Digitally signing `.cab` files is pretty much the main security mechanism for ActiveX controls, since once they are installed on the client, they are exactly like any other COM component on the system.[14] ActiveX controls and COM objects in general are just program modules installed on the client computer. They can be invoked and used by the Web browser and other programs, unlike Java applets, which can be used only in the context of a browser.

Summary

When building Web applications, important consideration must be given to the use of business logic on the client. First, the distinction between what is business logic and what is presentation logic needs to be clear. Business logic is the rules and processes that contribute to the shaping of the business state of the system. It is field validations and data computations. Presentation logic is centered on making the user interface easy for the user. It

---

12. OCX, the original name for the first generation of COM components, is another file name extension valid for COM components.

13. Of course, Java applet access to client computer resources could be increased with the use of signed JAR files. Even still, ActiveX controls have more access to client computer resources.

14. ActiveX controls downloaded by Internet Explorer are by default placed in a special directory (windows\occache); however, this can be overridden by the setup configuration file.

may accept any data that contributes to the business state of the system, but it is not responsible for it. By keeping the distinctions clear, system analysts and designers can build systems that meet the needs of the business, and user interface designers and Web page authors can concentrate on delivering that ability within the confines of the Web browser.

A number of technologies and mechanisms bring business logic to the client. These same technologies can also be used to enhance the user interface. For the most part, they fall into one of two categories: scripted or compiled. All of them share some common features:

- They are associated with the Web page and can access and modify its content.
- They are automatically deployed (downloaded) to the client computer as needed.
- They address specific security concerns.

When only minimal business logic needs to be used on the client, scripting is often an easy yet powerful mechanism to use. When truly sophisticated logic needs to run on the client, building Java applets, JavaBeans, or ActiveX controls is probably a better approach, since those environments are more structured and powerful. ActiveX, however, is an option only when the client computers are Windows based. In an intranet environment, this could very well be the case, and such an environment could take advantage of the increased performance of natively coded modules.

Client-side enabling technologies can be sophisticated and very object oriented if done properly. This depth of functionality is very important to keep in mind when designing client-side activity. When giving the client a role in the business, it is important to do so in a way that is consistent with the rest of the system.

In keeping with the theme of this book, it is important to recognize that the technologies used to bring business logic to the client need to be well understood and incorporated into the overall application model. Just because an element of the application uses some JavaScript to perform some simple calculations on the client and the rest of the system relies on distributed C++ objects and CORBA ORBs doesn't mean that the script isn't important. If it implements a business rule or process, it needs to be included in the model.

Chapter Summary

❏ Web applications implement business logic. Business logic is a rule or process that affects the business state of the system.

❏ The Document Object Model (DOM) is a platform-neutral interface to the browser and the HTML or XML documents it's rendering.

❏ The browser is responsible for executing client-side scripts.

❏ Dynamic HTML (DHTML) is a vendor term that describes a combination of HTML, style sheets, and scripts that allow documents to be manipulated in a Web browser. It is not a W3C specification or recommendation.

❏ JavaScript is the most common scripting language supported in browsers today.

❏ JavaScript resembles Java but does not have its static typing and strong type checking.

❏ A custom JavaScript object is an attempt to create "objects" with JavaScript. It involves the bundling of discrete functions with generic JavaScript object instances.

❏ JavaBeans, small reusable components that can be used to build larger Java programs and applets, have brought Java into the component world.

❏ The use of Java on the client is usually in the form of an applet.

❏ ActiveX controls are the Microsoft solution to distributing custom components inside Web pages.

❏ An ActiveX control or COM object is a complete executable module that is executed by the browser.

Chapter 4
Beyond HTTP and HTML

The basic architecture for Web systems includes a client browser, a web server, and a connecting network. The principal protocol for communication is the HyperText Transfer Protocol (HTTP). The principal language for expressing the content between the client and the server is the HyperText Markup Language (HTML). For many Web applications, these are enough on which to base a robust and sophisticated Web application. Internet applications especially benefit from this simplicity, since requiring sophisticated software and high-speed connections on clients is not always possible.

With the recent successes of Web applications, more and more architects are choosing this architecture for their next generations of systems. The significant advantages of easy deployment and minimal client configuration are well suited to organizations that maintain a varied array of computer types and models. This increased use of the Web as an architectural platform, however, has stretched the limits of the ability for HTTP and HTML to deliver the functionality required in relatively sophisticated software systems. This chapter discusses the limitations of and extensions to these two principal elements of Web applications: HTTP and HTML.

Distributed Objects

From an object point of view, one of the biggest disadvantages of HTTP is its connectionless nature. Object-oriented architects and designers have been working for years with distributed object systems and are familiar with their overall architecture and design patterns. If we consider how most Web applications work, we know that a client browser navigates a system's Web pages, with each containing a certain content, either active or passive. At one level of abstraction, the pages in a Web application can be considered objects. Each possesses content (state) and may execute scripts (behavior). Pages have relationships with other pages (hyperlinks) and objects in the system (Document Object Model, database connectors, and so on). The fact that pages are distributed to clients, where they are executed, in a sense makes the simple Web system a type of distributed object system. In fact, the principal goal of this book is to show how to model the pages of Web applications and other Web-specific components in an object-oriented manner, consistent with the models of the rest of the system.

It should therefore be no surprise that architects and designers of Web applications have a natural affinity for distributed object systems. They have certain advantages, including the ability to truly distribute the execution of the business logic to the nodes in the system that are the most appropriate to handle it. But because of the connectionless nature of HTTP, many of the existing distributed object design patterns are difficult to apply directly to Web applications. Most distributed object systems depend on a consistent network connection between client and server.[1]

In addition to the connection issue, there is a limit to how much functionality can be delivered with plain HTML, client-side scripting, even with applets or ActiveX controls. In many cases, the bandwidth to the server is too severely restricted by HTTP for sophisticated objects to perform business tasks on the server.

A classic example is the basic address collection interface. Many software systems that require the collection of personal and business addresses allow the user to enter in a zip (postal)code, and have the system populate the state and city fields of the address automatically. For a Web application to do this, either the entire postal code list needs to be accessible on the client or downloaded to the client, or the system must make an additional server request for the information. Neither solution is well suited for the Web, since the zip code list itself might be many megabytes in size and take several minutes just to download to the client, and an extra server trip is itself lengthy (on the order of several seconds). Additionally, the usability issues related to a several-second discontinuity in the data entry process of a common address block will prevent most designers from pursuing this route.

The solution for this common problem is beyond the ability of HTTP to solve. What is needed is a quick, efficient way for the client to query the server for the city and state of a given zip code. In a distributed object system, this is not a problem; a client object just obtains a reference to a server-side object that can answer the query. The server-side object will have access to a database of postal codes and city/state mappings. The response time in such a system will probably be on the order of milliseconds, depending on network bandwidth, instead of the seconds that a full HTTP page request would require. See Figure 4-1.

Using distributed objects in a Web application can solve a lot of functionality and performance issues that are often encountered in Web application development. There are costs, however, the most obvious being an additional order of magnitude of complexity in the

---

1. This discussion of distributed objects does not mean to ignore the existence of message-based systems, whereby communications between client and server objects are managed by message queues. Since the use of distributed objects in Web applications is typically promoted for its speed of execution, object-based messaging systems do not immediately provide the answers to the problems that distributed objects solve in Web applications. Despite this assertion, it is my opinion that message-based systems and architectures will, in the near future, become increasingly associated with Web-based architectures—to their mutual benefit.

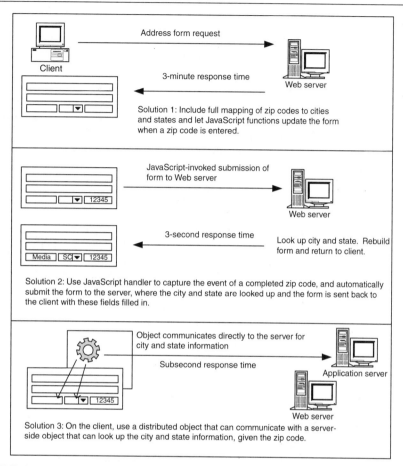

FIGURE 4-1   Mechanisms for implementing a smart address form

architecture of the system. The key to the use of distributed objects in a Web application is
to incorporate the distributed object system without losing the main benefits of having a
Web architecture in the first place. The most notable benefit of the Web is its ease of deployment. For a Web application to effectively make use of distributed objects, there must
be a way to automatically send to the client the necessary objects and interfaces needed
for it to participate in the system without having the user stop the application and install
special software.

Another benefit of Web architectures is the ability to leverage heterogeneous and minimally powered clients. Depending on the choice of distributed object infrastructures, there
may be an impact on the types of clients that can participate in the system. In addition to
the requirements on the client computer, using distributed objects in a Web application
requires a reliable network, since managing and designing for spotty network connections
is often more trouble than it is worth.

At the time of this writing three principal distributed object infrastructures are associated with Web application development: Java's RMI (Remote Method Invocation), OMG's CORBA (Common Object Request Broker Architecture), and Microsoft's DCOM (Distributed Component Object Model). The RMI and CORBA approaches are merging and even today are interoperable in some implementations.

The goal of all of these approaches is to abstract out the details of distributed communications and to make it the responsibility of the infrastructure, not the class designer or implementer. These approaches work on the principle of location transparency, which states that the object designer/implementer should never need know the true location of a given object instance. That decision is left to the architect or the deployment individual. Ideally, the designer of a particular class should not care whether a given instance of a class is located on the same machine or not. The reality of distributed object design, however, is that the location can be important, especially when designing to meet certain performance requirements.

The approaches taken by these infrastructures are for the most part the same. Each of them uses proxies, or stubs, as interfaces between the distributed object infrastructure and objects that use and implement the business functionality. Both provide naming and directory services to locate objects within the system, and both provide a set of security services. Bridges can even be built that allow objects from one infrastructure to communicate with objects in the other; however, these are subject to severe functional limitations and performance consequences.

What follows is a brief overview of these infrastructures and how they are leveraged in Web applications.

RMI

Remote Method Invocation (RMI) is the Java standard for distributed objects. RMI allows Java classes to communicate with other Java classes that are potentially located on different machines. As a set of APIs and a model for distributed objects, Java RMI allows developers to build distributed systems easily. The initial release of the RMI API used Java serialization and the Java Remote Method Protocol (JRMP) to make method invocations across a network look like local invocations. JRMP is the transport protocol for remote method invocations; in the latest version of RMI, support has been added for CORBA's IIOP transport protocol (discussed later in this chapter).

From the designer's point of view, the underlying transport protocol should have nothing to do with the design of the system's classes. This is not always the case, however. When IIOP (Internet Inter-ORB Protocol) is used as the underlying transport protocol, special care must be made when designing operation signatures. Most CORBA implementations limit operation parameters to basic primitive types. Operations that accept Java object references as parameters might not be usable in IIOP-based systems. Also, the present release of the Java Development Kit (JDK) does not support the use of output and input/output parameters on operations. It is conceivable that existing CORBA objects might have operations that expect or require such parameters, and so it would be difficult for Java-based clients to use them.

RMI introduces two new types of objects: stubs and skeletons. The stub is a client-side object that represents the remote object and executes on the client machine. The skeleton is responsible for managing all of the details of being remote—that is, responding to communications from objects on another machine—and exists on the server machine. The best part about these two objects is that you don't have to write the code for them yourself. They are automatically generated from a special compiler, `rmic`, which creates the stub and skeleton classes from business objects that implement certain interfaces. For example, the `rmic` command would take the Java class `MyObject` as an argument and produce class files of the form `MyObject_Skel.class` and `MyObject_Stub.class`.

The goal is, again, to insulate the designer and the developer as much as possible from the details of remote communication. Figure 4-2 shows an overview of the layered architecture for RMI.

To use a remote object, a client must first obtain a reference to it. This means that the client will need to know the remote object's name and location. This information can be expressed in terms of a URL. For example, a `CityStateServer` object existing on a machine called `myhost.com` would have the URL

```
rmi://myhost.com/CityStateServer
```

The `rmi:` part of the URL indicates its type or protocol. Clients wishing to communicate with an instance of this object use the Java naming and directory interface to look up and obtain a reference. Obtaining a reference and using an instance of a `CityStateServer` object in an applet is as simple as

```
CityStateServer cs = null;
cs = (CityStateServer) Naming.lookup("rmi://myhost.com/CityStateServer");
aCity = cs.getCity(zip);
aState = city.getState();
```

The `Naming` instance is itself a well-known remote object that connects to the remote server and requests an instance of the object. It returns the object stub, which the client program uses to invoke methods on.

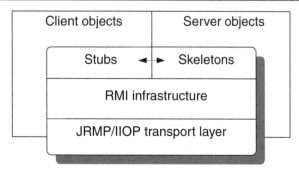

FIGURE 4-2 RMI layered architecture

One of the most significant features of RMI is that if the stub for the remote object doesn't exist on the client, it will automatically be downloaded to the client in accordance with the policies of the security manager. Every instance of an RMI-enabled program must install and run a security manager object. Applets, however, have the option of defaulting to the existing `AppletSecurityManager` instance.

On the server, an interface is defined for the remote object as follows:

```
package myapp.CityStateServer;

import myapp.Address.*;
import java.rmi.Remote;
import java.rmi.RemoteException;
public interface CityStateServer extends Remote {
 City getCity( String zip ) throws RemoteException;
}
```

Each method call of the remote object must throw a `RemoteException`. All parameters passed to remote methods must be serializable, since they will eventually get sent over the network.

Setting up a remote object server involves three steps:

1. Start a security manager class so that the server itself can accept stub classes from other machines and, in effect, become a client to another machine.
2. Create one or more instances of the server object.
3. Register at least one of the server objects with the RMI naming registry so that it can be found by client programs.

Presently, only Java applications, not applets, can be remote object hosts. The following code fragment for an application's main function shows the `CityStateServer` getting registered on a host.

```
public static void main( String [] args ) throws
     RemoteException, java.net.MalformedURLException,
     RMISecurityException
{
     System.setSecurityManager( new RMISecurityManager() );
     CityStateServer css = new CityStateServer();
     Naming.rebind("rmi://myhost.com/CityStateServer", css );
}
```

The designer and the implementer are not completely isolated from the RMI infrastructure; remoteable server objects must implement a certain interface and throw special exceptions. Clients must catch these exceptions and handle them gracefully. Additionally, all parameters passed as arguments to the interface's functions must be able to send their states out in a stream. There are also other responsibilities on the part of the implementer; for the most part, however, they do isolate the designer and the developer from the complex issues of remote procedure calls, networking, and deployment.

When used in a Web application, RMI is typically used as a communication mechanism between an applet and an application server. The applet is delivered as part of a Web page that the user navigates to. All that is required on the part of the client is a Java-enabled Web browser. All of the classes necessary to invoke and to use remote objects will be downloaded to the client as necessary. Once the client applet is run, it can contact the remote server, request a remote object instance reference, and begin to invoke methods on it as if it were a local object instance. All of the marshaling of protocols is handled by the stub and skeleton classes and the RMI infrastructure. Figure 4-3 shows how applets and remote objects work together.

CORBA

The Common Object Request Broker Architecture (CORBA) is not a product but rather a specification of the Object Management Group (OMG),[2] a group of industry vendors that publishes specifications that individual vendors can use to make interoperable and compatible software. The latest version of the CORBA specification is version 2.2; however, at the time of this writing, CORBA 3.0 is expected to be released soon. CORBA is a specification that defines how objects can communicate with one another—participate in collaborations—over a network and execute methods on one another even if they are located on different machines.

The big difference between CORBA and RMI or DCOM is that CORBA is just a specification. It relies on individual vendors to provide implementations. Because the specification is the result of an industry consortium, it gives vendors significant opportunities to add value to the specification. Vendors can then compete in the marketplace, based on additional features or other added values, yet still interoperate.

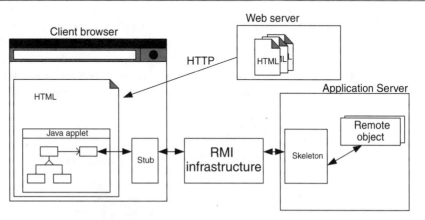

FIGURE 4-3 Applets using RMI

---

2. The OMG Web site: www.omg.org.

The major goal of CORBA is to allow developers and designers to build distributed object systems without concern for the details underlying the network communications and implementation languages. CORBA, unlike RMI, allows objects to be written in any vendor-supported language in which there are bindings. CORBA accomplishes this by defining a language-independent interface definition language (IDL) in which object interfaces can be described in a language-neutral way. Individual vendors provide the infrastructure and the tools to allow objects in any particular language to support it. A language binding is the mapping of a particular language's syntax to IDL. The OMG provides language bindings for Java, since all Java implementations are identical. Other languages, however, such as C++, may have subtly different bindings, depending on the compiler vendor and the operating system.

The middleware that CORBA defines for the communication of objects on different machines is called an object request broker (ORB). ORBs manage the sending and receiving of method invocations across the network. An ORB is installed on the client and the server. Client applications create instances of remote objects, using CORBA services, and invoke methods on them. These invocations are then marshaled through the network to the remote object, and the return value is sent back to client (Figure 4-4).

CORBA defines two types of interfaces that can be used by clients wanting to invoke a remote object's methods: stubs and dynamic invocation. Stubs, as in RMI, represent a hard-coded interface to a specific object. The methods of the stub are identical to the public interface of the object implementation that performs the object's behavior. Interfaces for stubs are defined in IDL, which defines the operations and the parameters that a particular object can implement.

Dynamic invocation, on the other hand, is a generic interface to an object. Instead of being published as an IDL file, object interfaces are added to an interface repository service, which represents the components of an interface as objects, allowing runtime access to them. This service can be used by a client to invoke methods on any type of remote object. Clients specify the object to be invoked, the operation to be performed, and the parameters for the operation through a sequence of calls to the dynamic invocation interface. Both the IDL used to describe stubs and the interface repository have the same expressive power.

ORBs from various vendors interoperate by using the same transport protocol. For TCP/IP-based networks, this is the Internet Inter-ORB Protocol (IIOP), which allows client ORBs from one vendor to interact with server ORBs from a another vendor. Additionally,

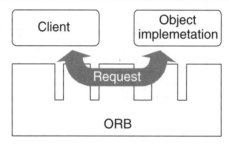

FIGURE 4-4   CORBA ORB

the client and server objects can be implemented in any language. As long as server objects implement the interface defined by the IDL, client applications written in any language or using any vendor's ORB can interoperate.

CORBA-based distributed object environments are more complex than RMI-based ones. CORBA, which has had a longer history than RMI, has a richer security model and offers many other services not found in RMI. CORBA supports multiple languages. Language bindings and ORB services can also vary, depending on the vendor. CORBA's naming and directory services and security services are also more sophisticated. All of this makes CORBA both more difficult to use yet more powerful and potentially more useful for certain applications.

CORBA is a viable distributed object technology infrastructure for Web applications because the latest Java Development Kit, version 1.2, includes a CORBA ORB. So you can write Java CORBA code without having to license and to install another vendor's ORB on the client. The one limitation remains, however, that all client code must be implemented in Java. When CORBA is part of a Web application, the client-side functionality is typically delivered in the form of an applet, and the server can be implemented with any ORB vendor and in any language. Figure 4-5 shows an overview of the use of CORBA in a Web application. This figure is similar to the use of RMI in a Web application, and it should be. The goal of both RMI and CORBA is to make the use of distributed objects easy and transparent to the implementer.

DCOM

Microsoft's solution to the problem of distributed objects is to extend the popular Component Object Model (COM) with Distributed COM (DCOM). Microsoft describes DCOM

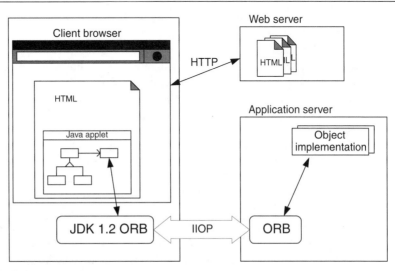

FIGURE 4-5   CORBA used in a Web application

as just COM with a longer wire. Most of the effort in making COM objects distributed is in their deployment and registration.

Just as RMI does, DCOM isolates the object developer from the details of distributing an object. DCOM goes even further by providing facilities to make COM-only objects live on remote servers. Unlike RMI, in which server objects must implement certain remote interfaces, DCOM gives the object developer complete independence from the distributed object infrastructure.

COM object implementations are assigned special class identifiers (CLSID). Clients wanting instances of a particular COM object request them with the CLSID from the operating system. When the client machine has the DCOM-supporting facilities installed, it is possible for these object to be located on a remote server. When a client creates an object instance, the following steps occur.

1. The client calls `CoCreateInstance()` on a CLSID supported by a local server.

2. The DCOM runtime, working together with the SCM (service control manager), determines whether the requested local server is already running and can be connected to.

3. The client is provided with a reference to an interface proxy to the object. If an existing instance of the object is available, it will be used; otherwise, a new instance is created.

The principal responsibility for locating objects rests with the service control manager. The SCM will locate or create the object instance on the local machine or across the network, if necessary.

Once a client obtains an object reference, the client can invoke operations on it. In normal COM, the communication between the client and server objects that are in different process spaces is managed by the distributed computing environment's (DCE) remote procedure call (RPC) mechanism. When the objects are located on different machines, the DCOM infrastructure enters the picture and marshals the messages and replies over the network.

DCOM uses a scheme similar to RMI and CORBA, creating proxy and stub objects to act as interfaces between the client program or server object implementation and the COM infrastructure. The existence of these objects is invisible to the implementer and is provided by DCOM. Figure 4-6 shows an overview of the DCOM architecture.

The principal strategy for deploying these objects is either to manually install the object proxies on the client or to use the code-downloading capabilities of Internet Explorer (IE) to do it for you. IE versions 3 and greater are capable of requesting and downloading COM components from servers. The download is, of course, subject to the security policies set up on the client. The objects that are downloaded are complete COM objects that can run completely on the client. This means that if it is possible to download a COM object, it is also possible to download proxies for remote objects.

When DCOM is used in a Web application, Web pages contain ActiveX controls that are downloaded to the client and executed. Along with these controls, proxy objects can be downloaded and registered to point to implementation objects on the appropriate application server (Figure 4-7).

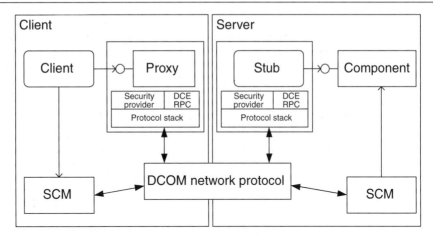

FIGURE 4-6 Overview of DCOM architecture

The biggest disadvantage of using DCOM instead of RMI or CORBA is the client requirement of running Windows. Even though COM and DCOM are public specifications, the reality is that only Windows-based operating systems support them. Additionally, Microsoft's Internet Explorer is the only major browser that has native support for COM. For intranet applications, however, this may not be a problem.

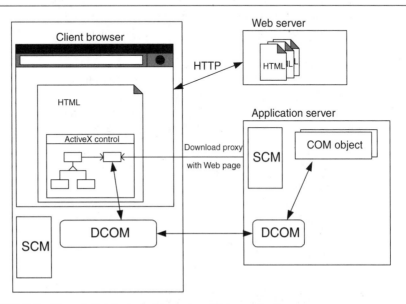

FIGURE 4-7 Use of distributed objects in a Web application

XML

The Extensible Markup Language (XML) does for HTML what distributed objects do for HTTP. XML is the creation of the W3C,[3] which also controls the evolution of HTML. XML offers Web application developers another way to express Web page content. One of the principal problems with HTML is that content and presentation details are interwoven in the same document. XML documents don't contain presentation information; instead, a separate document formatted with the Extensible Stylesheet Language (XSL) or a cascading style sheet (CSS) document is referenced in order to render the document in a browser. In most situations, XML documents are not rendered just in browsers but are used as a cross-platform way of managing and communicating data between systems.

A lot of hype surrounds XML, and there is a lot of confusion as to what XML is and how it relates to Web applications. It is true that XML is powerful and will be a significant player in the next generations; however, it is not a technological silver bullet. XML is just a language, or rather a metalanguage. It requires an agreement by all parties using it.

Basically, an XML-formatted document is a hierarchical collection of elements. An element is one document part that usually contains a textual value. An element can have child elements and hence form a hierarchy. Every XML document begins with one root element. Elements can be enhanced with attributes, which are just key/value pairs.

The beauty of XML, and the reason that so many people are interested in it, is that you can define your own element types and associate your own semantics with it. In effect, XML offers the basic rules for formatting generic documents so that simple parsers can read and validate their contents.

Most of the content of an XML document is textual; however, elements of the document can point to nontextual resources, such as images or applications. By describing documents with XML, generic XML parsers can be used to extract the document's structure. Individual applications will still have to apply semantic meanings to the elements. A document that obeys XML formatting rules is considered *well formed* and can be parsed by any generic XML parser.

XML, like HTML, has its roots in the Standard Generalized Markup Language (SGML), the mother tongue for a whole group of document-formatting languages. XML formats its content with tags. An XML element is expressed with a pair of tags: a beginning tag and an ending tag. The following XML document could be used to express a postal address.

```
<?xml version="1.0" encoding="UTF-8"?>
<address>
    <street>123 Pine Rd.</street>
    <city>Lexington</city>
    <state>SC</state>
    <zip>19072</zip>
</address>
```

---

3. The World Wide Web Consortium: www.w3.org.

A proper XML document begins with a heading that indicates the version of XML used and the encoding character set. As in HTML, tags are surrounded by angled brackets (< >). White space outside of tags is optional, so the indenting of the address's child elements is strictly for human reading. Space between an element's tags is not ignored, however. Ending tags are denoted by a slash as the first character, followed by the tag name. The text between these tags is the element's value, which can be any combination of text or child elements. In the preceding example, the <address> element has four child elements, each of which contains textual information.

Unlike HTML, XML elements cannot have open-ended or overlapping tags. Every beginning tag must have an ending tag, or the tag can be constructed in a shorthand form:

```
<pobox/>
```

The tag for pobox is both a beginning and an ending tag. This particular tag on its own doesn't convey much information except for its existence. Additional information can be tied to an element through the use of element attributes. For example, the tag pobox might have the attributes of id and rural defined:

```
<pobox id="1234" rural="false"/>
```

When these attributes are included, the usefulness of the pobox tag becomes clearer.

The trick to successfully using XML in an application and across applications is in obtaining agreement on the structure and semantics of the documents that will be used. The preceding address element is intuitive to a human being—at least to U.S. residents— but an automated application must be explicitly programmed to accept address information in this form. Take as an example a healthcare provider that has an application that exchanges patient information with an insurance company. The insurance company might expect address information in the preceding form, but the healthcare company might supply addresses in the following form:

```
<?xml version="1.0" encoding="UTF-8"?>
<patient-address>
    <street>
        <line1>123 Pine Rd.</line1>
        <line2></line2>
    </street>
    <city name="Lexington"/>
    <state abbrev="SC"/>
    <zip base="19072" plus4=""/>
</patient-address>
```

In this case, the insurance company application will not automatically associate the proper semantic meaning to the document, and it will not be able to use it. In order for XML to be used as a general data interchange medium, a mechanism to help coordinate and define their construction is needed. The answer lies in a DTD.

A document type definition (DTD) is a document that defines the syntax for a particular type of XML document. DTDs are used to determine whether any given XML document is *valid*; that is, its structure is defined by a DTD. A DTD is a document that can either be embedded in an XML document or be a file on the network and just referenced in the document. DTD syntax rules are a little different from those of XML.

A DTD is not required for a parser to read the document. The first XML address document example is a well-formed document that can be read and parsed; however, it is unclear whether it is also a valid document. For this, it must be checked against a DTD. If the DTD was included with the first version of the address, the XML document would be as follows:

```
<?xml version="1.0" encoding="UTF-8"?>
<!DOCTYPE address [
    <!ELEMENT address (street, city, state, zip)>
    <!ELEMENT street (#PCDATA)>
    <!ELEMENT city (#PCDATA)>
    <!ELEMENT state (#PCDATA)>
    <!ELEMENT zip (#PCDATA)>
]>
<address>
    <street>123 Pine Rd.</street>
    <city>Lexington</city>
    <state>SC</state>
    <zip>19072</zip>
</address>
```

The DTD, beginning with the keyword !DOCTYPE, specifies five element types. The root element—and name of the document type—is specified to contain four child element types. All four contain only parsed character data (#PCDATA), or text that does not contain special markup character, such as <, >, or &. This XML document, with embedded DTD, can be validated with a validating XML parser.

Instead of embedding a DTD in every XML document, it is possible to just reference it and to give the parser the option of fetching it or use a cached copy to perform the validation. The second address XML document could be constructed with a referenced DTD:

```
<?xml version="1.0" encoding="UTF-8"?>
<!DOCTYPE patient-address SYSTEM "http://dtd.mycompany.com/paddress.dtd">
<patient-address>
    <street>
        <line number="1">123 Pine Rd.</line>
        <line number="2">Apt B116</line>
    </street>
    <city name="Lexington"/>
    <state abbrev="SC"/>
    <zip base="19072" plus4="4501"/>
</patient-address>
```

In this document, the DTD can be obtained with the URL specified after the SYSTEM keyword. This particular URL happens to also specify the machine name and the protocol that can be used to obtain the document.

It is expected that industry groups will get together to collectively define DTDs for their specific industries. For example, the healthcare industry might define a set of DTDs to exchange patient health care records. This standardization of information interchange has the potential to breathe new life into electronic data interchange (EDI), making it easier on software developers, who can rely on off-the-shelf parsing and navigation software to process this information.

As XML becomes more popular and as standards become defined, there is a greater chance that element names might collide. Since anyone can create an element, it is possible that a banking application might define the element <state> to mean the state of the account (open, closed, pending, and so on). Another application dealing with psychological things might define state to mean "normal," "depressed," "schizophrenic." As long as these elements remain in their own documents, there is not much of a problem. A problem arises for the designer of the Mental Health Home Banking application. The situation might be contrived, but it does illustrate the possibility of instances when multiple XML documents might get packaged together and when name collisions might occur in this document. The element <state> could now have three possible meanings: part of an address, account status, or mental condition. This reuse of the element <state> would be very confusing for a validating parser.

To help parsers resolve this dilemma, the W3C has recently defined a namespace mechanism. A namespace can be defined in an XML document, allowing us to continue to use the element name of <state>; in each instance, we can define the namespace it belongs in. Each namespace is identified with the special attribute (xmlns) and requires a unique identifier, which is usually a common URL. For example, our address element might define a default namespace for the document.

```
<?xml version="1.0" encoding="UTF-8"?>
<address xmlns="http://mycom.com/postaladdress/" >
    <street>123 Pine Rd.</street>
    <city>Lexington</city>
    <state>SC</state>
    <zip>19072</zip>
</address>
```

In this example, a default namespace is defined for all of the elements of address (the root element). Namespaces can be qualified and multiple namespaces used in a single document. For example, our banking application might use a document like this:

```
<?xml version="1.0" encoding="UTF-8"?>
<client xmlns="http://crazybanking.com/accounts/"
        xmlns:mental="http://mymind.com/mental/"
        xmlns:postal="http://mycom.com/postaladdress/" >
    <name>jim conallen</name>
    <accountno>123456789</accountno>
    <mental:mind>
        <mental:state>normal</mental:state>
    </mental:mind>
    <postal:home>
        <postal:street>123 Pine Rd.</postal:street>
```

```
        <postal:city>Lexington</postal:city>
        <postal:state>SC</postal:state>
        <postal:zip>19072</postal:zip>
    </postal:home>
</client>
```

In this example, three namespaces are defined, with one as the default. When referencing an element that is not part of the default namespace, the element name is prefixed with the namespace. With the namespaces defined, a validating parser has a much better chance of understanding and validating the document against a DTD.

Although DTDs are useful in Web applications, they have plenty of shortcomings.

- DTDs don't allow the specification of data types such as numbers or dates.

- DTDs can't be reused or combined to form new document definitions.

- The grammar of a DTD is different from that of XML and can be difficult to understand, especially by new users.

- It is not easy to expand the DTD with new features.

Several movements are under way to replace DTDs with other mechanisms, with the aim of providing an even richer description of an XML document's structure and content. XML schemas, introduced by Microsoft, are probably in the forefront of these efforts. An XML schema is a document that describes the structure of an XML document. It also happens to be a valid XML document in its own right. In addition to describing a valid XML document, an XML schema can go further to define element data types.

The XML schema that describes the second version of the postal address might look like this:

```
<Schema name="patient-address-schema"
    xmlns="urn:schemas-microsoft-com:xml-data"
    xmlns:dt="urn:schemas-microsoft-com:datatypes">
<ElementType name="patient-address" content="eltOnly" order="seq">
    <description>Postal address of a patient</description>
    <element type="street" />
    <element type="city" />
    <element type="state" />
    <element type="zip" />
</ElementType>

<ElementType name="street" content="eltOnly" order="many">
    <description/>
    <element type="line">
</ElementType>

<ElementType name="line" content="textOnly" dt:type="string">
    <attribute type="number">
</ElementType>

<ElementType name="city" content="textOnly" />
<ElementType name="state" content="textOnly" />
<ElementType name="zip" content="textOnly" dt:type="int" />
</Schema>
```

The details of the syntax are beyond the scope of this book and are subject to change; however, it is important to note that this entire schema is itself a valid XML document. The same parser that parses XML documents can also be used to parse the schema document. In this document, data types are specified for some of the elements. There is also a place to include element descriptions, which can be captured by the parser. (Comments in DTDs are often skipped over by parsers and don't have obvious connections the elements they describe.)

Two other emerging specifications that are likely to have a big impact on how XML will be used in Web applications are the Extensible Linking Language XLink (XLL) and the Extensible Pointer Language XPointer (XPL). XLink specifies how XML documents can reference other documents and resources, similar to the anchor tag <a> in HTML.

XLL and XPL are languages for expressing relationships among XML documents. Both are powerful languages that allow a document to locate and to reference subelements in other documents. The current recommendations for XLink and XPointer are still in flux and likely to change before they are official. For the most part, XLL provides a richer way to reference other documents or resources in the network. XLL allows additional information to be specified about the link that a host application might make use of.

XPL is a language that expresses how to capture part of a referenced document. For example, many FAQs on the Internet use one document to outline all of the questions and another to break up the answers to the questions. When a user clicks on a question that is augmented with an HTML anchor tag, the browser navigates to the answer page and scrolls down to the specified bookmark. In the case of HTML, the entire page must be loaded, even though the user was interested in the answer to only the one question. XPL allows you to specify just that one part of the document you are interested in. XPL has a rich set of capabilities that allow you to "point" to specific parts of a document in a number of ways. For example, you can specify the third <address> of the second <customer> in a document. XLL and XPL have potential to be very expressive and useful in Web applications that use XML as a principal communication mechanism.

XML is an emerging technology, one that is evolving very quickly. The discussions of XML in this chapter are just to introduce the topic and to place it in the context of building Web applications. XML, like RMI, CORBA, and DCOM, are all topics that are important to the Web application architect and designer. They may or may not be appropriate for any given application. All of these technologies are evolving, and it is likely that in the future, most Web applications will need to consider some of these technologies as a means to meet the increased functional demands being placed on them.

Chapter Summary

❏ HTTP and HTML are the principal protocol and language in use on the Internet today. They form the backbone of a Web application's architecture.

❏ Web applications can be augmented with distributed objects that enable objects on the client to communicate directly with objects on the server, without using HTTP or going through the Web server.

❏ Remote Method Invocation (RMI) is a Java-based distributed object infrastructure that can be delivered in the form of applets to new clients.

❏ The latest release of Java comes with an implementation of a CORBA ORB.

❏ RMI is capable of using IIOP as its transport protocol, giving it the ability to work with CORBA systems.

❏ CORBA is a language-independent, vendor-neutral distributed object infrastructure.

❏ DCOM, or COM on a longer wire, is Microsoft's infrastructure for distributing objects on different machines.

❏ XML, like HTML, is an SGML-based language for expressing content in Web pages.

❏ The Extensible Stylesheet Language (XSL) defines formatting instructions for rendering XML documents on displays.

❏ You can define your own tags in XML. This gives designers the ability to tag document elements with special semantic meanings.

❏ A document type definition (DTD) defines the structure of a specific type of XML document. XML documents are validated against a DTD.

❏ XML documents can be combined and managed with namespaces.

❏ DTDs can be embedded in an XML document or referenced in an XML document.

❏ The Extensible Pointer Language (XPL) and Extensible Linking Language (XLL) are emerging standards for referencing other XML documents and resources in the system.

Chapter 5
Security

If you are building an Internet application, security is a concern. Even if you are building only an intranet application, one protected behind a company firewall, security should still be a concern. The term security describes the protection of our data and system. A secure system is a properly functioning software application that does only what it is supposed to do, without compromising the integrity of our data to those who are not authorized to have that information.

If our systems did only what they were supposed to do, security would not be an issue. So why is security a problem? Because our software and business processes often do things that we don't want or intend them to do. Unscrupulous individuals with even limited access to your system will take advantage of any side effect of the system to gain access to potentially valuable information, such as customer profiles and credit card numbers, or will simply bring your system down as a test of personal skill and pride. The threat is very real, and with Web applications taking on more mission-critical roles in corporations today, the need to understand the security risks and to manage them is even more critical.

The alt.security newsgroup FAQ[1] summarizes the issues of security by answering the common question:

Q: What makes a system insecure?

A: Switching it on. The adage usually quoted runs along these lines: "The only system which is truly secure is one which is switched off and unplugged, locked in a titanium lined safe, buried in a concrete bunker, and is surrounded by nerve gas and very highly paid armed guards. Even then, I wouldn't stake my life on it."

---

1. This FAQ is maintained by Alec Muffett (Alec.Muffett@uk.sun.com), with contributions from numerous others.

This paints a bleak picture for system architects and designers, but as in all forms of engineering, compromises need to be made, and a delicate balance of functionality versus security requirements needs to be maintained. This balance is unique to each and every software project and is not something that can be dictated by a book such as this.

Instead of presenting a complete security strategy suitable for all Web applications, this chapter attempts merely to introduce the issues and nature of security risks specific to Web applications. Since security is a huge topic and the subject of many texts,[2] a full discussion is beyond the scope of this book. This chapter will, however, outline the security issues and topics that every Web application architect and designer needs to be familiar with.

One of the best sources of current information on security can be found on the Internet. The Usenet newsgroups are a valuable source of current information regarding security issues, for both the new and experienced. In particular newsgroup FAQs are an excellent way to get introduced issues facing a Web system architect. Much of the information used in this chapter has come from reading these FAQs, and it is highly recommended that Web application architects and designers make a regular habit of monitoring the activity in these newsgroups.

Types of Security Risks

To understand the areas of risk in our application, we need to understand where our systems are vulnerable. The basic Web architecture, being a variant of a client/server architecture, has three principal architectural elements: the client, the network, and the server. Each is vulnerable to attack (see Figure 5-1).

- Our clients are at risk from software that damages the client's system or compromises private client-side resources, such as personal information and files.

- Our servers are at risk from unauthorized access to the server, which may result in the capture of confidential information, the execution of potentially damaging programs in the server, or even the temporary disabling of server functions.

- Our networks can be monitored, and data communications between the client and the server can be intercepted.

It is the job of the chief architect and designers to understand and to manage these risks. Managing security risks in a software application happens at two levels: technical and procedural. Technical risk, the focus of this chapter, deals with risk presented by the hardware and software components of the system and is the domain of the architect. This type of risk is managed by a better understanding of the system and its deployment and by adding to the design certain technical measures that make it more secure.

---

2. Two excellent security reference books are Lincoln D. Stein, *Web Security: A Step-by-Step Reference Guide* (Reading, MA: Addison Wesley Longman, 1998), and Simson Garfinkel and Gene Spafford, *Web Security & Commerce (Nutshell Handbook)* (Sebastopol, CA: O'Reilly & Associates, 1997).

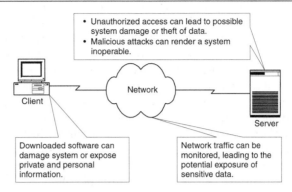

- Unauthorized access can lead to possible system damage or theft of data.
- Malicious attacks can render a system inoperable.

Client

Network

Server

Downloaded software can damage system or expose private and personal information.

Network traffic can be monitored, leading to the potential exposure of sensitive data.

FIGURE 5-1   Areas of risk in a Web application

Procedural risks, on the other hand, result from poor operating practices. As any security expert will tell you, many of the security holes in your system are a result of human error and confusion. According to a classic story told in security circles, a top-notch security expert was called in to examine the latest security precautions at a banking institution. The institution was proud of its security precautions, which were a comprehensive set of the latest and most advanced technologies available. The expert managed to gain access to the system by simply making a call to a new employee at the bank. The expert, claiming to be a member of the bank's IT department, asked the new employee for his name, office location, phone extension, and computer password, claiming to be updating the employee's status on the system. The new employee gave the expert the required information; within minutes the expert had gained access to the system.

This story emphasizes the point that security is more than just a technical issue. In order to maximize the security of our systems, we need to be aware of both the technical and human aspects of our system's vulnerabilities. Establishing proper security policies and training users are as important to a system's security as any technical component.

Technical Risk

To understand the technical security risks of a system, architects and designers need to understand the nature of these risks in order to better prevent them. The general nature of risks in our systems can be categorized into the following major areas:

- Improperly configured systems
- Buggy software
- Poor authentication (that is, insufficient password requirements)
- Lack of encryption in network traffic

The primary reason that any given part of a system is a security risk is improperly configured or buggy software. An improperly configured system or a system with a bug opens a security hole that can be exploited. One of the most famous security breaches has been chronicled by Clifford Stoll in his book *The Cuckoo's Egg*, in which he describes a detective-like story of the eventual capture of a successful West German cracker.[3] The cracker managed to gain privileged access to a number of systems throughout the world by exploiting a bug (unknown feature) in a common text-editing program. The program allowed users of the system to save a file to a particularly important area of the file system. Files in this directory were automatically executed with root-level privileges and considered normal parts of the operating system. Once there, the cracker's file was run, giving the intruder a secret and unmonitored account, which he used to anonymously examine the system for important information and as a jumping point to the next unconquered system. This particular bug has long since been fixed, along with many other bugs that have been discovered as a result of a security breach.

Anonymous attackers are not the only worry of a security-conscious designer. A disgruntled employee can cause even more damage to a system than can an outside intruder having only the most basic knowledge of the system. It is therefore important to establish the identity of the users of the system as best as practically possible. At a very minimum, separate user accounts and private passwords need to be established.

In a Web application, proper authentication of a system's users can happen at several levels. At one level, the client computer itself can be authenticated for use with the system. A Web application can be designed to allow only clients with certain IP addresses. My personal Internet service provider (ISP) uses this type of authentication to protect certain Web pages in the technical-support section of its Web site. Since I travel a lot, I often need to look up the local access numbers for the city I am visiting. This particular information is important to the ISP's customers but represents a minor potential for abuse from noncustomers (by tying up these lines trying to gain unauthorized access). This particular page is set up such that anyone whose IP address is one of the ISP's own addresses is allowed full access to this page; others are diverted to another page that contains only partial access numbers (just enough to determine whether an access line might be a toll call for a potential customer). This type of authentication is not perfect, but the complexity it adds to the system does balance out with the particular risks involved.

The most common form of authentication is a simple password. System users are given a log-on ID (a publicly known identification of the user), and a secret ID (password). To gain access to the system, the user must supply both. After the first access to the system, the user is usually prompted to change the password to something that only the user will remember. Passwords are usually the first line of defense in a system and help prevent interactive attacks on the system.

This type of authentication has many problems. From a purely technical point of view, a user ID and password tell the system only that a user who knows that combination is requesting access to the system, not necessarily that that person is supposed to have that knowledge. What a system is really authenticating is a user with knowledge of a valid user

---

3. Not to be confused with the term hacker; a cracker is someone who maliciously breaches a system's security, whereas a hacker is someone who is considered an authority on computer-related things.

ID and password combination, not the real identity of the person requesting access to the system.

This problem is further exacerbated by the practice in some organizations of creating "group" accounts, in which a number of individuals all use the same user ID and password combinations. In these situations, individual users' identities are never really known, and any given password often overlaps with the introduction and expulsion of employees. So it is likely that at any given time, valid user ID and password combinations are known by unauthorized individuals.

In Web systems, especially Internet systems, anonymous users are the norm, and a special account is often created for this type of user. Popular systems may have many thousands of simultaneous users, all using the same account ID.

In many situations, knowing a particular log-on account won't gain a cracker immediate access to all of a system's resources. Typically, user accounts are restricted to allow access to only those system resources necessary to perform the user's responsibilities. Of more interest to a cracker are the administration passwords (root or administrator). With this level of access, the entire system's resources are open for exploitation.

Administrator-level access to a system can be gained by obtaining a copy of the system's password file. The default configurations of many UNIX and NT systems allow this. The cracker can then use special software programs to "crack" the password file's encryption and thus obtain access to the more interesting administrator and root accounts on a system.

Simple passwords can be cracked with programs that repeatedly guess passwords from dictionary words and combinations of numbers or other common symbols. Short passwords are especially vulnerable, since there are fewer combinations of letters and numbers to try. The best passwords are those combinations of letters and numbers that are truly random. The problem with this is that a human is less likely to remember a completely random sequence of digits than one that has some semantic meaning to the user. Once a semantic meaning is placed in a password, it stops being purely random and is more likely to be cracked.

When creating passwords, you should not base your password on

- Your name or any part of your name
- Any part of a dictionary word or a proper name
- Acronyms

In general, any systematic way of producing a password is subject to being repeated by an unscrupulous cracker. The following passwords are all considered bad, since they can be easily cracked with common password-cracking software.

pba	Too short
jimc1	Based on user name
merlin	Dictionary name
bilbobaggins	Dictionary name
qwerty	Dictionary name and easy to see when typing
aaaaaa	Dictionary name and easy to see when typing

`4tune`	Prepending character to dictionary name
`tune4`	Postpending character to dictionary name
`hIho`	Capitalization in a dictionary word(s)
`c001`	Substitution of numbers for characters in dictionary word

The best passwords are those that the individual creates on a purely personal and random basis. The practical trick in password usage, however, is using passwords that can be remembered. I worked in one environment in which the passwords were distributed by the company's network administrator, who used a special piece of software that he believed produced very random and difficult-to-guess passwords. To further increase security (in his mind), he changed them every 3 months. He assigned passwords to users of the system, expecting us to quickly remember them and to destroy any written copies. They were very cryptic and difficult to remember. The result was that half of the users ended up writing down their passwords on Post-it notes and sticking them onto their monitors. In the end, this was not very secure, yet there was very little in the way that the common user could do.

The trick to the use of passwords is not to consider them the ultimate security tool but simply as a first line of defense. In order for passwords to be effective, they need to be as close to random as the user is capable of remembering. Additionally, users need to be the ones who create their passwords, as any systematic and organizationwide method of producing passwords is more likely to be cracked than are isolated and uniquely derived ones.

The final general category of security risks is the lack of encryption. In this type of risk, intruders monitor network traffic, collecting the dialogs of communication between clients and servers. The most common network protocols in use on the Internet today are TCP/IP. When designed, security was not foremost in mind. The Internet's being the world's largest public network does not prevent anonymous users from monitoring the general traffic passing through their systems. Crackers can use "sniffers" to monitor and to analyze the network traffic to a specific server or client and possibly to reconstruct important information useful in gaining further access to the system or simply picking up a few valid credit card numbers.

To counter this risk, the traffic between the client and the server can be encrypted. Encryption is discussed in more detail later in this chapter, but the general idea is to encode the network traffic between a specific client and server so that it cannot be understood by any listening third party.

One major use of network encryption is in virtual private networks (VPN), in which a public network, such as the Internet, is used as a private network. All members of the private network use encryption to communicate with other members of the private network. From the users' point of view, the network looks like a private network, as might be seen in a small business with a local area network (LAN) (Figure 5-2).

VPNs have the distinctive advantage of allowing small companies to give private network access, through the public Internet, to individuals who are remotely located, rather than through more expensive private leased lines. Using VPNs places most of the security responsibilities, such as network traffic encryption, on the infrastructure rather than on the individual applications. Some Web applications may use VPNs as part of their security measures. VPNs can be implemented with a combination of software and hardware or just as software.

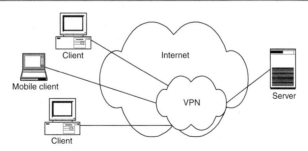

FIGURE 5-2   Virtual private networks

Server-Side Risks

Once placed on a network, a server is vulnerable to attack. When placed on a public network, such as the Internet, a server is even more likely to be attacked. The major goal of an attack is to either gain control of the server or extract valuable information from it. Achieving the first will make achieving the second trivial.

The specific risks of Web application servers (servers processing HTTP Web requests), like most systems, relate to improper configuration or bugs in the software. A cracker will exploit a bug in a server's software or an improperly configured system. The most common configuration mistakes involve the enabling of optional features not required for the application. For example, one common feature of a Web server is directory browsing. This features allows anonymous users to examine the contents of whole directories on the Web server instead of just the contents of the files it is supposed to serve.

A cracker uses as much information as can be obtained about a system to break into it. The more information a cracker has, the more likely the system can be cracked. Allowing directory browsing gives the potential cracker more information about the system. This information can include backup files of sensitive scripts that contain source code to the applications modules.

EMACS, the popular UNIX-based editor, by default maintains a backup copy of files that it is working on, usually in the directory where the original file exists. A sloppy developer might have used EMACS to correct a bug in a CGI PERL script on the production machine and forgotten to remove the EMACS-generated backup file. A cracker would recognize this file in a directory listing of the CGI directory and examine it. The file contains source code to the application and potentially valuable information about the Web application's server-side resources.

Allowing the use of symbolic links to directories elsewhere in the system is also a potentially dangerous feature. Symbolic links to sensitive areas of a server, such as /etc, are very dangerous. Unless the application requires the use of symbolic links, it is best to keep this feature turned off.

Another major security hole is the use of server-side includes (SSI). An SSI is a directive that is embedded in an HTML page. When a user requests this page, the Web server processes the embedded command(s) before sending back the HTML page. Some server-side includes allow the execution of general operating system commands or scripts. These "exec"-style directives are a major security hole, and should only be allowed when absolutely necessary. They open up the possibility of an attacker embedding a command that might e-mail out the system's password file or do other forms of malicious damage.

In addition to improperly configured servers, bugs in the Web server and associated software, even including the operating system itself, are a major security risk. Take, for example, one of the early versions of Microsoft's Internet Information Server (IIS) and Active Server Pages (ASP) running on a Windows NT 4.0 server. When the Web server used an NTFS formatted file system partition, clients could request the source code to all the Active Server Pages by simply appending :$DATA to a Web page request. In fact, clients could even request the raw contents of the special application configuration file (global.asa). This particular file often contains important configuration information normally hidden to users of the application.

One of my first ASP commerce applications was susceptible to this particular bug. My jaw virtually dropped to the floor when a friend e-mailed me the contents of my global.asa file, which contained important information on the structure of my application. Fortunately, neither that file nor the contents of any of the other dynamic files in the system alone was sufficient to allow the novice cracker unwanted access to the system. But the fact that the information was available was dangerous to the security of the system. Needless to say, Microsoft came out with a patch soon thereafter, and there were several workarounds posted to the net immediately after the bug became known.

When a company makes its first plunge into world of Internet commerce, the question often asked is, Are some operating systems and Web servers more secure than others? The simple answer is yes, qualified with "at any given time." It is impossible (and very impractical as well) for me to say here which operating systems are the most secure, since things could be completely different in a few months. In general, the older and more stable the operating system is, the more secure it is, since most of the obvious bugs have been discovered and patched. With each patch, of course, comes the potential for even newer bugs and incompatibilities to be introduced. This cycle of operating system patch and upgrades eventually leads to a refinement of the system, ideally one with greater stability. Unfortunately, the cycle resets itself each time a new set of features or significant upgrade is introduced.

Client-Side Risks

Clients, especially those on the Internet, are, like servers, at risk in Web applications. It is possible for Web browsers to unknowingly download content and programs that could open up the client system to crackers and automated agents all over the Net. Malicious programs could collect and send sensitive and private information from the client machine to Net programs and servers that collect such information.

As a general rule, pure HTML 3.2, without client-side scripting, is rather secure. A Web page designer can do little to extract or to breach a client's security. Client-side risk usually involves the use of the following technologies:

- Cookies
- JavaScript
- Java applets
- ActiveX controls
- Plug-ins
- MIME-type viewers

Except for cookies, each of these technologies is used by Web site and application designers to make the client itself more dynamic, such as animation, fly-over help, and sophisticated input controls. Cookies represent a risk only when Web application designers use them to hold sensitive information, such as private IDs and passwords.

Cookies

Cookies are little pieces of information that a server can request a client to hold on to and later request back from the client. Cookies can be either transient—ending with the browser session—or retained on a near-permanent basis. Typically, cookies are used by Web application environments to help the server keep track of a single client browser's session as it navigates the Web application's pages. Permanent cookies can be used as virtual admission tickets. When visiting a site for the first time, the user enters certain information to allow access; all subsequent access to the system requests the cookie, and if valid, immediately gives the client access.

Cookies become a risk only when one application gets access to another's cookies. An unscrupulous Web site might trick a browser into thinking it was another site and request the cookie for that site. If the cookies contained personal identification information (admission tickets), this would allow the Web site owners to impersonate a validated user of that system.

JavaScript

JavaScript—not to be confused with Java, which is a completely different technology discussed later in the chapter—is a potentially serious threat to the integrity of personal information on the client. Ever since its introduction, JavaScript bugs and security holes have appeared at a consistent rate. Most of the security breaches have been the ability for scripts to gain access to files on the client machine or to obtain sensitive information from the browser, such as navigation histories or information in other frames.

One of the many early bugs and security holes detected in the first-generation JavaScript-enabled browsers was the file upload hole. In this bug, it was possible for a script to trick the browser into uploading any file on the local system with a submission of a form to a server. Password files and other sensitive files could be unknowingly sent to servers.

Although not as obvious a threat to security, client scripts can collect information on the navigation histories of the user by monitoring a user's session. Some variants of this hole capture all of the URLs that a user visits, including any information used to fill out forms. Even though data or software located on the user's machine cannot be modified, the detailed knowledge that can be gained is a violation of a user's privacy.

Java

The use of Java on the client is typically in the form of applets.[4] Security issues relating to applets usually center on

- Reading and writing files on the client
- Making network connections to any machine other than the originating host
- Starting other programs on the client or making native operating system calls

In the original JDK, the security model was fairly restrictive, described by the sandbox model. Remote Java code was allowed access only to a restricted set of functions on the client. Essentially, it was allowed to play within the confines of a small sandbox.

In general, applets loaded over the Net are considered "untrusted" and are prevented from reading and writing files on the client file system and from making network connections except to the originating host. In addition, applets loaded over the Net are prevented from starting other programs on the client. Applets loaded over the Net are also not allowed to load libraries or to define native method calls. If an applet could define native method calls, it would thus have direct access to the underlying computer. Figure 5-3 shows the security model for the JDK 1.0 release.

For some applications, this model was too restrictive. Under pressure to provide more functionality, the JDK 1.1 security model was expanded to allow digitally signed applets to be treated as if they were local code (Figure 5-4). As discussed later in this chapter, a digital signature encrypts a software module such that it is possible to determine, with reasonable certainty, that the code originated from the specified author without modification by a third party. A certificate authority (CA) is a third-party organization that can be trusted by both the server organization and the client individual.

Signed applets, together with their signatures, are delivered to the client in JAR (Java Archive) files. JAR files combine multiple Java files into a single file, which can then be signed and delivered to the client (Figure 5-5). In JDK 1.1, unsigned applets still run in the more restrictive sandbox.

The user has the option of accepting signed applets and examining the signature to determine whether the source can be trusted. If accepted, the Java code will run as if it

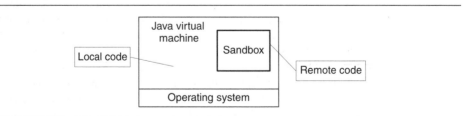

FIGURE 5-3   The JDK 1.0 security model

---

4. A good source of current security information related to applets and Java in general can be found on the JavaSoft Web site: http://www.javasoft.com/sfaq/.

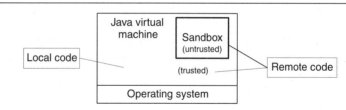

FIGURE 5-4   The JDK 1.1 security model

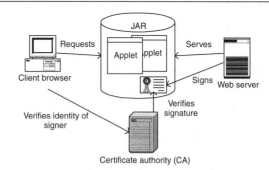

FIGURE 5-5   Delivery of digitally signed applets as JAR files

were local code and have all the privileges of any other application running on the client computer.

With the latest Java release (Java 2, or JDK 1.2), the security model has evolved to allow more control over which privileges any given component has access to. Even Java applications originating on the local machine are subject to implementation of custom security policies. The class loader is responsible for locating and fetching the class file, consulting the security policy, and defining the class object with the appropriate permissions (Figure 5-6).

Despite all of this attention to security by the Java designers, there is still the problem of bugs and poor implementation of the Java virtual machine, which can make even the most restricted applets dangerous. Since the most serious security bugs are in the implementation

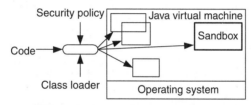

FIGURE 5-6   The JDK 1.2 security model

of the virtual machine, the security issues due to bugs are usually related to a particular operating system and version. One of the most glaring of these is the bug in the Windows NT 4.0 SP3 version of the virtual machine, which results in the infamous Blue Screen of Death (BSOD). It seems that when even an untrusted applet attempts to draw outside the bounds of a Java canvas, the entire operating system crashes.[5]

ActiveX

The issues related to security for ActiveX content are similar to those for Java applets. The risks to the client are generally damage to the system or theft of private information. An ActiveX control embedded in an HTML page is essentially just a compiled module, with free access to all of the resources on the client. The potential for serious damage to the client operating system is slightly more than with applets, since ActiveX controls execute only on Windows platforms,[6] and, consequently, more detailed knowledge about the client operating system is known.

ActiveX controls are just COM objects, and hence they are binary modules that execute directly on the operating system (Figure 5-7). There is no virtual machine as with Java applets to insulate operations and to provide a security buffer. The principal security mechanism for downloaded ActiveX controls is code signing. There are no restrictions to what the ActiveX control can do once it is loaded and executed on the client. All implementation of security measures happens at the point the component is being requested to load on the client. Some of the security precautions are implemented by the browser. Internet Explorer can be configured to automatically reject all requests to load ActiveX or Java components. These settings can be configured to prompt the user each time a control is loaded or to simply trust everything.

Internet Explorer also has the concept of security zones. A security zone is a network domain subset where the user can identify all of the hosts in it as trusted or not. For example, hosts on a company intranet can often be considered secure and hence ActiveX content on these hosts implicitly trusted. Hosts on the public Internet, however, are by default

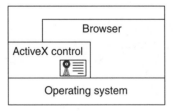

FIGURE 5-7   ActiveX security model

---

5. The details of this particular bug can be found at the Web site http://www.eyeone.no/KillerApp/KillerApp.htm.

6. Emulators may be available that can execute COM objects on non-Windows platforms, but the general rule remains: ActiveX content is for Windows-based clients.

considered untrusted. The user has the ability to identify certain regions of the Internet, using the domain name system (DNS), as secure. For example, I might trust Microsoft and set up my browser to implicitly trust all sites in the domain microsoft.com.

ActiveX controls are packaged in cabinet (.cab) files and digitally signed by the author. The signature, like those for JAR files, are verified by a trusted third party, such as VeriSign or Thawte Consulting, using public key encryption technology. It is very important to understand that code signing verifies only the identity of the author and that the module has not been tampered with. It does not impose any restrictions on its execution or imply that the component is safe for use on the machine.

Plug-Ins and MIME Types

A plug-in is an external program or module that is manually installed by the user to augment the functionality of the browser. Plug-ins were the original way to extend the browser feature set with Netscape's Navigator. Plug-ins are operating system dependent; hence separate versions of a plug-in are required for each operating system.

The most common use of a plug-in is to act as a viewer of special MIME types (Figure 5-8). MIME (Multipurpose Internet Mail Extensions) is a freely available set of specifications that enable e-mail and Web sites to work with media types other than text, such as images, sound, and video. Originally defined for e-mail, MIME extensions have been used widely on the Web. The list of public MIME types is continually increasing. For each MIME type, the client must either natively be able to render the information, as with GIF and JPG files, or have an external viewer installed and configured to render the information.

Plug-ins have the same security issues as do ActiveX controls, since they too are implemented as native executables. The principal security mechanisms for plug-ins are built into the plug-in itself. There is little that the browser can do to restrict a plug-in once it has been loaded and executed.

Depending on the plug-in itself, additional security issues might arise regarding the content it renders. For example, a PostScript viewer may be tricked into changing the password of a printer that has not been assigned one yet. All further requests to print will then be denied until the password can be reset manually. Other MIME types and viewers may have similar security concerns.

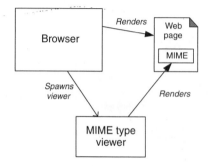

FIGURE 5-8 Plug-in used as a MIME type viewer

Security Strategies

In general, we make our systems more secure by

- Limiting access—through firewalls, passwords, and so on—to the system
- Understanding the system and security requirements
- Keeping up to date on the latest patches and security alerts

Of course, the easiest way to limit access to a system is to disconnect it from any public network, such as the Internet, and to physically secure all of the points where the network meets the real world. This type of security measure might be fine and appropriate for military systems, but for Internet e-commerce systems, it wouldn't do much to help business.

Another option to limit access to intranet-based Web applications is to establish a firewall between the intranet and the Internet. Most companies today maintain a firewall to insulate their internal systems from the external world, since they are relatively easy to install and to maintain. Firewalls, however, are no guarantee that an intruder or a disgruntled employee won't gain access.

Firewalls get their name from the steel wall between the driver's compartment of an automobile and the engine compartment. The idea is that a fire in the engine will have a difficult time spreading to the rest of the automobile. A network firewall is designed to prevent unwanted traffic from going into or out of an internal network (Figure 5-9). Typically, firewalls use a proxy server to monitor ingoing and outgoing traffic. Traffic can be limited a number of ways: by type—HTTP, FTP, or e-mail—by address—www.waste-employee-time.com—or by others.

Perhaps the most important precaution that you can take in protecting your system is to have a realistic password policy. This policy should also include training system users about what the basic security risks are and emphasizing the seriousness of keeping passwords private. All too often, passwords are shared and exchanged over the phone. The password policy must take into consideration the relative security risks and consequences with the personal considerations of the user. For example, requiring 30-character passwords not using dictionary words and updated every 2 weeks is certainly more secure than 8-character passwords left completely to the user's discretion and that never expire. However, 30-character passwords are often difficult to remember, especially for infrequent users of the system.

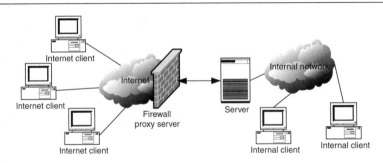

FIGURE 5-9   Firewall operation

Password requirements can be configured to require at least one numeric character, periodic changes, and no reuse of previous passwords.

In addition to complex password requirements, workers today are continually being requested to remember more and more unique passwords for various systems. I personally have to remember passwords for a half of dozen Internet sites, my company network account, my employer's human resources intranet application, and several e-mail accounts. Even though it is insecure to do so, I have little choice but to duplicate passwords or variants across systems just so that I can remember them. This is practical reality, and any password policy needs to consider this.

An additional option available to authenticate a user can be done with personal certificates. As with code signing, individual users of a system can be required to authenticate themselves with a digitally signed certificate. Personal certificates can be obtained from the major CAs for a small fee. Certificates presently are at two levels. At one level, the certificate verifies only that the person claiming to be a specific user name has applied and paid for a certificate. The other, more expensive level verifies that the CA has checked into the identity of the applicant and verified, usually via a government agency, that the person is who he or she claims to be.

Instead of relying on public certificate authorities, large organizations can distribute their own certificates to users of their system. These certificates, however, imply an existing trust relationship between the user and the company acting as its own CA. Distributing your own certificates is a very cost-effective way to authenticate users of intranet systems.

Encryption

Certificates and code signing all rely on digital cryptology. This same technology can be used to help secure the underlying network traffic in a Web application. Since many Web applications use the public Internet to connect clients and servers, it is possible for crackers to monitor and to decode network traffic and, with some effort, to determine access patterns and such confidential information as passwords and credit card numbers.

Client and server network traffic can be made more secure by encrypting it. The push to e-commerce has prompted the emergence of several schemes to protect confidential information over the Net. The two most promising ones are Secure Sockets Layer (SSL) and Secure Electronic Transaction (SET).

SSL was introduced by Netscape and is a low-level encryption scheme used to encrypt higher-level protocols, such as HTTP and FTP. SSL requires that the server present a certificate from a CA to verify its identity and can optionally require that a client present a certificate as well. SSL is implemented on most of today's browsers, and nearly all e-commerce applications use it to provide a measure of security for their users.

SET, a relatively new scheme to process credit card orders over the Internet, is being proposed by Microsoft, Netscape, Visa, and Mastercard. SET uses a complex system of CAs to verify the identities of everyone involved in the transaction: the customer, merchant, card issuer, and the merchant's bank. Unlike other schemes, SET goes to great lengths to protect the identities and information in the transaction from those whose don't need it. For example, the merchant doesn't have access to the type of payment the customer is presenting, only to the item, cost, and payment approval. Also, the card issuer has access only to the purchase price, not to the item purchased. This level of security helps protects the customer from being placed on specialized marketing lists, based on purchasing preferences.

Encryption technology today is based principally on the concept of public/private key pairs. A message is encoded by using a public key, which can be obtained by anyone from a CA or from the person who owns the key pair. Once the message is encoded, the only way to decode it is to use the special private key. Not even the original public key can be used to decode the message, thereby keeping it safe. The only way the message can be decoded is with the matching private key, which the owner should guard jealously (Figure 5-10).

The one disadvantage of public key technology is that the key is usually a long and cryptic code that can't be memorized by an individual. Hence keys are managed by copying and moving key files. So, just like physical keys, there is the possibility that a private key can be stolen or copied; its protection is only as good as the protection of your physical machine. For example, anyone who can gain access to my personal computer will be able to decode encrypted messages sent to me at that machine.

Best Practices

Relying on technology alone is no way to ensure the security of your application. Making a secure application requires continual attention and awareness all throughout the process of developing and maintaining the application. One of the first things that should be done when building a Web application is to create a written security policy. The fact that a policy is written down will help keep everyone involved aware of the issue.

A security policy should include at least the following:

- *Who* is allowed access to the system
- *When* are they allowed access
- *What* they are allowed to do with the system
- *How* new users get added to the system and how they get removed
- *System-monitoring procedures:* types of logs and frequency of review

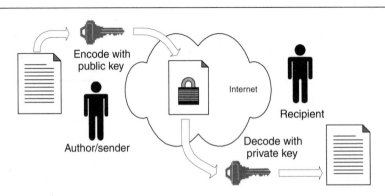

FIGURE 5-10   Public/private key encryption

The security policy needs to be kept simple and easy to read. The policy manual should be read by every member of the development team, as well as the users of the system. The intent is to make all of the issues related to the security of the system better understood.

When configuring a Web application system, it is always a good idea to make the server as lean as possible. This will typically increase execution speed, and mean fewer potential software bugs and security holes because of the unused modules and features installed on the server. For example, if the application doesn't use CGI, turn it off. If directory browsing is not part of the designed application, turn it off.

Proper management of user accounts on a Web application server is also very important. As a general rule, I create a number of accounts or groups for particular roles in the development and maintenance process. The privileges for each account need to be carefully examined to ensure that they are sufficient to complete the user's tasks, and no more than that.

During the development process, it is also useful to create a security view in the architecture model. A security view would contain such elements as users, policies, and authentication. As does any other model in the system, a security model abstracts part of the system into something more easily understood. For a typical e-commerce application, the model will contain entities for customers, account managers, certificate authorities, policies, and so on.

Keeping a system secure goes beyond its design. System administrators need to be ever vigilant and to actively monitor the popular security forums on the Web and Usenet newsgroups. The most up-to-date information regarding known security holes and software bugs can be found on the Internet.

Chapter Summary

- ❏ Every Web system architect, designer, and manager needs to be concerned with security issues.
- ❏ Usenet newsgroups are an excellent source for the discussion of the current security issues of interest to system administrators and maintainers of Web applications.
- ❏ Security risks are present in all parts of a system: client, server, and the network.
- ❏ The most common sources of security holes are improperly configured software or bugs.
- ❏ Passwords are the most common form of protection. Password policies need to be managed so that they are practical for both the system and the user.
- ❏ Virtual private networks and firewalls are one way to limit access to a network.
- ❏ Encryption technology can be used to authenticate users and to encode sensitive network traffic.
- ❏ Significant security issues must be understood when designing applications with dynamic client content.
- ❏ JavaScript, Java applets, ActiveX controls, and plug-ins all represent a certain degree of risk to the client and its information.
- ❏ The use of cookies to store important and private information, such as passwords, poses a significant risk.
- ❏ To manage the risks of security, best practices need to be implemented, including the creation of a security policy document and a security model, or view, of the system.

Part Two
Building Web Applications

Chapter 6
The Process

If you are looking for a cookie cutter recipe to success, forget it. Developing applications is hard work and relies heavily on the skill and ability of everyone involved. This is not to say that a strong process is not important. Heroic efforts on the part of a development team can often bring a project to maturity; however, heroic efforts and strong process can do so repeatedly and reliably.

A single chapter of a book is hardly sufficient to explain any software development process in detail, but it is enough to overview the process and to identify and to explain its key points. This chapter introduces the terms and concepts of a software development process applied to the development of a Web application. This process establishes the context for the remaining chapters of this book.

A software development process has four roles[1]:

- Provide guidance about the order of a team's activities
- Specify what artifacts should be developed
- Direct the tasks of individual developers and the team as a whole
- Offer criteria for monitoring and measuring the project's products and activities

A software development process might be packaged as a set of documents, or it could be an online hypertext system. The process defines the workflows, activities, artifacts, and workers' roles of the development process. A worker in this sense is a role performed by an individual in the process. In many projects, individuals perform the work of several workers.

---

1. Grady Booch, *Object Solutions—Managing the Object-Oriented Project* (Reading, MA: Addison Wesley Longman, 1996).

A workflow is set a of activities that ultimately produce a tangible and observable result. Workflows are such things as requirements gathering, use case modeling, analysis, design, implementation, testing, and deployment. Each workflow typically requires several workers to complete (Figure 6-1).

Workflows define a set of activities that the workers engage in. Activities are what the workers do to produce the output artifacts of the workflow. An artifact is any piece of information that is produced by the workers of the process. Artifacts can be models, model elements, or documents. An important property of an artifact is that it can be version controlled. Artifacts often undergo significant change throughout the process, and an accurate history of their evolution is critical to the process as a whole.

The process discussed here is based on the Rational Unified Process[2] and the ICONIX Unified Process.[3] Both are essentially a refinement of other, earlier, object-oriented processes and methodologies based on the work of Grady Booch, Ivar Jacobson, and Jim Rumbaugh,[4] who are also known as the "three amigos." The two processes are not the only formal processes in use today but rather are the ones that I am most familiar with, ones that I have used successfully (and unsuccessfully) in the past.

Both of these processes as well as others, are iteratively based (see Figure 6-2). This means that each phase—requirements, analysis, design, implementation, test, evaluation— of the process is repeated and refined until it ultimately meets the system's requirements

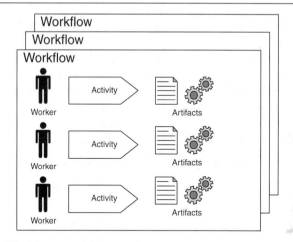

FIGURE 6-1   Workflows, activities, artifacts, and workers

2. An introduction to the process is provided by Philippe Kruchten, *The Rational Unified Process: An Introduction* (Reading, MA: Addison Wesley Longman, 1998).

3. Doug Rosenberg with Kendall Scott, *Use Case Driven Object Modeling with UML: A Practical Approach* (Reading, MA: Addison Wesley Longman, 1999).

4. A more recent view of their collaborative work, and a useful companion to the Rational Unified Process, is Ivar Jacobson, Grady Booch, and Jim Rumbaugh, *The Unified Software Development Process* (Reading, MA: Addison Wesley Longman, 1999).

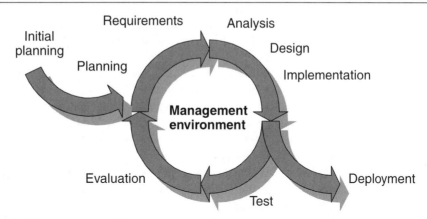

FIGURE 6-2　Iterative process (taken by permission from Philippe Kruchten, *The Rational Unified Process: An Introduction* (Reading, MA: Addison Wesley Longman, 1999, p. 7))

and is deployed. This is a significant departure from the traditional waterfall process, in which each phase of the project was completed before the team moved on to the next. Iterative processes came to be by simply acknowledging the fact that software just isn't created this way. In all but the most exceptional cases, each phase of the project discovered issues and circumstances that questioned, and even changed, decisions made in earlier phases. In the past, it was just dealt with informally. Today, it is acknowledged and even planned for in the process.

There are some differences in the two processes. The Rational Unified Process is

- Use case driven
- Architecture-centric
- Iterative and incremental

It suggests a use case style that is elaborate and encompassing. The ICONIX process strongly encourages the use of formal robustness analysis and advocates a larger number of smaller use cases. The differences between these two methodologies are subtle and for the most part insignificant when compared to the differences encountered when the process is put into use. In the real world, the software process becomes tailored for each and every organization that uses it. The process is even further modified to fit the specific type of application that is being built.

Processes that are taught or are found in a book are basically abstract processes. Implementing a development process is itself a process. It's very unlikely that you can walk into an organization, plop down a book and say, "This is our software development process; read it, and we begin tomorrow." It won't work: not for the obvious reason that a day isn't long enough for reading and digesting a book but for the fact that the process needs to take into account a number of factors not available to the authors. A process must consider the following in order to tailor itself for the task.

- *Makeup of the company and organization.* Large companies with large pools of specialized talent may be more successful with a strict process. In such organizations team members perform one role and a small set of activities that are particularly suited to their talents and experiences. Since the number of people involved is large, the need for formal communications among project team members is important. This means that the artifacts of the process need to be complete and comprehensive. A greater emphasis on the review process might be appropriate, since it is unlikely that team members will be participating in downstream activities and be able to provide explanations for earlier decisions.

  At the other end of the spectrum, small project teams may prefer a more relaxed process. Teams whose members have worked successfully together in the past and whose group dynamics include good communications may not need the rigor of an artifact-laden process. These types of organizational structure rely on the proven abilities of the individual team members. This does not mean that a strong process is not required. It just means that some aspects of the process, such as code reviews and formal meetings, play less of an important role.

- *The nature of the application.* What the application has to do can affect the structure of its development process tremendously. Human-critical applications, such as medical devices, spacecraft systems, and thermonuclear controls, obviously require a great deal of quality control. In these situations, a strong emphasis is placed on quality assurance (QA), which includes reviews and testing. The rhythm of iterations in the process is established by the successful completion of QA objectives over anything else.

  Given the present state of Web application technologies, it is unlikely that a human-critical Web application will be built soon. Still, other factors of the application can influence the process of building Web applications. For example, international applications may require significantly more effort up front during analysis than most others, placing a greater emphasis on the nonfunctional requirements and processes. Commerce applications have architectural and security implications that need to be monitored during the process, with additional reviews and exploratory prototypes. If the application's goal is to make use of a new technology ("We need a Web site to demonstrate our new WizBang™ product line"), defining strict requirements is not as important as allowing the team to take advantage of discoveries along the way.

  Certain process considerations can be applied to Web and e-commerce applications as a whole. Stan Ward of Context Integration and Per Kroll of Rational Software Corporation have done some excellent work in integrating the "creative" input into the software development process.[5] The basic idea is that because of some of the characteristics of e-commerce applications—greater emphasis on

---

5. "Building Web Solutions with the Rational Unified Process: Unifying the Creative Design Process and the Software Engineering Process," A Rational Software and Context Integration white paper: http://www.rational.com/products/rup/prodinfo/whitepapers/dynamic.jtmpl?doc_key=101057.

graphic design and the largely anonymous user base—the process itself can be tailored to incorporate the special activities and workers needed to handle them.

- *The skill level of the development staff.* When implementing a process, the team's skill level should be taken into account. Relatively inexperienced teams require a more defined process, one in which peer reviews are more prominent. For these types of teams, the development process is as much a learning process as anything else.

- *The relative priorities of feature set, time to delivery, acceptable defect count, and so on.* Whatever is important in the final system will obviously determine which elements of the development process are important. If getting the product to market first is the most important goal of the project, QA inspections might be lessened and the ability to change requirements—that is, remove requirements from initial release—be given greater importance. The development process in this situation is tailored for quick delivery. When a rich feature set is important, it is important to ensure compatibility, and this means greater emphasis on analysis.

It cannot be stated strongly enough that the software development process has to work with the people and the goals of the effort if it is ever to be successful. A process is no good if it is not used. Huge monolithic processes that fill volumes of shelf space often go untouched because they didn't consider the people who had to use them. If a process is to be successful, it must be accepted and used by the team.

The Model

Communication is a fundamental part of the process. One role of the system's model is to serve as a communication mechanism. The model is an abstract representation of the system to be built, the system being built, and the system that was built. The model therefore evolves with the system and is a major part of every phase of the project.

The model is a collection of artifacts, each one expressing a view of the system. The model is used by nearly every member of the team: from the stakeholders whose jobs will depend on the system to the implementers responsible for coding its components. Each worker in the development process uses or contributes to the model differently (see Figure 6-3). Communication is facilitated by everyone's using and contributing to the same model. Even though different workers have different views of the system, it is one model and one system that are being developed.

As systems become increasingly complex, they extend beyond the ability of any one individual to comprehend. Constructing an abstract model of the system helps manage this complexity. The model is used to answer questions about the system. A good model will be able to tell which components are associated with which use cases and in what capacities. The model can also help to predict the relative impact that change requests might make to the system.

Another key feature that the model supports is traceability, the ability to start with one element of the model and trace its collaborations and connections to other parts of the model.

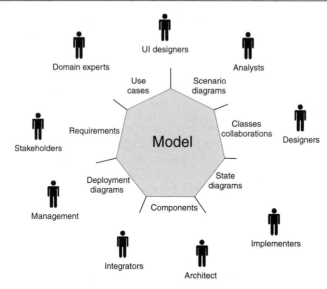

FIGURE 6-3   The model as a central artifact of the process

For example, use cases in the model are associated with use case realizations and sequence (scenario) diagrams, which in turn are associated with the key classes and collaborations that realize the scenario. The classes are traced to the components that implement them. The components deployed in the system can be captured in the deployment diagrams. The use cases also form the basis for the automated test scripts. Defects can be traced to the classes and components that participate in the scenario and be further correlated with the deployment schedule to help determine when the defect was introduced. Traceability enables project managers to navigate the model to help find answers and solutions to problems encountered during the development process.

Workflows

The basic workflows of the software development process are project management, requirements, analysis, design, implementation, test, deployment, configuration, and change management.

Project Management

The project management workflow is responsible for the overall management of the application and includes the typical responsibilities of managing people and budgets, as well as acting as the external spokesperson for the project. The project management workflow also contributes to the project's artifacts through

- Project planning
- Iteration planning
- Risk management
- Progress monitoring

The principal worker for the project management workflow is the project manager, who is responsible for ensuring that the process is being executed properly. The project manager is directly responsible for several key artifacts of the project:

- Configuration and change management plan
- Project glossary
- Vision and business case
- Project plan
- Iteration plans
- Iteration evaluations

The configuration and change management plan (C/CMP) is the detail plan of how change is managed in the process. For an iterative and incremental software process, change management is critical. This plan describes how change requests are made and handled and defines the configuration management tools and processes, which include artifact version control, reporting, and metric gathering. A solid C/CMP enables project managers to establish traceability and accountability throughout the entire project. When changes and decisions are made, they are recorded and tracked. This information is used by the project manager to help gauge risk. If an area of a project undergoes frequent changes, especially ones that waffle, it is a sign that there is some serious risk ahead and prompts some risk management activities on the part of the project manager. Configuration and change management is so important to an iterative project that is a workflow itself. On large projects, it even has a dedicated team perform it.

Another important part of the process is the early involvement with QA. QA is not a team or worker but rather a role that every member of the team plays. QA is continual self- and peer evaluation of the artifacts in the process. One consequence of this is that nothing should be planned or completed unless it can be verified and validated.

The results of each iteration are monitored and evaluated. The testing team contributes to the evaluation by providing a detailed report of the executable release, but the project manager also needs to evaluate the artifacts against the iteration and project plans. Project metrics, such as billable hours, resource usage, and technical discoveries, need to be evaluated with respect to the iteration plan. The project manager assesses the iteration and makes adjustments to the next increment's plan and to the project plan. Depending on the results, timetables may need adjusting, or features might need to be dropped.

What usually starts off a project is the vision statement. This document, which can be completed by the project manager or by a system analyst, describes in very broad terms the goal of the project. The vision statement contains the very high-level (and often non-technical) requirements of the system and is meant to give the reader a sense of what the system is all about. The vision document, read and used by nearly every member of the team, is the basis for producing the business case, an economic assessment of realizing the vision.

Vision statements are often used to obtain funding. For this reason, they often exaggerate what the system will do. This is bad, since these claims can threaten the success of the project as a whole. (Believe me; I've been there.) When writing vision statements, the project manager should make sure that the vision is realistic, not futuristic.

It is vital that a clear and understandable statement of the overall purpose and plan for the project be made. It must never be open ended. Visions that include such statements as; ". . . to utilize the latest technologies in establishing a competitive position" are a recipe for disaster. Perhaps the most important piece of the vision statement is the definition of success criteria. Concrete examples, such as ". . . a gain of 15 percent of the marketplace" or ". . . a 50 percent reduction in the processing of paper forms" are very tangible success criteria and make for a clearer vision statement.

It's a fact of human nature that everyone has an agenda. At this early stage, it should be made clear what the goals and expectations of all the stakeholders are. When constructing the vision, be careful about specifying the technology before the requirements are sufficiently understood. Too often, a VP reading a magazine article will come up with a great idea to use a particular piece of technology for its own sake.

The project glossary, which starts with the vision statement, is continually updated and refined throughout the project and can often be very contentious. Never underestimate the value of a good glossary of terms in a project. The glossary should be easily accessible by all. Establishing a project team's own internal Web site is an excellent way to manage an evolving glossary.

There is only one project plan per project, yet it, like most of the other artifacts of the process, evolves and refines itself. The project plan contains the major and minor milestones: the start and delivery dates. The plan contains a first guess at the iterations and their dates and goals. It is a broad and sweeping view of the entire lifecycle of the project. The early parts of the plan should be relatively accurate. Further down the plan, however, they are mostly educated guesses. These need to be refined with each iteration. The idea is that by continually refining the plan, you will always have relatively accurate assessment of the next milestone.

Iteration planning is a key artifact. Iteration plans are the individual plans of each iteration and include sufficient detail to direct all of the other workflows and activities of the process. Iteration planning includes the staffing and goals of each team, as well as the artifacts that are expected to be completed and when. At any given time, there are always "two" iteration plans: the active one and the next iteration's plan. The active one, the current iteration that the team is working on, is referenced by team members and measured by the project manager. The next iteration plan is modified and improved with the information gained from evaluating the results of the present and any previous iterations. The goal is to continually refine and refocus the direction of progress toward the ultimate satisfaction of the requirements.

Requirements Gathering

A requirement is a statement of what the system should do. The collection of all of the requirements of the system is the requirements specification. Anyone who has ever written software for someone else knows that defining a system's requirements is not easy. The mental pictures that everyone has about the proposed system are often very different from one another early on. Even from a common vision statement, various users and system stakeholders will view it differently. Most importantly, the developers of the system itself might view it differently.

The overall goal of requirements is to unambiguously express what the proposed system should do: not how to do it; just what it should do. The "hows" are answered by the analysis and design workflows. A key component of expressing requirements in a way that all concerned can understand them is use cases. A somewhat formal mechanism, use cases express usage scenarios of the system in the language of the domain. The requirements-gathering workflow and use cases are discussed in detail in Chapter 8.

Analysis

Analysis is often mentioned in the same breath as design, yet I prefer to separate the two workflows conceptually. Often, the same individuals contribute to these workflows, yet the activities and motivations are distinctly different. Analysis is the process of examining the requirements and making a conceptual model of system to be built. The analysis artifacts include detailed classes and collaborations, sequence diagrams, state diagrams, and activity diagrams. These are the same artifacts used and elaborated during design; however, the main difference is that the architecture is not applied yet. The artifacts of analysis represent the system abstracted from the architecture. Analysis artifacts can often be discussed with domain experts and educated users of the system, whereas once the architecture is applied in design, these artifacts often become too technical for the casual domain expert. A more detailed look at analysis is found later in Chapter 9.

Design

The design workflow takes the artifacts produced during design and applies the architecture to them. The principal goal of design is to make the analysis model of the system realizable in software. It is the first time that the realities of software are introduced to the abstract business concepts. In some situations, the application of an architecture affects the model so much that two conceptually separate models of the system are maintained: the analysis model and the design model. These two models are just different views of the same system. When separate models are maintained, even more responsibility is placed on the configuration and change management workflows to ensure that these two models remain consistent with each other. Web application design is discussed in detail in Chapter 10.

Implementation

The implementation of a software system is more than just writing and compiling the code, although that is a large part of the workflow. Implementation takes the artifacts of design and applies software development tools to them. The tools are typically editors and compilers. CASE tools can provide some automation to map model elements into code elements; however, the level of CASE tool technology limits this to mostly structural elements, leaving the implementation of the dynamics of the application completely up to the implementer.

Web applications often involve a number of technologies that need to be managed. The programming languages and skills for client-side development are principally HTML, JavaScript, Java, ActiveX, and, possibly, some distributed object technologies. The languages and technologies on the server have a greater range and involve typical third-generation and object programming languages (C/C++, Java, Smalltalk, Ada, Eiffel), as well as component technologies, such as JavaBeans and COM. The server side also deals with the traditional database and transaction-processing monitor (TPM) technologies. On the server, a Web application is pretty much just like any other client/server system. Details on the mapping of UML model elements into Web application–specific code are covered in detail in Chapter 11, Implementation.

Test

The test workflow focuses on the evaluation of the executable artifacts of the system. Test is separate from quality assurance (QA), since QA affects every part of the system, whereas testing is done only to the executable (or nearly executable) parts of the system. The RUP doesn't even define a QA worker, since it is expected that everyone in the process is involved with QA activities as part of the normal workflow.

Many different tests of the system are made. Each test tries to determine one quality of the system. A performance test accesses the system's ability to function quickly and under heavy loads. Load testing specifically stresses the system and establishes the breaking point of the system or just the performance curves under load. Functional tests determine whether specific functions, as defined in the requirements specification, have been implemented properly. Functional tests often are derived directly from use case specifications.

In addition to testing for specific qualities of the system, there are tests for certain stages of the system.

- *Unit test:* the test that the implementers perform on small system units they have developed. Often, these tests are made on a singular component or small collaboration of components. Each implementer is responsible for unit testing his or her own work.

- *Integration test:* the test that validates the individual component interfaces and their ability to work with one another. Such tests are made when certain parts of the system are connected together but before the entire system is assembled.

- *System test:* the test to verify that all the requirements have been satisfied. This test is conducted when all components of the system are assembled, to validate the system as a whole.

- *Acceptance test:* a formal test that the user community performs on the system. If the system passes this test, the user community accepts the system and is ready for it to be deployed.

In addition to testing at various stages, regression testing is very important in an iterative development process. Regression testing is the retesting of a system that has potentially changed. Even though traceability in the model makes it easier to determine which use cases are affected with which code changes, there is always the possibility that a change to one part of the system will affect another, seemingly unrelated, one. Regression testing helps mitigate this risk by continually re-applying the same tests to the system. If a discrepancy is found, it might be an indication of an unknown connection in the model and needs to be explored.

Testing Web applications is pretty much carried out in the same manner as for other systems. Often, the test team regards the system as a black box: What is inside is unimportant; how the box behaves, however is important. Depending on the nature of the Web application, testing may need to be carried out on a number of client platforms and browser configurations. Internet applications need to consider all of the various browsers that might be used, even the platforms they run on. This fact alone is enough to limit the design of most Internet applications to just the bare essentials.

Deployment

Deploying a Web application can be either real easy or very complicated. The simple intranet application that runs on one server and leverages an existing network can be very easy to deploy. Only the server needs to be set up. Clients probably already have suitable browsers. If the application is designed to use only the most basic client capabilities there is nothing more to do.

But if the application is to deal with security issues and heavy loads on the Internet, a significant amount of deployment planning is required. The handling of failover issues and load balancing as defined by the architecture often involve the use of a number of third-party and off-the-shelf components that need to be integrated. Internet applications also need careful planning of network resources and feeds. Most large Internet applications have redundant Internet connections and off-site backup systems. Deployment in these types of applications requires careful planning and management.

Configuration and Change Management

Configuration and change management is a workflow unto itself because it plays such a vital role in an iterative process. The workflow manages change so that it can be introduced and monitored in a controlled way. The ability to incorporate changes into the ongoing process is the very heart of an iterative process. Each change is a small adjustment in the overall direction in which the project is heading. A sailing ship is more likely to get to its destination by continually adjusting for the elements than is a ship with a fixed rudder, regardless of how much planning went into the ship's launch.

Monitoring change gives the project manager information necessary to assess the quality of any section of the project. Areas that experience frequent and unexpected change are indications of high-risk areas and probable lack of up-front analysis. Configuration and change management is one way in which risk is managed by the process.

Risk

One of the important goals of this process is to address risk early. Risk is the unknown; it is the proposed application's areas that rely on new, unproven technology or areas in which the development team is unfamiliar. Early in the process, the project manager, architect, and key members of the team review the current set of requirement artifacts, which include the use cases, and look for signs of risk.

Instead of letting risk pop up uncontrolled, the process actively seeks out risky areas of the system and implements them first. The mechanism for this is to let use cases drive the process. Use cases are a resource for nearly every activity in the process. Every worker typically reviews the use cases to validate decisions made during work activities. The use case–driven approach helps manage and attack risk by providing the focus for development.

Use cases or sets of use cases that are determined to contain the most risk are targeted for early development. One by one, these use cases are elaborated and implemented. As they are, they contribute to the incremental delivery of the system (see Figure 6-4). Since they are delivered as an executable—or at the very least, as a set of semifunctional Web pages—they can be evaluated by the testing team. The testing team uses the iteration plan and the current state of the use cases and requirements to prepare test plans and scripts to evaluate each iteration delivery. The project manager assesses the results and uses them to make adjustments to development schedules or to reassess the minimal set of requirements needed to make the project a success. Behind all of this is a conscious QA effort.

A project manager experienced in this type of development process will realize that the first few use cases will typically take the longest to develop, as they are often the learning

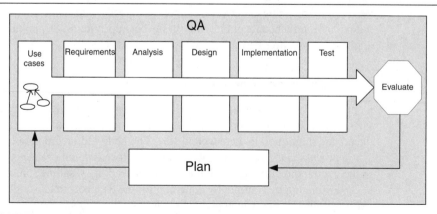

FIGURE 6-4   Driving the process with use cases

mechanism for the team's junior members. Once the first few iterations are complete, the project's rhythm is established. Establishing a rhythm is crucial. The project's rhythm is a periodic delivery of incremental pieces of the system and also the periodic project activities that contribute to the creation of the system's artifacts, including the weekly status meetings, the daily "stand-ups," the nightly builds, the morning's testing reports, and any other periodic team activity. The rhythm is important because inevitably, something will go wrong. A date will slip or a technology will falter, and the natural reaction of an unseasoned team is to panic. With an established project rhythm, enough inertia will be built up to make it more difficult to toss away the process while concentrating on fixing the "big" problem.

Nearly every organization starts off with a process. The real test of a successful process-oriented organization is the continued use of the process even in the face of slipping schedules. I've seen it too many times. The organization starts off right by defining a process (or at least accepting one) and for the most part follows it. Technical problems pop up, requirements get changed, and eventually the schedule starts slipping. The natural reaction of the team, still unsure about the process, is to temporarily drop it and concentrate on coding, the hope being that a last-minute Herculean effort will bring the project back on schedule. What usually happens is that the team makes that one milestone on time but is left with a model and a set of project artifacts in such disarray that they are virtually unusable and out of date and unable to help meet the next impending milestone. The cycle repeats, and the project continues to slip.

Ironically, such situations require an even stronger commitment to the process. In an incremental process, slippage is considered an artifact of the process. Slippage is captured as an important metric that is used to help guide future iteration plans. Slipping schedules and significant defects rates are key metrics monitored by the process. They help guide the planning of iterations.

Iteration

Planning iterations is key to the process. Iterations don't just happen; they are planned in advance. After determining the areas of risk that need to be addressed, the project manager, architect, and key members of the team first develop an initial iteration plan. This plan details the short-term goals of each member of the team and establishes artifact deliverable dates.

The first iteration is, for the most part, the definition of the vision. The vision statement and the business case are the principal artifacts of the initial iteration. The first iteration may also involve putting into place the C/CMP procedures and establishing the environment. The first iteration could also include preliminary use case modeling, or defining the top-level use case packages. In some situations, the choice of a Web application architecture is obvious—for example, a live cut roses company wishing to sell on the Internet is obviously going to build some kind of Web-based e-commerce system. The architect will be examining possible architectural strategies for the system and, possibly, some prototypes.

The iteration is complete when the vision and the business case are completed, the project plan and glossary have been started, and the next iteration's plan has been completed. Each iteration's milestones represent a new executable version of the system. In the first iteration, however, the only executable would be the prototypes.

In subsequent iterations, the results of the previous iteration are examined and used to refine the project and iteration plans. The process's executable artifacts, including storyboards and scenarios, are tested. Delivery dates and staffing resources are assigned. Incrementally, the system is being built.

For example, consider a hypothetical live cut rose company: Roses Alive! Senior management has decided to start selling roses over the Internet. A project manager is assigned, and management makes an initial commitment for the project. The project manager produces an initial project plan. The outline of the project plan is given in Appendix D. (The real project plan is much too detailed to be shown here.) The goal of this outline is not to provide a detailed map of every activity to come but to provide the team with an idea of what to expect and when. The outline attempts to establish the project's rhythm, something very important to do early on. This plan is, of course, an initial one and is evaluated and updated at every iteration milestone. The 2-week period for iterations is arbitrary; however, I have found that 2 weeks is a good and fast pace for relatively small projects like this.

The first-generation Web applications have, for the most part, been created in the absence of any real process. They were the products of small teams (even teams of one) and had a limited scope of functionality. It was possible, and some would say even practical or optimized, to create these early projects without a strong process. Current Web applications, however, are becoming more complex and inserting themselves into more mission-critical roles. All this means that the development teams are becoming larger and team members' skills specialized. Developing these types of applications without a strong and understood process would be foolish.

Chapter Summary

❑ Developing applications is hard work. A strong process helps bring a project to maturity repeatedly and reliably.

❑ A software development process has four roles:

- To provide guidance to the order of the team's activities
- To define the artifacts of the process
- To direct the tasks of the teams
- To offer criteria for monitoring and measuring the project's progress

❑ The process described here is iterative, is use case driven, and relies on a strong architectural foundation.

❑ Iterations don't just happen; they are planned in advance.

❑ An important goal of the iterative process is to address risk early. Use cases representing potential risk are targeted for early elaboration.

❑ Establishing a rhythm helps build project inertia.

❑ Every process needs to be tailored for the specific application and organization that uses it.

❑ The software development process has to work with the people and the goals of the project if it is ever to be successful.

❑ QA needs to be involved early. Nothing should be planned or completed unless QA can verify and validate.

❑ The model is an abstract representation of the system to be built, the system being built, and the system that was built.

❑ The model serves as a communication mechanism for the project team.

❑ The model supports traceability throughout its elements and artifacts.

Chapter 7
Defining the Architecture

As the requirements team gathers the requirements and builds the use case model, the architect or architecture team is examining the use case model and exploring possible system architectures. The architect is responsible for defining a software architecture that is capable of meeting the requirements and realizing the use cases.

The term architecture itself may have various meanings. In the context of this book, I define the architecture as the highest-level views of the architecturally significant components in the system. A component in this sense is a self-contained entity with a public interface. Architecturally significant components are those appearing in the highest-level views of the system. Those components or collection of components typically can't be grouped or packaged with other, similar components. The nature of the specific components will, of course, depend on the specific view.

The idea of using sets of different views to express an architecture was put forward by Philippe Kruchten in a paper entitled "The 4+1 View Model of Architecture."[1] The four views of the architecture are logical view, implementation view, process view, and deployment view. The one view that ties them all together is the use case view; it binds the other views of the architecture to the original reason for system in the first place. If a component in any of the views can't point to a component in the use case view, its existence in the architecture should be questioned.

The four views mentioned in the original article are not the only views allowed. Other views can be included to express the architecture. In an Internet commerce application, for example, a security view should be included. As a huge public network, any Internet monetary or

---

1. Philippe Kruchten, "The 4+1 View Model of Architecture," *IEEE Software* 12 (6), November 1995, pp. 42–50.

identity transactions should be secure. The security view of such an application would contain such components as SSL, SET, certificates, and certificate authorities.

Examining the Use Cases

One of the activities of the architecture team is to examine the use case model from a technical viewpoint. The use case model, as a view of the desired system's dynamic behavior, is prioritized according to perceived risk. The process is to address the use cases with the most risk early and thus prevent unwanted "gotchas" later. A risky use case might involve the use of a technology or require a high degree of performance. Take, for example, an Internet-based commerce application. The use case writers might describe the collection of customer information in the following way:

> The system then prompts the customer for name and address information. The customer enters in his or her first and last name, then tabs to the address section of the screen. The customer enters in a street address. The customer may enter in a city and state or go directly to the zip code field and enter in a five-digit zip code. When the customer enters in a zip code, the system automatically fills in the city and state fields (if not already filled in).
>
> When the address is completed, the customer clicks the Next button to move on to the next step in the order process.

Aside from the obvious implications that this Internet application is limited to U.S. addresses, this use case fragment describes some particularly risky dynamic behavior. Reviewing the use case means partitioning the behaviors into one of the system's tiers: client, server, or other tier. But since this is an Internet commerce application, we can make the assumption that no special software is loaded on the client and that, for the most part, the activities described in this use case are happening in an HTML form on the client. The use case specifies that the customer can enter in a zip code and have the system identify the correct city and state. If this is all happening on the client, it implies that the mapping of zip codes to cities and states must reside there as well. This is a problem because this mapping is not only continually changing but also huge, about 100,000 records! This amount of information would take minutes just to get to the client over normal Internet connections.

Since the use of client-side scripts is not a possible solution, the determined architect might consider the use of a Java applet or ActiveX control that could asynchronously communicate with a server to get the city and state for a zip code and then update the HTML form fields. A small server process would manage the zip code information and provide the simple service of mapping zip codes to cities and states. But even this solution presents a certain amount of risk, because a new technology is being incorporated. Additionally, if the requirements state that this application should work on a broad range of browsers, some of which might not have ActiveX or Java capabilities, it too is not a possible solution. In this particular situation, the architect should reaffirm the priority of this feature; it's most likely that this is not a critical requirement, and a small rewrite to the use case is perhaps the least risky solution.

Arch decision

There are other situations in which the experienced architect might detect risk in the use case yet be constrained to keep and overcome it in the application. For example, an account management application might allow users to open and view several accounts simultaneously in different browser windows. Depending on the details of the architecture or proposed architecture, this may cause difficulties in the management of the client state by the server.

Web application development environments, such as Microsoft's Active Server Pages, use cookies to help manage client state. Cookies are key/value pairs that are to be placed in a browser when it first contacts the Web server. Cookies can persist beyond the single servicing of a browser's page request and offer a convenient mechanism for tackling the client state problem. The cookie usually contains a value that can be used as an index into a dictionary of objects and values: the client state. The architectural risk is that in some instances, a new browser window will inherit the originating window's cookie. This creates an instance in which two simultaneously open browser windows are sharing the same client state on the server.

The disaster scenario might take the form of an account manager opening up a customer's profile, ready to make a slight change in it. The manager remembers that another customer has similar values and proceeds to open up another, and simultaneous, browser window. This second window inherits the first's cookie and hence client state. As far as the server is concerned, the singular browser instance just switched to a new customer profile. The manager views the second customer's information and then switches to the first browser window, makes some changes, and submits them to the server. If the client state contained the primary key to the customer, the server might update the second customer's record with the first customer's data.

These specific scenarios don't represent limitations on the technologies; there are ways around the problems of both. At this stage of the process, it is important to simply recognize that the seemingly innocent use cases as applied to certain architectures may represent a risky aspect of the application. Therefore, they need to be addressed earlier rather than later.

Web Application Architecture Patterns

After a careful analysis of the requirements and use cases, the architect proposes an architecture in the form of a software architecture document, which expresses the architecture as through a set of views. Since this book is dedicated to Web application development, all discussions of architecture assume that a Web application architecture will best meet the needs of the project.

Web application architectures are diverse. It's no wonder, given the sheer number of Internet-related products and technologies on the market today. When the Internet finally registered on corporate radar screens, there was a mad rush to be part of this phenomenon. Everything on the shelf was either modified or marketed for the Web and the Internet. As a result, we have is a wide array of products and technologies that can be part of the architecture of a Web application, with some a natural fit and others not so.

Web applications grew out of Web sites. Basically, a Web application extends a Web site by enabling its user to invoke business logic and subsequently to change the state of the business on the server. This definition of a Web application implies that, at a minimum, there are three significant architectural components to a Web application: the client browser, the Web server, and the application server. It is also most likely that the Web application will also use a database server.

To be more specific, we define a Web application as a client/server software system that has, at a minimum, the following architecturally significant components: (1) an HTML/XML browser on one or more clients communicating with a Web server via HTTP, and (2) an application server that manages business logic. This stricter definition does not mean that a Web application cannot use distributed objects or Java applets; nor does it imply that the Web server and application server can't be located on the same machine. These commonly used technologies enhance the basic Web application architecture.

At a very high level, we can identify several Web application architectural patterns that exist today. An architectural pattern expresses a fundamental structural organization schema for software systems. It provides a set of predefined subsystems, specifies their responsibilities, and includes rules and guidelines for organizing the relationships among them.[2]

The three most common patterns are as follows:

1. *Thin Web Client,* used mostly for Internet-based applications, in which there is little control of the client's configuration. The client requires only a standard, forms-capable Web browser. All of the business logic is executed on the server.

2. *Thick Web Client,* meaning that an architecturally significant amount of business logic is executed on the client machine. Typically, the client uses dynamic HTML, Java applets, or ActiveX controls to execute business logic. Communication with the server is still done via HTTP.

3. *Web Delivery,* whereby, in addition to use of HTTP for client and server communication, other protocols, such as IIOP and DCOM, may be used to support a distributed object system. The Web browser acts principally as a delivery and container device for a distributed object system.

This list cannot be considered complete, especially in an industry in which technological revolutions seem to happen annually. This list does represent, at a high level, the most common architectural patterns of Web applications. As with any pattern, it is conceivable to apply several to a single architecture. For example, an Internet-based e-commerce system may use the Thin Web Client pattern for its consumer sales use cases but use the Thick Web Client or the Web Delivery pattern for the back-office maintenance use cases. This is likely, since there is a degree of control of the client's configuration when you own the client but not so when you are soliciting business from Internet users all over the world.

The remainder of this chapter explains in more detail each of the architectural patterns that can be applied to a Web application.

---

2. See Frank Buschmann, Regine Meunier, Hans Rohnert, and Peter Sommerlad, *Pattern Oriented Software Architecture: A System of Patterns* (New York: Wiley, 1996).

Thin Web Client

The Thin Web Client architectural pattern is useful for Internet-based applications, for which only the most minimal client configuration can be guaranteed. All business logic is executed on the server during the fulfillment of page requests for the client browser.

Applicability

This pattern is most appropriate for Internet-based Web applications or for those environments in which the client has minimal computing power or no control over its configuration.

Known Uses

Most e-commerce Internet applications use this pattern, as it doesn't make good business sense to eliminate any sector of customers just because they do not have sufficient client capabilities. A typical e-commerce application tries to reach the largest customer pool possible; after all, a Commodore Amiga user's money is just as good as a Windows NT user's.

Structure

The major components of the Thin Web Client architecture pattern exist on the server. In many ways, this architecture represents the minimal Web application architecture. The major components are as follows:

- *Client browser:* Any standard forms-capable HTML browser. The browser acts as a generalized user interface device. When used in a Thin Web Client architecture, the only other service it provides is the ability to accept and to return cookies. The application user uses the browser to request Web pages: either HTML or server. The returned page contains a fully formatted user interface—text and input controls—which is rendered by the browser on the client display. All user interactions with the system are through the browser.

- *Web server:* The principal access point for all client browsers. Client browsers in the Thin Web Client architecture access the system only through the Web server, which accepts requests for Web pages—either static HTML or server pages. Depending on the request, the Web server may initiate some server-side processing. If the page request is for a server scripted page, CGI, ISAPI, or NSAPI module, the Web server will delegate the processing to the appropriate script interpreter or executable module. In any case, the result is an HTML-formatted page, suitable for rendering by an HTML browser.

- *HTTP connection:* The most common protocol in use between client browsers and Web servers. This architectural element represents a connectionless type of communication between client and server. Each time the client or the server sends information to the other, a new and separate connection is established between the two. A variation of the HTTP connection is a secure HTTP connection via Secure Sockets Layer (SSL). This type of connection encrypts the information being transmitted between client and server, using public/private encryption key technology.

- *HTML page:* A Web page with user interface and content information that does not go through any server-side processing. Typically, these pages contain explanatory text, such as directions or help information, or HTML input forms. When a Web server receives a request for an HTML page, the server simply retrieves the file and sends it without filtering back to the requesting client.

- *Server page:* Web pages that go through some form of server-side processing. Typically, these pages are implemented on the server as scripted pages (Active Server Pages, Java Server Pages, Cold Fusion pages) that get processed by a filter on the application server or by executable modules (ISAPI or NSAPI). These pages potentially have access to all server-side resources, including business logic components, databases, legacy systems, and merchant account systems.

- *Application server:* The primary engine for executing server-side business logic. The application server is responsible for executing the code in the server pages, can be located on the same machine as the Web server, and can even execute in the same process space as the Web server. The application server is logically a separate architectural element, since it is concerned only with the execution of business logic and can use a completely different technology from the Web server.

Figure 7-1 shows a diagram of the logical view for the Thin Web Client architecture.

The minimal Thin Web Client architecture is missing some common optional components, most notably the database, that are typically found in Web applications. Most Web applications use a database to make the business data persistent. In some situations, the database may also be used to store the pages themselves; this use of a database, however, represents a different architectural pattern. Since Web applications can use any number of

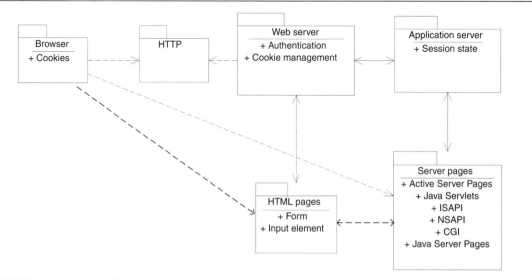

FIGURE 7-1   Minimal Thin Web Client architecture

technologies to make business data persistent, the architectural component is labeled with the more generic term persistence. The persistence component also includes the possible use of a transaction-processing monitor (TPM).

The simplest way to connect a database to the system is to allow the scripts in the server pages direct access to the persistence component. Even this direct access uses standard data access libraries, such as Remote Data Object (RDO), ActiveX Data Objects (ADO), Open Database Connectivity (ODBC), Java Database Connectivity (JDBC), and DBLib to do the dirty work. In this situation, the server pages are knowledgeable of the database schema. *pattern* For relational database systems, they construct and execute the necessary SQL (structured query language) statements to gain access to data in the database. In smaller and less complicated Web applications, this can be sufficient. For larger and more robust systems, however, the use of a full business object layer is preferred.

A business object component encapsulates the business logic. This component is usually compiled and executes on the application server. One of the advantages of having a business object architectural component is that other Web or client server systems can use the same components to invoke the same business logic. For example, an Internet-based storefront may use server pages and the Thin Web Client architectural pattern for all consumer activity; the billing division, however, may require more sophisticated access to the data and business logic and prefer to use a client/server system rather than a Web-based one. The billing division's system can use the same business components on the same application server as the Web front yet use its own, more sophisticated client software.

Since relational databases are the most common type of database in mainstream businesses, an additional architectural component is usually present between the application server and the database. This component provides a mapping service between objects and relational databases. This mapping layer itself can be implemented in a number of ways. Detailed discussions of this component are beyond the scope of this book.[3]

Other options commonly added to this architectural pattern are integration with legacy systems and, for e-commerce applications, a merchant account system. Both are accessed via the business objects or the application server for those systems without a formal business object component. Legacy systems could represent an accounting system or a manufacturing scheduling system. The merchant account system enables an Internet Web application to accept and to process credit card payments. Many merchant account systems are available for small businesses wanting to get into the online market. For larger businesses, this component would most likely be an interface to an existing system capable of processing credit card requests.

With these optional components in place, the logical view of the Thin Web Client architectural pattern becomes more complete. The logical view is shown in Figure 7-2.

Much of a Web application's server components can be found on non-Web-based applications as well. The design and architecture of a Web application's back end is not unlike the design of any mainframe or client/server system. Web applications use databases

---

3. See Scott Ambler, *Building Object Applications That Work* (New York: SIGS Books, 1998) for an excellent object-to-relational-mapping scheme.

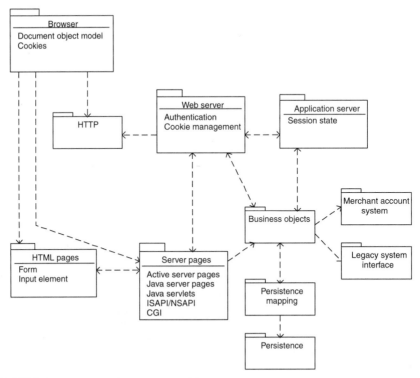

FIGURE 7-2 Thin Web Client Logical View

and transaction processing monitors (TPM) for the same reasons that other systems do. Enterprise JavaBeans and Microsoft's Transaction Server are new tools and technologies that, even though they were introduced with Web applications in mind, are equally suited for use in other application architectures.

The architecture and design of a Web application's server-side components are treated exactly like those of any client server system. Since this architectural pattern focuses on the Web and the components specific to Web applications, a detailed review of possible back-end server architectures is beyond the scope of this pattern.

Dynamics

Underlying the dynamics of this architectural pattern is the principle that business logic gets executed only in response to a Web page request by the client. Clients use the system by using HTTP to request Web pages from the Web server. If the requested page is an HTML file on the Web server's file system, the Web server simply fetches the page and sends it back to the requesting client.

If the page is scripted, that is, one with interpretable code that needs to be processed before it can be returned to the client, the Web server delegates this action to the application server. The application server interprets the scripts in the page and, if directed to, interacts with server-side resources, such as databases, e-mail services, legacy systems, and so on. The scripted code has access, through the application and the Web server, to special information accompanying the page request. This information includes form field values entered by the user and parameters appended to the page request. The ultimate result is a properly formatted HTML page suitable for sending back to the client.

The page may also be an executable module, such as an ISAPI or NSAPI DLL. A DLL, or dynamic link library, is a compiled library that can be loaded and executed at runtime by the application server. The module has access to the same details about the page request (form field values and parameters) that scripted pages have.

The key point of the dynamic behavior of this pattern is that business logic is invoked only during the processing of a page request. Once the page request has been fulfilled, the result is sent back to the requesting client, and the connection between the client and the server is terminated. It is possible for a business process to linger on after the request is fulfilled, but this is not the norm.

Consequences

This type of architecture is best suited to applications whose server responses can be completed within the acceptable response time expected by the user and within the timeout value allowed by the client browser. This is usually on the order of no more than a few seconds. This may not be the most appropriate architecture pattern if the application needs to allow the user to start and monitor a business process that lasts a long time. Push technologies, however, can be used to allow the client to monitor long-running processes. For the most part, push technologies just use periodic polling of the server.

Another major consequence of this architectural pattern is the limited ability for sophisticated user interfaces. Since the browser acts as the entire user interface delivery mechanism, all user interface widgets and controls must be available via the browser. In the most common browsers, and in the HTML specifications, these are limited to a few text entry fields and buttons. On the other hand, it could be argued that such a severely limited user interface is a plus. Sparse user interface offerings prevent the development team from spending effort on "cool" and "neat" interfaces, when more simple ones would suffice.

Thick Web Client

The Thick Web Client architectural pattern extends the Thin Web Client pattern with the use of client-side scripting and custom objects, such as ActiveX controls and Java applets. The Thick Web Client pattern gets its name from the fact that the client can execute some of the business logic of the system and hence becomes more than just a generalized user interface container.

Applicability

The Thick Web Client architectural pattern is most appropriate for Web applications in which a certain client configuration and browser version can be assumed, a sophisticated user interface is desired, or a certain amount of the business logic can be executed on the client.

Much of the distinction between the Thin Web Client and Thick Web Client patterns is in the role the browser plays in the execution of the system's business logic.

The two strong motivations for Thick Web Client usage are enhanced user interface capability and client execution of business logic. A sophisticated user interface could be used to view and to modify three-dimensional models or to animate a financial graph. In some instances, the ActiveX control can be used to communicate with client-side monitoring equipment. For example, healthcare equipment that can measure blood pressure, sugar count, and other vital signs could be used by an agency that needs to monitor geographically remote patients on a daily basis and be able to reduce their personal visits to twice a week.

In some situations, business logic can be executed on the client alone. In these situations, all of the data required to carry out the process should be available on the client. The logic may be as simple as validating entered data. Dates can be checked for accuracy or compared with other dates; for example, the birth date should be before the date first admitted to the hospital. Depending on the business rules of the system, some fields may or may not be enabled, depending on the currently entered values.

Known Uses
The most obvious use of client-side scripts, applets, controls, and plug-ins is on the Internet in the form of enhanced user interfaces. JavaScript is often used to change the color or the image of a button or a menu item in HTML pages. Java applets and ActiveX controls are often used to create sophisticated hierarchical tree view controls.

The Shockwave ActiveX control and plug-in is one of the most common user interface components in use on the Internet today. This component enables interactive animations and is used primarily to spice up Internet sites with attractive graphics, as well as to display simulations and to monitor sporting events. Several Internet sites use Microsoft's agent control to accept voice commands and to execute actions in the browser that assist the user navigating the Web site.

Off the Internet, a healthcare software company has developed a Web-based intranet application to manage patient records and billing. The Web-based user interface makes heavy use of client-side scripting to perform data validations and to assist the user in navigation of the site. In addition to scripts, the application uses several ActiveX controls to manage XML content, which is used as the primary encoding scheme for information.

Structure
As in the Thin Web Client pattern, all communication between client and server is done with HTTP. Since HTTP is a "connectionless" type of protocol, most of the time there is no open connection between client and server. Only during page requests does the client send information. This means that client-side scripting, ActiveX controls, and Java applets are limited to interacting only with objects on the client.[4]

The Thick Web Client pattern uses certain browser capabilities, such as ActiveX controls or Java applets, to execute business logic on the client. ActiveX controls are compiled

---

4. Direct communication between client and server-side objects is discussed in the Web Delivery architectural pattern.

binary executables that can be downloaded to the client via HTTP and invoked by the browser. Since ActiveX controls are essentially COM objects, they have full access to client-side resources and can interact with both the browser and the client system. For this reason, ActiveX controls, especially those on the Internet, are typically "authenticated" by a trusted third party.

The most recent versions of common HTML browsers also allow client-side scripting. HTML pages can be embedded with scripts written in JavaScript or VBScript. This scripting capability enables the browser to execute, or rather interpret, code that may be part of the business logic of the system. The term "may be" is used because client scripts commonly contribute to only extraneous aspects of the user interface and are not part of the business logic. In either case, there are potentially architecturally significant elements—scripts—that are embedded inside HTML pages that and need to be expressed as such.

Since the Thick Web Client pattern is really just an extension to the Thin Web Client pattern, most of the architecturally significant elements are the same. But the Thick Web Client pattern does introduce some additional elements, as follows:

- *Client script:* JavaScript or VBScript embedded in HTML-formatted pages. The browser interprets the script. The W3C has defined the HTML and Document Object Model interface that the browser offers to client scripts.

- *XML document:* a document formatted with the Extensible Markup Language (XML). XML documents represent content (data) without user interface formatting.

- *ActiveX control:* a COM object that can be referenced in a client script and "downloaded" to the client, if necessary. Like any COM object, it has full access to client resources. The principal security mechanism for protecting client machines is through authentication and signing. Internet browsers can be configured to not accept or to warn the user when ActiveX controls are about to be downloaded to the client. The authentication and signing mechanisms merely establish the identity of the author of the control through a trusted third party.

- *Java applet:* a self-contained and compiled component that runs in the context of a browser. For security reasons, the applet has limited access to client-side resources. Java applets are used both as sophisticated user interface elements and for parsing XML documents or to encapsulate complicated business logic.

- *JavaBean:* a small single-purpose Java component that implements a certain set of interfaces, enabling it to be easily incorporated into larger, more complex systems. ActiveX is the analog to the JavaBean in Microsoft-centered architectures.

Figure 7-3 shows a diagram of the logical view for the Thick Web Client architecture.

Dynamics

The principal dynamics of the Thick Web Client pattern include those of the Thin Web Client pattern, along with the ability to execute business logic on the client. As with the Thin Web Client pattern, all communication between the client and the server is done during page requests. The business logic, however, can be partially executed on the client with scripts, controls, or applets.

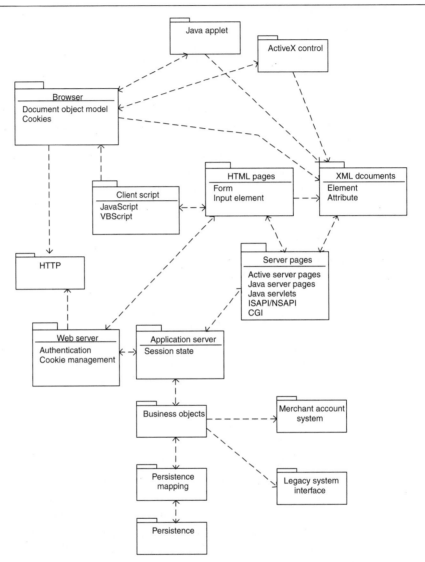

FIGURE 7-3 Logical view of the Thick Web Client architecture pattern

When sent to a client browser, a page may contain scripts, controls, and applets, all of which may be used simply to enhance the user interface or to contribute to the business logic. The simplest business logic uses are field validations. Client scripts can be used to check for valid input not only in a single field but also across all fields in any given Web page. For example, an e-commerce application that allows users to configure their own computer systems may use scripts to prevent incompatible options from being specified.

In order for Java applets and ActiveX controls to be used, they must be specified in the content of the HTML page. These controls and applets can work independently of any scripts in the page or be driven by scripts in the page. Scripts in an HTML page can respond to special events sent by the browser. These events can indicate that the browser has just completed loading the Web page or that the user's mouse just moved over a specific region of the page.

The events have access to the browser's Document Object Model (DOM) interface. This interface is a W3C standard for giving scripts, controls, and applets access to the browser and HTML content in pages. Microsoft's and Netscape's implementation of this model is dynamic HTML (DHTML). DHTML is more than just an implementation of the DOM interface; in particular, DHTML includes events, which at the time of this writing are not part of the DOM Level 1 specification.

At the core of the Document Object Model is a set of interfaces that specifically handle XML documents. XML is a flexible language that enables designers to create their own special-purpose tags. The DOM interface enables client scripts to access XML documents.

The use of XML as a standard mechanism of exchanging information between client and server is enabled by the use of special components on the client. ActiveX controls or Java applets can be placed on the client to independently request and send XML documents. For example, a Java applet embedded in an HTML page could make an HTTP request from the Web server for an XML document. The Web server finds and processes the requested information and sends back not an HTML document but an XML-formatted one. The applet, still running in the HTML page on the client, would accept the XML document, parse it, and interact with the current HTML document in the browser to display its content for the user. The entire sequence happens in the context of a single HTML page in the client browser.

Consequences

By far the biggest consequence of this pattern is portability across browser implementations. Not all HTML browsers support JavaScript or VBScript. Additionally, only Microsoft Windows-based clients can use ActiveX controls. Even when a specific brand of client browser is used exclusively, there are subtle differences in implementations of the Document Object Model.

When client scripting, controls, or applets are used, the testing team needs to perform the full set of test scenarios for each client configuration to be supported. Since critical business logic is being performed on the client it is important that it behave consistently and correctly for all browsers involved. Never assume that all browsers behave the same. Different browsers can behave differently with the same source code, and even the *same* browser running on different operating systems might show anomalous behavior. For instance, we have seen the same browser (Internet Explorer 4.01) behave slightly differently on Windows 95 and Windows NT 4.0.

Web Delivery

The Web Delivery architectural pattern is so named because the Web is used primarily as a delivery mechanism for an otherwise traditional distributed object client/server system.

From one viewpoint, this type of application is a distributed object client/server application that just happens to include a Web server and client browser as significant architectural elements. Whether such a system is a Web application with distributed objects or a distributed object system with Web elements, the ultimate system is the same. The fact that these two viewpoints are of the same system and that distributed object systems have always been seen as systems requiring careful modeling further emphasizes the theme in this book that Web applications need to be modeled and designed like any other software system.

Applicability

The Web Delivery architectural pattern is most appropriate when there is significant control over client and network configurations. This pattern is not particularly suited for Internet-based applications, for which there is no or little control over client configurations, or when network communications are not reliable.

The greatest strength of this architecture is its ability to leverage existing business objects in the context of a Web application. With direct and persistent communications possible between client and server, the limitations of the previous two Web application patterns can be overcome. The client can be leveraged to perform significant business logic to an even greater degree.

This architectural pattern is unlikely to be used in isolation. More realistically, this pattern would be combined with one or both of the previous patterns. The typical system would use one or both of the first architectural patterns for those parts of the system not requiring a sophisticated user interface or where client configurations are not strong enough to support a large client application.

Known Uses

One of the busiest news sites on the Net is the CNN Interactive Web site. Most of its public access is done with conventional browsers and straight HTML 3.2; however, behind the Web site is a sophisticated CORBA-based network of browsers, servers, and distributed objects. A case study of this system was published by *Distributed Computing*.[5]

A healthcare software company has created a Web application to manage patients, health records, and billing. The billing aspects of the system are used only by a significantly small proportion of overall user community. Much of the legacy billing systems were written in FoxPro. The new Web-based system leveraged the old FoxPro legacy code and, through the use of some conversion utilities, built ActiveX documents for the user interface and business logic. The resulting system is a Thick Web Client–based Web application for patient and health records, integrated with a Web Delivery–based Web application for billing operations.

5. Al Issa, "CNN Interactive: CORBA Scales to the Mass Market," *Distributed Computing,* 1 (8), August 1998, pp. 24–30.

Structure

The most significant difference between the Web Delivery and the other Web application architecture patterns is the method of communication between the client and the server. In the other patterns, the primary mechanism was HTTP, a connectionless protocol that severely limits the designer when it comes to interactive activity between the user and the server. The architecturally significant elements in the Web Delivery pattern include all of those specified in the Thin Web Client pattern, as well as these additional ones:

- *DCOM:* Distributed COM is Microsoft's distributed object protocol. It enables objects on one machine to interact with and invoke methods on objects on another machine.

- *IIOP:* Internet Inter-ORB Protocol is OMG's CORBA protocol for interacting with distributed objects across the Internet or any TCP/IP-based network.

- *RMI (JRMP):* Remote Method Invocation is the Java way of interacting with objects on other machines. JRMP (Java Remote Method Protocol) is the native protocol for RMI but not necessarily the only protocol that can be used. RMI can be implemented with CORBA's IIOP.

Figure 7-4 shows a diagram of the Logical View for the Web Delivery Architecture pattern.

Dynamics

The principal dynamic of the Web Delivery architectural pattern is the use of the browser to deliver a distributed object system. The browser is used to contain a user interface and some business objects that communicate, independently of the browser, to objects in the server tier. Communications between client and server objects occur with IIOP, RMI, and DCOM protocols.

The main advantage of using a Web browser in this otherwise distributed object client/server system is that the browser has some built in capabilities to automatically download the needed components from the server. A brand-new computer to the network needs only a compatible Web browser to begin using the application. Special software does not need to be manually installed on the client, since the browser will manage this for the user. Components are delivered and installed on the client as needed. Both Java applets and ActiveX controls can be automatically sent to and cached on the client. When these components are activated as a result of loading the appropriate Web page, they can engage in asynchronous communication with server objects.

Consequences

By far the biggest consequence of this pattern is portability across browser implementations. The use of this pattern requires a solid network. Connections between client and server objects last much longer than do HTTP connections, and so sporadic loss of the server, which is not a problem with the other two architectures, poses a serious problem to be handled in this pattern.

constraint   *

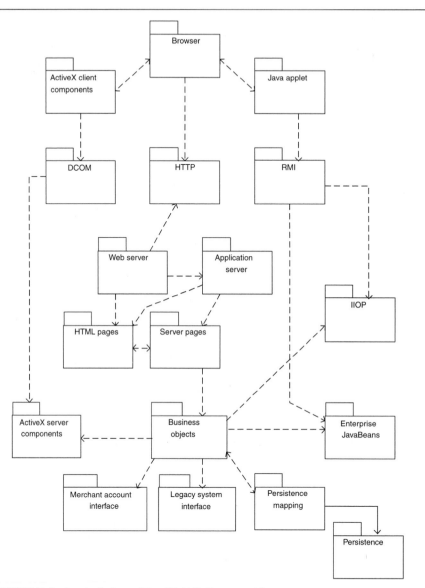

FIGURE 7-4   Logical view of the Web Delivery architecture pattern

Chapter Summary

❑ Software architecture is the highest-level view of the architecturally significant components in the system.

❑ The architecture team examines the use case model from a technical viewpoint and prioritizes each use case according to perceived risk.

❑ The three most common architectural patterns for Web applications are Thin Web Client, Thick Web Client, and Web Delivery.

❑ Thin Web Clients rely on only the most basic browser capabilities. Most of the business logic is executed on the server.

❑ Thick Web Clients allow business to be executed on the client though scripts, applets, or ActiveX controls. A significant amount of business logic is executed on the client.

❑ In a Web Delivery system, the client participates in a distributed object system. In this architecture, the client communicates directly with object servers, bypassing HTTP.

Chapter 8

Requirements and Use Cases

Requirements

A requirements specification, a collection of documents and models, attempts to unambiguously describe a software system to be built. Each document usually includes a description of the document's purpose, version number, contributors, and other administrative information, in addition to a list of specific system requirements. The specification can consist of a single document for small systems or be distributed over multiple documents, each expressing one category of requirement. The requirements specification needs to be made available to nearly everyone connected with the project. An excellent way to do this is to make it available on an intranet via a Web server. If the application is going to be a Web application, the infrastructure for doing this is probably already in place.

A requirement, or constraint that the system must observe, is typically expressed as a statement that begins with a phrase like "The system shall . . . ." The purpose of a requirement statement is to express a behavior or a property that the system should have. More important than the phrasing, however, is its goal: to express the need for one very specific system behavior, in clear and easy-to-understand language. Requirements need to be understood by the development team and validated by the stakeholder and user communities. Making requirements difficult to understand doesn't help anyone.

A feature of a system is like a high-level requirement—a statement—but it tends to have a broader definition. Feature statements are things that find their way into marketing materials and overhead slides. The details of features and those things that can be objectively verified by the testing group are expressed by several requirement statements. One very important quality of a good requirement statement is that it can be verified by the testing team when delivered. If a requirement can't be objectively verified, it doesn't belong in the requirement specification.

In general, requirements can be categorized as functional or nonfunctional. Functional requirements express an action that the system should perform and usually define both the stimulus and the response, or input and output. Functional requirements, the most common type of requirement, identify the things that the system can do, usually in response to external input. Examples of functional requirements are

- "The system should be able to compute international shipping charges for all products available for sale."
- "The system shall automatically produce a summary report of all sales made for each week."

Nonfunctional requirements can be further categorized to make them easier to understand and track.

- *Usability:* Usability requirements refer to those general aspects of the interface between the user and the system. These types of requirements are often related to user interface standards. For example, an obvious usability requirement might be "The system shall adhere to the company user interface standards document." If it is known that the application is to be a Web application, the usability requirements might include the minimal browser configuration that is to be used or which HTML elements are to be used. For example, a Web-related usability requirement might be "The system interface shall not use HTML frames" or "The system shall be accessible by any forms-capable browser that supports the use of the <table> tag."

- *Performance:* Performance requirements describe system execution performance and are usually related to time. A common requirement for Web applications is to specify a maximum load time for a page. For example, "Web pages should not take longer than 15 seconds to load in the browser during normal system usage."

- *Robustness/Reliability:* All mission-critical applications need to clearly state the degree to which the application must be available. Most of these requirements affect only the architecture decisions. It would be nice if we could just say that the system needs to be fully functional $24 \times 7 \times 52$ (24 hours a day, 7 days a week, 52 weeks a year), but building in that level of reliability is going to be costly. What is more likely is a realistic expectation of maximum acceptable down time. It is not unreasonable for most applications to schedule 1 hour a week of down time for maintenance and upgrades. Robustness and reliability are also concerned with backup and storage issues. For example, a system requirement might be something like "The system should enable access to data on weekly backup tapes within a 2-hour window."

- *Security:* Security requirements tend to specify levels of access to the system and often map to human roles of the business. Security requirements should also include access to the system by other "external" systems, if used. A typical security requirement might be stated as "The system will ensure that all confidential information provided by customers via the Internet shall be encrypted with at least SSL version 3 or later."

- *Hardware:* Hardware requirements often state the minimal hardware required to implement the system. For example a sophisticated internal intranet application that uses multimedia, such as video or VRML (Virtual Reality Modeling Language), may require that the system be capable of running on the company's standard client configuration: Pentium 133, 16MB RAM, SVGA $800 \times 600 \times 16$, and so on. As with the reliability and robustness requirements, the hardware requirements are used mostly by the architect and help constrain the architecture.

- *Deployment:* Deployment requirements describe how the application is delivered to the end users. It provides constraints on how the system is to be installed, maintained, and accessed by maintenance staff. A deployment requirement for a Web application may require all client software to be downloaded and installed from the browser and not require the client to reboot or to perform a manual setup.

This list is by no means complete. Depending on the system's purpose, other categories might also be appropriate. With so many categories, it is common for some requirements to naturally fit into more than one. For example, the hardware requirement specifying a minimal 800×600 pixel display is also a usability requirement. It's best to keep requirements in one place and to avoid duplicates in the requirements specification, whenever possible. This makes it easier to maintain, especially if they are subject to change later in the process.

It would be nice if it were possible to unambiguously specify a real system completely. In practice, however, it is most likely that some requirements are missing, overstated, or even wrong. This stems, in part, from an "impedance mismatch" between the problem space (world of the domain) and the solution space (the world of the software system). Whenever you attempt to translate from one language to another, there is always some loss of meaning.

The requirements specification is a contract that binds the stakeholders to accept a system that meets the criteria specified in the requirements documents. This sounds simple, and it can be. However, the realities of software development always lead to downstream changes that affect nearly every aspect of the process and its artifacts. More often than not, the requirements specification is a living artifact that evolves with the rest of the system. This recognition of the fact that requirements can change, even though we would rather they not, is at the heart of an iterative development process.

Now, before you take what has just been said the wrong way, it needs to be stated that we write requirements down, expecting and hoping that they will not change. If the requirements team has done a good job, there should be very little change in the requirements of the system throughout the process. In fact, a very important metric of the process is measured by the amount of change made to the requirements. If the requirements change significantly or waffle throughout the process, it is a sign that the requirements-gathering process is in need of some help.

Gathering Requirements

Requirements gathering is typically done by groups. It is not recommended that only one person define the requirements of particular part of the system, even if that person is the undisputed authority on the subject. Minimally, a requirements team is made up of a representative of the user or stakeholder community and a technical member of the development staff. The requirements are, after all, a contract between these two groups of people, and proper representation by both sides is important. Additional skill sets can complement the team. If the team has been appointed to examine the reporting and data-mining aspects of the system, a database expert should join the team.

The formatting of the document is not of much concern, but the ability to tag or to identify each requirement is important. Each specific requirement of the system should have a unique identifier that is used for traceability. The identifier might be something as simple as the chapter, section and subsection numbers in an outline-formatted document. For example, the following is a simplified fragment of a small system's requirements document.

3. Performance Requirements

This section describes the system's performance requirements. These requirements usually relate to the execution speed and capacity of the individual components of the system.

3.1 Web server performance

The Web server performance section describes the expected performance of the Web server and network of the system.

3.1.1   Each Web server in the system shall be able to handle at least 150 simultaneous user sessions.

3.1.2   The system shall require no more than 3 seconds to retrieve and to respond to a client's request for a static Web page.

3.1.3   The system shall require no more than 8 seconds to respond to a dynamic page.

Note that, in this fragment, descriptive text introduces the sections and subsections. A requirements document should be a self-explanatory document, one that can be given without additional explanation to any member outside of the development team. Each requirement is by default assigned a unique ID. For instance, the requirement "3-second page response" would have an ID of 3.1.2. This ID is part of the traceability of the model. As the process goes on and the system gets designed, each element in the model traces back to at least one requirement. This is a key aspect of the process. Each and every element in the model must be able to point to a requirement item to support its existence.

Take, for example, the zealous object-oriented practitioner who insists that certain areas of the model need to be modeled and implemented more abstractly. Instead of modeling a customer as a class with a set of attributes that include name, e-mail, address, and so on, the analyst might insist on modeling it as an entity whose properties are captured by an aggregation or a qualified association of string objects. The argument for this is that it enables the system to dynamically add attributes to customers in the system without having to redesign. In this way, the system could be able to add a tax ID attribute to customers without having to recode the system. The feature is nice, but unless it states somewhere in the requirements that this feature is *required*, it should not be built.

During design reviews, elements—classes and packages—of the design model are checked to ensure first that they point to at least one requirement and second that they really do capture the spirit of the requirements they point to. A reviewer might look at the abstracted design mentioned earlier and compare it to the requirements that it points to. Those requirements might simply state that the system needs to capture customer demographic information and even explicitly state the information to be captured. The reviewer then must raise the question: "Isn't this overkill?"

It is entirely possible that the designer has realized something that the requirements team has missed. Perhaps the design team's experience in the domain has noted similar situations in the past and has a workable solution. In this situation, discussions between the analysis/design team and the requirements teams need to take place. If it turns out that this feature is desirable and seems as though the additional effort to implement it is minimal, the change control process kicks in. This process ensures that the appropriate people (or departments) are notified and consulted of the pending change. Depending on the scope of the change, this may affect a large number of people, and its impact needs to be examined and scheduled by the project manager. The ability to manage such things is a key aspect of the incremental and iterative development process.

The requirements fragment mentioned earlier contains some pretty specific knowledge about the architecture. For example, it references Web servers and the use of Web pages explicitly. Unless the use of a Web application was stated elsewhere in the requirements, these sets of Web-specific requirements probably evolved from others or were introduced during a later increment. For example, the requirements in the usability section for the first increment might have just mentioned that the user interface response time should be less than 3 seconds.[1] In a later increment, when it was realized that a Web architecture was going to be applied, the requirements were refined to include those items specific to Web applications.

Whenever it is determined that Web applications are involved, you will probably find new sets of requirements appearing, especially in the hardware section. Once the architecture has been tentatively settled on a Web application, refinements and additions can be made to the requirements documents. Remember that artifacts in an incremental and iterative development process change, and we just have to get used to the idea. The key, of course, is expecting, managing, and minimizing those changes.

Guidelines for Writing Good Requirements

When writing a requirement statement, you should keep a few things in mind.

- Each requirement should be clear and concise. Avoid wordy descriptions that can be interpreted in a variety of ways.
- A requirement statement should focus on one point. The finer granularity enables better traceability though the model.

---

1. In a realistic requirements document, this requirement would probably have gone on to say that operations taking longer should provide a visual display to the user that the operation was still active and that this display should change at least every 3 seconds. The use of progress bars is the preferred way to indicate the progress of long operations.

- Every requirement must be verifiable. "The UI must be intuitive" cannot be objectively tested and so is not a verifiable requirement statement.

Prioritization

Before the requirements can be used in any downstream phase of the process, they must first be prioritized. It would be nice if all of the requirements specified in the requirements documents were built into the system exactly as requested, but the realities of software development often force compromises between functionality and time to delivery. By prioritizing a system's requirements, both the stakeholders and the development staff know where it is important to spend valuable effort. Prioritization also helps resolve conflicting requirements. For example, one requirement of the system might specify that the application be functional on client computers with only a monochrome 640 × 480 pixel display. Another requirement might require all invalid field validations to be identified with a red background to the user. Clearly, if the system were used with a monochrome client, invalid fields would never be identified.

The requirements team would probably have made the screen-resolution requirement a relatively high priority, since another goal of the system is to leverage existing computing equipment in the organization. Using red to display invalid field values would probably have a lower priority, since the use of specific colors in a user interface is often problematic. During the requirements review process, these inconsistencies would be noted. Having them prioritized makes it easier to decide how to handle the conflict.

Most systems can prioritize requirements with just a few levels: low, medium, and high are often sufficient. A high-priority requirement would be a "must-have" requirement. The system would not be functional without it. A medium-priority requirement might mean that it is strongly desired but that it could be put off until the second release of the product. A low-priority requirement, of course, might mean that it is desired but optional. The system would be functional without it but would be a better system with it in. Of course, the definition and the number of priority levels varies with each development organization.

Determining the priority structure is nowhere as difficult as determining individual requirement priorities. This particular part of the process is probably one of the most stressful activities of the process, and some words on human nature need to be said. It's a rather powerful feeling that one can get when defining requirements for a system. With seemingly little effort, our ideas can become pseudoreality. We can see it in our heads, and everything is perfect. In a subconscious way, these requirements or features of the system become owned by their creators. When it comes time to prioritize the requirements, their creators tend to rate their requirements high, whereas others think otherwise. The psychological battles ensue.

I can remember one experience of my own. This was my first "real" object-oriented (OO) project. We were gathering the requirements for the customer demographics section of the application. The system was to replace an older DOS and file server–based system. I had suggested that instead of capturing in three separate attributes a customer's street address (Line 1, Line 2, and Line 3), we use a multiline edit box. Multilined addresses would be entered in the same control, by just pressing the Enter key to create a second line. From the system's point of view, it was just a single attribute of the Address object that, optionally, had line feeds in it. It caught on with my fellow requirement team members at the time, and we all agreed that the application might be simpler that way. That was my only unique contribution to the team's efforts, and I was prepared to defend it. Eventually, the team reversed the requirement, and we ended up using three separate street address attributes, due in part to my junior status and in part to other, higher-prioritized requirements for deployment and legacy system compatibility. In retrospect, it was the best outcome for the system, and I learned a little about myself and the politics of requirements.

Even experience alone is not enough to ensure proper prioritization of requirements. In another personal experience, the project manager and chief architect of a Web-based application had defined these two requirements: (1) "All users of the system will exclusively use browsers for system access," and (2) "There will be a common source code repository across all platforms." These were prioritized as the two most important requirements of the entire system, even over every functional and usability requirement! This became a problem only when applied to the off-line component of the system. Part of the system needed to be implemented with laptops and palm top computers that would be temporarily disconnected from the main Web server. Since being a Web application and having a common source code repository were the top two requirements, it meant that a complete Web and server had to be put on the portable devices. It was another case of envisioning the technology before understanding the full scope of the problem. Despite the arguments of nearly every other member of the development team, these two requirements remained a top priority. In the end, the application was never created. The constraints placed on the development team by these two seemingly laudable requirements meant, in the end, the death of the application.

It is important to objectively prioritize every requirement. If necessary, refer back to the original vision statement of the project. Ask how important this requirement is in realizing the original vision of the system. Most requirements of a system are good and should be worked toward; however, there are often tradeoffs to be considered, such as development time, complexity, and compatibility. They need to be weighed with the benefit that the requirement adds to the system. For example, one requirement might improve data entry speed significantly but increase the development time and complexity. Look at the project's vision statement. If it emphasizes or discusses the importance of speeding up the process, it just might be a high-priority requirement. If the vision statement doesn't mention the need for fast data entry, prioritize it lower, and let it become part of the system without endangering other parts.

When dealing with requirements and especially the prioritization of requirements, we need to keep in mind the human factor. A good team will be able to bring these issues out in the open early, when there is still time to accommodate everyone. Improper prioritization of requirements can lead to disastrous results later on. Proper prioritization of requirements can mean the difference between meeting or missing the delivery date.

Use Cases

Writing down simple statements is an excellent way to capture and to prioritize performance, hardware, deployment, and usability requirements but is a little lacking for capturing functional ones. Functional requirements describe how the system behaves in response to user and external system input. They tend to be more dynamic and often require more detail in order to clearly understand them. Use cases are a powerful technique for capturing and expressing detailed system behavior. Use cases were first put forward by Ivar Jacobson.[2] Another excellent resource on use cases is the work of Alistair Cockburn.[3]

Use cases are a formal way to capture and to express the interaction and dialog between system users (called actors) and the system itself. Since a full discussion of use cases is beyond the scope of this book, I will concentrate on the highlights and most interesting points as they relate specifically to Web-based applications.

Jacobson uses the term *actor* to represent a generic role of user. The term *user* is reserved for instances of people using the system. Users may play the part of many actors of the system. An actor's name should represent the type of role it plays with the system. A typical actor of an e-commerce system might be *Online Customer*, someone who uses the system to purchase items by using a browser and the Internet.

A use case, a textual description of the interaction between an actor and the system, contains a narrative description of a specific usage scenario, one in which an actor supplies input and the system exhibits an observable output. A use case may contain more than one scenario; however, there is always one main scenario. The other scenarios are called alternative scenarios, or alternative paths. Appendix B contains an example of a typical use case description for an e-commerce application.

A use case is written to express what a system should do, without constraining how it should do it. A use case describes the behavior of the system as viewed from the outside. All of the behavior is in the form of observable results. Of course, they don't have to be displayed on the user's screen; they could be in the form of a database change or cutting a bank check at the home office. The point is to maintain focus on the input and output behavior of the system and to leave the details of applying the architecture and creating a workable design to the analysts and designers who will use the use case later on.

Each use case is named, and its name reflects its purpose, or goal. It is also helpful to uniquely number use cases for traceability, since even use case names are subject to change. In addition to the required name and scenario description, most use cases capture other key information:

- *Unique ID:* Ideally, an automated number or a numbering system that will enable a use case name to evolve and yet maintain traceability throughout the process. The ID can be an intelligent key with the use case category (package) or other understandable information.

- *Goal statement:* A simple one-line, if possible, statement that summarizes the goal of the entire use case. This goal, like a vision statement, is useful for

---

2. Ivar Jacobson, Magnus Christerson, Patrik Jonsson and Gunnar Övergaard, *Object-Oriented Software Engineering: A Use Case Driven Approach* (Harlow, England: Addison-Wesley, 1992).

3. Alistair Cockburn, "Structuring Use Cases with Goals," *Journal of Object-Oriented Programming,* September-October 1997 and November-December 1997. More references for Cockburn's work can be found on his Web site: http://members.aol.com/acockburn/

referring to as the use case evolves. If actions in the use case don't support the goal, their inclusion in the scenario should be questioned.

- *Authors:* The names of the requirements team members who have directly contributed to the text in the use case. Depending on how cynical you are, it could mean the people to contact when clarification needs to be made or the people to blame when things go wrong.

- *Priority:* The overall priority of the use case. This value will help project managers determine how much effort is justifiable for the use case. A high priority will ensure that the use case is completed early, probably by senior staff. A low-priority use case might be handled by junior staff or completed later in the process.

- *Risk:* A risk assessment that identifies the relative likelihood that something might go wrong during its implementation, or the level of inexperience the development (or business) team has with it. Risky use cases are usually targeted for early completion. The risk, together with the priority assessments, help the project manager schedule and assign the work.

- *Assumptions:* A textual description of things that are assumed, that is, the state of the system. The assumptions do not constrain the system, but are simply things that the use case writers assumed to be true while writing the use case.

- *Preconditions:* A textual description of conditions that must be met before this use case can be performed. Unlike the assumptions, preconditions must be satisfied before the use case can begin.

- *Postconditions:* A textual description of conditions that must be met before this use case can be completed. Postconditions typically refer to a state the system must be in for the use case to end, such as no outstanding error conditions.

- *Outstanding issues:* A collection of items that need to be resolved before the use case can be elaborated in analysis and design. This particular section of a use case should be used only during its construction and should be blank by the time it is used in any downstream process.

- *Requirements satisfied:* A list of requirement identifiers that this particular use case is supposed to satisfy. Usually, the requirements are feature points of the system—"able to compute international shipping charges," "capable of maintaining individualized customer settings"—that don't fit neatly into their own use case, that is, are not easily expressible as an interaction between an actor and the system.

The formatting of the scenario is very flexible, and there is no one right way to do it. Use cases can be very structured, with tightly controlled phrasing and plenty of section headings and enumerations to identify ordering. At the other extreme, use cases can be very relaxed and appear to be more like a story. I have worked with use cases at both extremes, and I can't say that I favor one over the other. The right style of use case is usually related to the type of application being developed and the dynamics of the organization building it.

A use case is written in the language of the domain. Remember, use cases are just a technique to express requirements, and a requirement is a contract between the stakeholders/

users and the development staff. Both parties need to be able to clearly understand what is captured and meant by a use case. Use cases are also used by the technical writers as the basis for a user manual. In a well-managed project, user documentation should be complete about the same time as the software is, since both the software and the user's manual are directly based on the use cases. Some processes even stress that use case descriptions be written in the form of a user's manual. For the testing group, use cases are the basis for the majority of the test scripts. Nearly every member of the development team makes use of the use cases for one reason or another. Use cases are a central artifact of the process and drive all other aspects of the process.

I had one experience in which the initial requirement teams consisted mainly of an analyst/developer, a database-oriented developer, and a domain expert (end user). We constructed a use case model and use case descriptions that were more or less as they were presented in the original text by Jacobson. The style was a compromise between the two extremes, and we all seemed to be happy with how they were formatted.

About a month after we had begun, the testing team had finally been assembled. Its members looked at our use cases—something that every new member of a development team should do—and determined that the use cases needed to be a little more explicit for developing automated test scripts from them. We revised our use case descriptions, and they became progressively structured to the extreme. The phrasing and terminology were so rigid and explicit that when one domain expert was asked whether this use case was what she wanted the system to do, she had to say, "Well, I think so; I'm not sure now, since I really don't understand most of it anymore."

That raised a flag, and we immediately reassessed how structured we wanted our use cases to be. In the end, we had another compromise. We kept the general structure (numbered steps and simple sentences) but dropped a lot of the technical phrases and references to specific user interface elements. In the end, we had use cases the domain experts could read and, with some help from the design artifacts, something the testing team could read and build test scripts around.

A use case often contains multiple scenarios. One of them is always the main scenario, or "happy path." The other scenarios represent alternative paths through the use case. These alternative paths may be exceptions or infrequently used options in the scenario. An exception would be something like the actor deciding to cancel the use case part way through it. An infrequently used option might be the capturing of additional information, required only for international customers. The common theme among all scenarios is the intent of the actor to accomplish the goal statement. Even an actor canceling a use case started it with the intent mentioned in the goal statement. In a use case document, the alternative scenarios are clearly indicated as alternatives, and when appropriate, additional information is supplied to help connect them to the main scenario. The main scenario may similarly refer to the alternative scenarios when appropriate in the narrative.

Use cases can have varying formats and lengths. The Rational Unified Process (RUP) suggests creating use case descriptions that are about 5–10 pages in length.[4] These scenarios

---

4. See Philippe Kruchten, *The Rational Unified Process: An Introduction* (Reading, MA: Addison Wesley Longman, 1998).

tend to be elaborated and formatted more strictly and usually contain multiple sections. The ICONIX Unified Process (IUP), on the other hand, recommends shorter use cases, tending to have more of them in the use case model than the RUP.[5] The one unifying aspect of all use cases, however, is that they contain a descriptive scenario—a dialog between an actor and the system—that is written in the language of the domain. This is what a use case is all about.

The Use Case Model

The typical use case contains a narrative flow of events that constitutes a specific use of the system. A very common use case in client/server systems is the log-on use case. The goal of this particular use cases is to enable an actor to have access to the system. Most Log-on use cases describe the entering of user ID and password information. Once that goal has been completed, the use case ends. Anything else the actor does with the system is detailed by another use case. In order for this to make sense, we need a way to connect two use cases, such that they would represent an even more detailed flow of activity between the system and the actor.

Relationships among use cases are documented in a use case diagram. The complete collection of use cases, actors, and diagrams forms a use case model. Like individual use cases, the use case model is just one part of the system's requirements specification.

In a diagram, a use case is rendered by an oval with the use case name printed in or just below it. An actor is rendered as a stick figure. Figure 8-1 shows a simplified use case model that includes the Log-on use case.

In this diagram, the actor, called Online Customer, represents a role that a user can play with the system. The actor is associated with the Log-on use case. This means that the actor can "invoke" this use case and participate in the scenario described in it.

An additional use case in the diagram, Update Profile, is shown connected to the Log-on use case with an arrow. Next to the arrow is the word "extends" inside a pair of

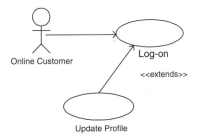

FIGURE 8-1   Simple use case diagram

5. Doug Rosenberg with Kendall Scott, *Use Case Driven Object Modeling with UML* (Reading, MA: Addison Wesley Longman, 1999).

guillements (« »). In the UML notation, this is read as the use case Update Profile *extends* the use case Log-on. Extending the Log-on use case means that the actor participates and follows the scenario described in Log-on but can also move on and participate in the Update Profile use case.

This same scenario can be expressed with another relationship: *includes*. Figure 8-2 shows another use case diagram with the same use cases but with different relationships. This relationship is read in UML as Update Profile *includes*[6] the Log-on use case. This means that the actor that invokes the Update Profile use case may also be invoking the Log-on use case, presumably if the actor has not already logged on. For the most part, these two use case diagrams are equivalent. I have found it useful to stick to one method of associating use cases whenever possible, and either one is sufficient.

The use case model shows the structural relationships among use cases. It does not show dynamic relationships, or workflows. Dynamic behaviors are expressed with interaction diagrams (sequence, collaboration, and activity). It is important to keep that in mind when drawing use case diagrams. It's easy to start constructing use case diagrams as if they were workflow diagrams, since use case names often reflect major activities of the business workflow. Most associations between use cases in a diagram simply imply that one invokes the other.

This simplistic explanation of use case modeling is sure to raise the eyebrows of the seasoned professional. The art of use cases has received an unusual amount of criticism ever since they were introduced. I believe that this is due partly to the fact that when they were introduced, no rigid template or structure was required. Most object-oriented practitioners agree that use cases are generally good things. It's the details that seem to get everyone's blood boiling. The «uses» versus «extends» discussions alone could fill a book. This book, however, is dedicated to building Web applications, and detailed discussion of use case modeling is beyond its scope. All I can do is point out that experienced use case modelers may (and probably should) have strong opinions on the details of the structure of

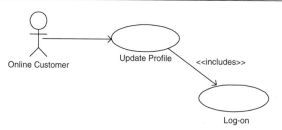

FIGURE 8-2   An equivalent use case diagram

---

6. In Jacobson's original description of use case modeling, this type of relationship was called *uses*. A uses relationship means that one use case makes use of another. For most purposes, the *includes* relationship conveys the same meaning. There may be deeper subtleties involved in the choice of terms, but since this is a book on Web applications and not use case modeling, we'll stick to the simple explanations.

use case modeling. This book just covers the essentials, enough to establish the framework necessary to analyze and to design Web applications.

In the first iteration of the requirements-gathering phase, most of the attention is focused on the overall structure of the use case model. Even the smallest application will have a significant number of use cases, so many that they need to be organized a little further. The idea of breaking a problem into smaller, more easily managed ones is not new. A use case model is often divided into packages, each of which owns a set of use cases or even other packages. A package is a UML mechanism for breaking a model into more manageable pieces. In a diagram, a package is rendered as a tabbed folder. Figure 8-3 shows a set of four folders, three of which are inside a larger one. The Storefront package owns the three other packages. A dashed arrow indicates that the Order Placement package depends on the Catalog Browsing package. This usually means that a use case in the Order Placement package «includes» or «extends» a use case in the Catalog Browsing package.

As the use case definition activity progresses and a top-level use case diagram is completed, the project manager can assign separate packages and use cases to different requirements teams to complete. Careful coordination is needed for those teams with packages and use cases that have relationships with those owned by other teams. In the initial iteration, this is usually accomplished by completing the goal statements of all of the use cases involved and leaving the individual teams to fill in the use cases' details later. The goal statement becomes a temporary contract between the teams. During reviews, of course, every use case owner will look carefully at all of the available details of those use cases that they depend on.

In the early iterations, requirements teams usually own packages and not individual use cases, since many of the system's use cases have not even been defined yet. Each team treats the package as its own isolated system. The system, of course, has relationships with other systems (via package and use case relationships), but the focus is on the set of goals and use cases owned by the package.

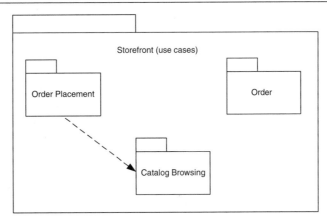

FIGURE 8-3 Simple use case model diagram

Sequence Diagrams

Once a use case and its dependent use cases are near completion, it is time to begin diagramming the scenarios. A sequence diagram, a specific type of interaction diagram, expresses the interaction between an actor and the system, with a special emphasis on the time line. Each scenario in a use case should be diagrammed. The diagram is not necessarily for the consumption of the domain experts, since it's more technically oriented. I suggest creating these scenarios during use case construction and not deferring them for later, when a different team could potentially be responsible for them, since the sequence diagram can help verify the completeness of a use case scenario.

Sequence diagrams begin by placing the scenario text in the diagram. If the style of the text is elaborate and descriptive, it's better to paraphrase the key points of the scenario. Each step in the scenario should be placed separately in the diagram, starting with the first step at the top and continuing down the left side of the diagram. The vertical axis of the diagram represents the time dimension; the top is the beginning of the scenario, and the bottom is the end. The two major players of the scenario—the actor and the system—are placed in the diagram at the top. The actor is rendered as a stick figure and the system simply as a rectangle. Dashed vertical lines, called object lifelines, are drawn down the page from the actor and system icons. A blank sequence diagram is shown in Figure 8-4.

In this diagram, the use case text is either taken verbatim or paraphrased. What is shown in the figure represents a first pass at the use case. It is probably an incomplete use case, since the details of an e-commerce checkout can get quite involved. Subsequent iterations will elaborate the use case and include all of the necessary behavior expected by the system. The goal of this use case is to check out of an e-commerce shopping session. The use case begins with the actor's sending a message to the system, indicating that the actor is ready to check out. In a client/server system, this might be implemented by clicking a user

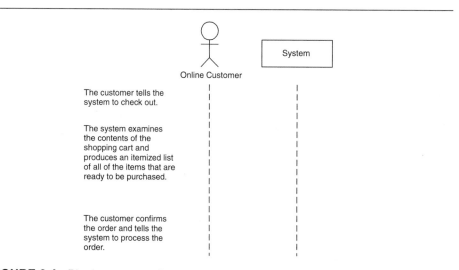

FIGURE 8-4   Blank sequence diagram

interface button. In a Web application, it might be implemented with a hyperlink to another Web page. The important point, however, is that the actor's intent is described in the scenario, and not in the implementation mechanism. The implementation mechanism is decided by a combination of the system's architecture and the designer. The decision of the architecture, of course, depends on the entire requirements specification, not just a few isolated use cases.

The analyst completes the sequence diagram by adding on the diagram interactions between the actor and the system. System input, supplied by the actor, is indicated by drawing arrows between the actor's line and the system's. System responses, as seen by the actor, are indicated with arrows going back to the actor. These interactions are essentially messages sent from one object to another. The messages are ordered sequentially from top to bottom and can be numbered for clarity as well. In addition to messages sent from one object to another, an object can send a message to itself. This type of action can be thought of as calling a subroutine, or breaking up a complex reaction into smaller ones. The text displayed atop the arrows identifies the name or the intent of the message. Figure 8-5 shows the completed sequence diagram for the use case fragment. The rectangular boxes running down the lifelines are called the focus of control, which shows the period of time that the object is in control.

Sequence diagrams are not meant to show the structural relationships among objects in the system, just the dynamic ones. Therefore, a sequence diagram contains only one scenario. If multiple paths are navigated in the scenario, only one of them is shown in a diagram. That is the strict interpretation. In practice, small deviations in the path can sometimes be displayed in a sequence diagram without making it unreadable.

In Figure 8-6, for example, a clerk is entering a new customer profile. There is a slight branch in the flow if the customer is a reseller. In those instances, the clerk must get additional information and enter it into the system. For all other customers, this step is skipped.

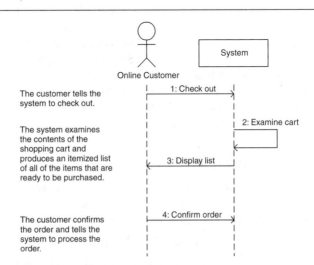

FIGURE 8-5   Completed sequence diagram for use case fragment

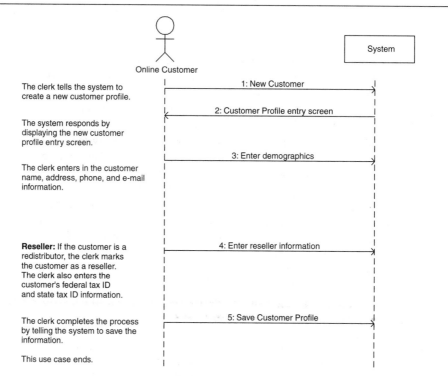

The clerk tells the system to create a new customer profile.

The system responds by displaying the new customer profile entry screen.

The clerk enters in the customer name, address, phone, and e-mail information.

Reseller: If the customer is a redistributor, the clerk marks the customer as a reseller. The clerk also enters the customer's federal tax ID and state tax ID information.

The clerk completes the process by telling the system to save the information.

This use case ends.

FIGURE 8-6 A sequence diagram with a branching scenario

The branch is indicated by the narrative text. A boldface heading for Resellers is an extra cue to alert the reader to something unusual.

Although not as flexible as use cases, sequence diagrams do allow some freedom in expressing a scenario. The few diagram elements shown in Figure 8-6 are sufficient for diagramming use case scenarios. Sequence diagrams can get much more involved, with a rich set of elements and semantics that closely map to a design and implementation. Use case scenarios are written in the language of the domain and typically don't contain too much technical information; therefore, the full set of sequence diagram elements is not really needed in this phase.

Use Case Analysis

Use case analysis is another activity that is done when the use cases near completion. In the ICONIX process, this is called robustness analysis and is an integral part of that process. The goals of use case analysis are to

- Identify the classes and objects that will perform a use case's flow of events
- Identify the responsibilities, attributes, and associations of the classes
- Note the usage of architectural mechanisms

In the RUP, the principal outputs of use case Analysis are a set of use case realizations and analysis-level objects. Each use case realization is the set of sequence diagrams, class diagrams, and textual descriptions that describe how a given use case is performed in the system in terms of the objects. A use case realization is a stereotyped use case that realizes a normal use case. The stereotyped relationship «realizes» links a use case to its use case realization (Figure 8-7). All of the sequence diagrams and class collaborations that describe how the use case gets performed in the system belong to the realization, not to the original use case.

A separate use case realization allows the base use case to be implemented by multiple systems. Take as an example a use case that describes the browsing of a store catalog. The same use case can be realized in terms of a client/server system that supports the telesales department. The use case might also be realized by a Web application system, which would be used by Internet customers. A separate use case realization provides a layer of independence from requirements of the system and its implementation while still maintaining a link in the chain of traceability.

Use case analysis begins with the elaboration of the base use case's sequence diagrams with analysis-level objects. Analysis objects are instances of analysis classes that represent the major "things" in the system that have responsibility and behavior. Class diagrams capture these classes and their relationships to one another. These classes are the early prototypes of the design-level classes. For the most part, the names of these classes should have relevant meanings in the vernacular of the domain. Such class names as `UnOrderedSetIterator` probably don't belong in an analysis model. Instead, the analysis model should have classes with such names as `Customer`, `Order`, `LineItem`, and `Product`.

Analysis classes can be stereotyped into three types: boundary, entity, and control.

1. *Boundary objects* represent the interface between the actor and the system. Instances of these objects are typically entry screens or special user interface controls. In Web applications, these may represent whole Web pages.

2. *Entity objects* are those things that are described in the use case but that will outlast it. Orders, customers, products, and payroll are entity objects whose instances may appear in many invocations of use cases.

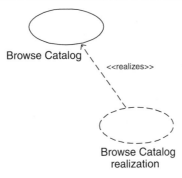

FIGURE 8-7   Browse Catalog realization

3. *Control objects* represent processes. These objects represents system activities that can often be named. Compute payroll, process and invoice, recatalog inventory are all processes that are significant enough to be named. Control objects direct the activities of the entity and interface objects.

As with any class, these analysis-level classes have relationships with one another. The classes and their relationships are drawn on class diagrams. Actors can also be displayed on the diagrams, to help differentiate which interfaces are appropriate for which roles. The associations among the objects are governed by certain rules.

- Actors can interact only with boundary objects.

- Entity objects can interact only with controller objects.

- Controller objects can interact with any object, including other instances of controllers.

One way to begin use case analysis is by examining the use case text for key nouns and verbs. The nouns are a candidates for entity objects; the verbs, for controllers. A first pass at the New Customer scenario of Figure 8-6 yields the diagram of Figure 8-8.

The diagram in Figure 8-7 is oversimplified. Most analysis diagrams contain many entity and controller objects and often multiple interface objects. If the creation of Reseller customers were significantly complex, the robustness diagram might look like that shown in Figure 8-9.

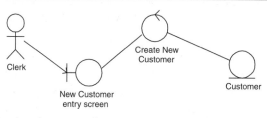

FIGURE 8-8   A simple robustness diagram

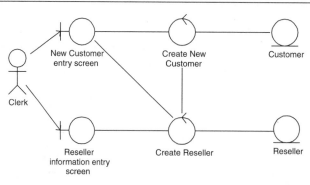

FIGURE 8-9   More complex robustness diagram

The results of use case analysis will help the requirements team better understand what the use case is saying, especially on the technical side. These two artifacts are not necessarily for the domain expert's use but are valuable to the technical members of the team. If they are not done during the use case definition process, they will ultimately be done later. If inconsistencies or problems are discovered then, it will require much more effort to resolve them than if they had been discovered during the requirements phase.

Use case realizations are a primary source of links in the chain of traceability throughout the models of the system. This chain of responsibility begins with the use cases and requirements of the system and threads its way through every other artifact of the process. Each link in the chain connects artifacts from one process or activity to another. Use case realizations provide a link from the world of the domain, as expressed by use cases, to the world of the system, as expressed by analysis-level objects.

Chapter Summary

- ❑ A requirements specification is a collection of documents and models that attempt to unambiguously describe a software system to be built.
- ❑ A requirements specification needs to be made available to nearly everyone connected with the project.
- ❑ A requirements specification is a contract that binds the stakeholders to accept a system that meets the criteria specified in the requirements documents.
- ❑ A requirement, a constraint that the system must observe, is typically expressed as a statement that begins with a phrase like "The system shall . . . ."
- ❑ It is important to objectively prioritize every requirement.
- ❑ Use cases are a powerful technique for capturing and expressing detailed system behavior. A use case is a textual description of the interaction between an actor and the system.
- ❑ A use case may contain more than one scenario; however, there is always one main scenario.
- ❑ A use case is written to express what a system should do, without constraining how it should do it.
- ❑ A use case is written in the language of the domain.
- ❑ Use cases are a primary input to testing activities.
- ❑ A sequence diagram is a type of interaction diagram that expresses the interaction between an actor and objects of the system, with a special emphasis on the time line.
- ❑ Use case analysis identifies classes and objects that perform a use case's flow of events.
- ❑ A use case realization is a special use case that describes a use case in terms of the system's architecture. The realization is a set of analysis-level objects and sequence diagrams.

Chapter 9
Analysis

The activities of analysis and design help transform the requirements of the system into a design that can be realized in software. Analysis and design can be done separately or combined as part of the same set of activities.

Analysis comprises those activities that take the use cases and functional requirements to produce an analysis model of the system. The analysis model is made up of classes and collaborations of classes that exhibit the dynamic behaviors detailed in the use cases and requirements.

The model represents the structure of the proposed system at a level of abstraction beyond the physical implementation of the system. The classes typically represent objects, such as shopping cart, order, line item, or product, in the business domain (problem space). The level of abstraction is such that these same classes could be applied equally to architectures other than Web applications. Important processes and objects in the problem space are identified, named, and categorized during analysis.

Analysis focuses on the functional requirements of the system, ignoring for the moment the architectural constraints of the system. The emphasis is on ensuring that all of the functional requirements, as expressed by the use cases and other documents, are realized somewhere in the system. Ideally, each requirement item and use case is linked to the classes and packages that realize them. This link is important in establishing the traceability between requirements and use cases and the classes that will realize them.

Design, on the other hand, is primarily a refinement of the analysis model. Design uses the nonfunctional requirements of the system and the constraints of the architecture to refine the analysis model into something that can be coded. The designer must take into consideration that nothing happens in zero time, that computers have limited memory, and that on occasion things can go awry. The designer is often the pragmatist of team.

When analysis and design are done as separate activities, two models are produced: an analysis model and a design model. Since the analysis model is a direct input to design, it can either be kept as a separate model, and maintained separately, or can evolve into the design model.

A separately maintained analysis model is useful when the system is being designed for multiple target architectures. If the system is very complex, the additional abstraction layer provided by a discrete analysis model may be useful in understanding the system. The abstraction is especially useful for answering some of the "Why did we ever do it that way?" questions that always seem to pop up late in a project.

The benefits of a separate analysis model must be weighed against the cost of maintenance. Often, the design activities and realities of software development need to change things so they can be realized in software. Design activities almost always drive the evolution of the model of the system away from the idealized "analysis view." Maintaining the analysis model means evolving it with the design model. Eventually, the finer details of the analysis model will be lost, so even if it is maintained, it is best to keep only the most important domain classes and relationships. Once the analysis model becomes significantly out of sync with the design model, its usefulness is limited.

Iteration

The analysis and design activities usually get started with a somewhat complete use case model and set of requirements. In an incremental development process, the entire use case model or set of requirements artifacts do not need to be completed before activities in subsequent phases of the development process can take place. This is not to imply that you can code while you're still gathering requirements and analyzing the problem. It just means that when a fair understanding of the requirements is known and certain packages of the use case model completed, it is possible to begin analysis and design on them. It is important to understand that the more complete the use cases and requirements are, the less likely that the analysis and design will have to be reworked.

Another important aspect of iterative development is the opportunity to address risk early on. Risk is that unknown void in which the team knows it has to tread but is unsure of the terrain. Risk is usually identified through the experience—or lack of experience—of the senior members of the team. Often, the unknowns are related to nonfunctional requirements, such as performance, security, or external system interfaces. For some organizations venturing into new domains, however, the risk might be in the business processes themselves. Often, it is the architect who identifies the risky areas; however, any member of the team should be able to point out areas of uncertainty.

For example, the architect of an e-commerce system may have identified the integration of the billing system with the external merchant account system as being particularly risky. Perhaps the architect has never used this particular online merchant account system or has had troubles with it before. In an iterative development process, this would be one of the areas in which the requirements and uses cases would be completed first and in which the analysis and design activities could begin before some of the other parts of the system had completed their use cases.

When working in an iterative and incremental development process, it is important to have a solid change control process in place. In risky areas of the problem space, important discoveries are often made that affect certain assumptions made in previous phases. When this happens during analysis, the use cases or requirements need to be questioned. For example, the requirements might state that new customers are automatically assigned a new ID that is a composite of their last name and phone number. The requirements might also state that every customer must have an ID. Yet elsewhere, the requirements might state that getting a new customer's phone number is optional. In practice, this simple scenario would most likely have been caught during requirements gathering, but if not, the analysis activities most certainly would have caught it, and this would be reason to call for clarification of the requirements. "Does the ID have to use the phone number, or could any unique number do?" or "Is it unreasonable to require each customer to provide a phone number?" should be answered by the requirements team. No member of the development should be shy about asking questions that could simplify the system.

Packages

One of first activities of the analysis team is to create the package hierarchy of the analysis model. As with any complex system, one natural way to attack the task of representing the problem and solution space in a comprehensible way is to "divide and conquer." The UML mechanism for this is the package. A package is nothing more than a "chunk" of the model: small enough that one can understand its purpose and significance in the model. Packages contain elements of the model; classes, diagrams, components, interfaces, and so on. Every element in the model is owned by exactly one package. This does not limit model elements from appearing in the diagrams of other packages or from participating in relationships of elements in other packages. Classes in a package can be made public or private. A public class in a package is visible to and can be used by elements outside of the package. In a way, these classes represent the public interface of the package and should be chosen carefully.

Packages themselves can be further subdivided into more packages; hence, it is possible for a model to be represented by a hierarchy of packages. The most important property of a package is that it should be comprehensible. A person should be able to understand and to comprehend a package's purpose, significance, major elements, relations, and relations to elements owned by other packages.

A package is rendered graphically as a tabbed folder. A package has a name that is unique throughout the model. Each package forms a namespace, meaning that two elements can have the same name as long as they are owned by two different packages.

Packages can have relationships with one another. The two types of relations are dependency and generalization. A dependency relationship typically means that one package depends on, or has structural knowledge of, elements in the other. This relationship is drawn with a dashed line and an arrowhead pointing to the package that the other depends on.

A generalization relationship is like generalization in classes; the subpackages represent specializations of a package. For example a User Interface package might have two subpackages: ActiveX-Enabled UI, and Java-Enabled UI. Both contain elements that support the goal of providing a user interface, but each subpackage does so with a different architecture.

Throughout the process, the package can also be used to denote ownership. Typically, a package is "owned" by one analyst or designer. The public classes of the package are that package's interface to the other packages of the system. The designer is free to add additional classes or to alter the methods of private classes in the package without impacting the rest of the team. Changes in public classes and operations, however, need to be agreed on. A properly maintained model should be able to quickly answer the question, "Who uses this class's public interface?" Since they are "owned" by team members, packages make for a convenient unit of version control and are checked out of the configuration management system by the analyst or designer when being worked on.

Defining the Top-Level Model

Subsystems? →

During the use case definition activities, the use case model was divided into packages. During analysis, the same package hierarchy could be used to model the structural view of the system. It has been my experience, however, that the hierarchy of the dynamic view of the system (use cases) may provide an initial start but usually falls short for defining the structural view of the system (classes). The reason is that certain objects likely participate in a large number of use cases and packages and logically can't be assigned to a single use case package.

At the highest level, the packages are often the same; at the lower levels of the hierarchy, however, there are often better ways of dividing the packages. For example, the top-level use case view of an e-commerce system might comprise the following packages: Storefront, Billing, Inventory, and Site Administration. The top-level use case diagram is shown in Figure 9-1.

This same diagram also could be used for the top-level analysis model. At the lower levels—for example, in the Storefront package—there may be additional packages to separate the principal functions of the system as available to the on-line user. The subpackages of Storefront (Figure 9-2) in the use case model might include packages for placing orders, tracking orders, and browsing the catalog.

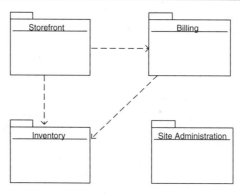

FIGURE 9-1 Top-level use case view of e-commerce application

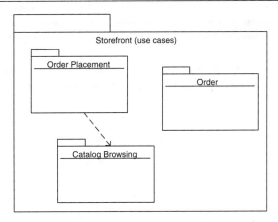

FIGURE 9-2   Storefront use case package

As shown in Figure 9-3, on the other hand, the Storefront package for analysis model might be very different, with the following packages: Catalog, Shopping Cart, Customer Profile, and Product Customizations for engravings, color, and size. In the analysis model, the packages tend to represent things rather than actions. Dividing up the analysis model to make it more manageable tends to place like things (objects) together instead of behaviors.

A good way to start the analysis model is to begin with the top-level use case diagram packages. From that point on, it is best to examine the use cases and functional requirements from a fresh viewpoint and to divide up the model according to similar things (classes of objects).

One of the most important things to remember when creating the initial package hierarchy is this: The *reason* we use packages is to help us manage the size and the complexity

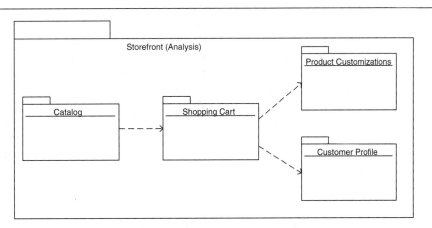

FIGURE 9-3   Structural view of Storefront package

of the "model" itself, not what we are "modeling." A package does not represent an abstraction of the business, nor does it mimic the structure of the system. A package is merely a mechanism to divide the "model" into more manageable pieces. Too often, we define the package hierarchy according to an abstraction of the business: functional, user, and so on. Try to avoid making the package hierarchy match the semantics of the business, and instead use packages as a means of managing the model.

Ultimately, the use of packages make the model understandable. When defining packages you should strive to make them

- *Comprehensible:* An individual is expected to be able to comprehend the package's semantics, reason for existence, major elements, and responsibilities.
- *Cohesive:* Logically speaking, the classes belong together. At some level of abstraction, all of the classes in the package form a natural group.
- *Loosely coupled:* Generally, each class has more relations with classes in the same package than with classes outside the package.
- *Hierarchically shallow:* Deep hierarchies tend to be difficult to understand, since each level carries its own meanings. It is best to keep the number of levels down to two or three.

Starting with a good package hierarchy is important. Since the top level and, possibly, second levels of the hierarchy are important for all members of the analysis and design team to understand, this particular activity should be done as a group and with an experienced member of the team leading. Throughout the analysis process, team members will be creating more packages, and some packages may, early on, get rearranged.

Analysis

Whether you are building Web applications, or distributed object systems, the activities of analysis are pretty much the same. Since analysis focuses on the functional requirements of the system, the fact that some or all of the system will be implemented with Web technologies is beside the point. Unless the functional requirements state the use of a specific technology, all references to architectural elements should be avoided.

Analysis begins with the analysis team's examining the use case model, the use cases and their scenarios, and the system's functional requirements that are not included in the use cases. The team identifies objects and classes of objects that can collaborate to perform the required behavior of the system. Since so many books discuss objects, classes, and the principles of object-oriented software, this one will not attempt to introduce these concepts here.

If a robustness analysis[1] has been done, an initial set of classes and major operations or processes has already been defined. In addition to robustness analysis, several other mechanisms can be used to help identify classes and collaborations.

---

1. See *Use Case Driven Object Modeling with UML*, Doug Rosenberg with Kendall Scott (Reading, MA: Addison Wesley Longman, 1999).

CRC (Class-Responsibility-Collaboration) card exercises are a simple, low-tech way of identifying classes and their responsibilities.[2] A CRC card is just an index card that contains the name of a class, its responsibilities, and its collaborations, or relationships with other classes. A CRC card exercise is really a team brainstorming exercise; members of the team come up with potential classes and define their responsibilities rather than their attributes and operations. Classes are matched up to produce collaborations that achieve the goals mentioned in the use cases and requirements. For some, it is an excellent way of beginning the process of class discovery; for others, not. If you are having a difficult time discovering classes or are getting bogged down with too many classes and their details, CRC exercises might be helpful.

Role playing is another team-oriented activity useful in identifying and elaborating classes in a system. Team members "play" the roles of a part of the system. The roles can be users, the system itself, other systems, or even entities in the system. The group walks through scenarios in the use cases and discussses how the work of the system gets done. All members take notes on the responsibilities of the roles they play. Role playing is often done along with CRC card exercises.

Noun analysis is another technique for identifying classes and objects. Use case and requirement texts are scanned for important nouns. These nouns indicate possible classes of objects. Verbs, on the other hand, indicate possible operations and processes. For example, consider the following use case fragment:

> . . . The customer tells the system that he is ready to check out. The system examines the contents of the shopping cart and produces an itemized list of all of the items that are ready to be purchased. The customer confirms the order and tells the system to process the order.

There are many important-sounding nouns that would make good classes in the system: "customer," "shopping cart," "order," and so on. The verbs "check out" and "process" are also significant actions in the use case and are likely to be identified as operations on some of the objects.

 Ultimately, analysis identifies a preliminary mapping of required behavior onto structural elements—classes and collaborations—in the system. The UML defines the notation whereby these structural elements can be represented visually in a diagram. Figure 9-4 shows the three principal classes that make up an online shopping cart. Since this is part of the analysis model, only the major public properties and operations are shown. During design, when the model gets refined, more properties and operations will be added.

---

2. Kent Beck and Ward Cunningham, "A Laboratory for Teaching Object-Oriented Thinking," from *OOPSLA 1989 Conference Proceedings,* October 1–6 1989, New Orleans, LA and the special issue of *SIGPLAN Notices,* 24(10), October 1989. Available at http://c2.com/doc/oopsla89/paper.html. And Rebecca Wirfs-Brock, Brian Wilkerson, and Lauren Wiener, *Designing Object-Oriented Software* (Englewood Cliffs, NJ: Prentice Hall), 1990.

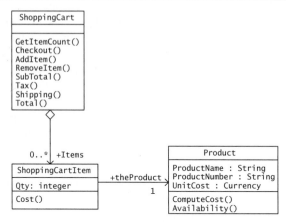

FIGURE 9-4   A class diagram in the analysis model

Sequence Diagrams

The structural view of the system is only one of the artifacts of analysis. Expressing the collaboration among classes is as much a part of analysis as is class definition. The UML mechanism to express the dynamics of class collaboration is the interaction diagram, which is the generic for several types of diagrams: collaboration, sequence, and activity. These diagrams express the dynamic behavior of the system, using the structural class and relationship elements of the model.

Sequence and collaboration diagrams, in particular, provide a critical link of traceability between the use case scenarios and the classes' structures. These diagrams can express the flow in a use case scenario in terms of the classes that will eventually implement them.

During requirements gathering and use case definition, simple scenarios were defined and expressed with interaction diagrams. These diagrams, however, showed only two objects interacting, the actor and the system. Figure 9-5 shows a scenario fragment that corresponds with the earlier use case fragment.

The diagram contains paraphrased use case text (on the lefthand side in Figure 9-5), which narrates the activity in the diagram. A major activity of analysis is to elaborate the sequence diagrams created during use case modeling with the structural elements in the analysis model. This merging of dynamic and structural elements of the model is a key link in the traceability of the model and should be taken very seriously. Through sequence and collaboration diagrams, methods and classes can be traced to scenarios, which are part of use cases, which support requirements of the system. A properly kept model should be able to answer questions such as, "Will we violate any requirements if we modify this operation?" or "What classes are affected if we modify this business process expressed by this use case?" or "We've discovered a problem in the computation of a date in this class; which use cases do we need to retest, and which test scenarios need to be revisited?" Accurate and timely answers to these types of questions can return the investment of any additional effort in modeling and are sometimes priceless.

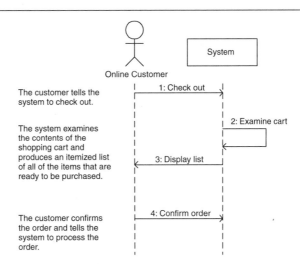

FIGURE 9-5   Simple sequence diagram from use case scenario

During analysis, the Checkout scenario fragment of Figure 9-5 might get elaborated into the diagram of Figure 9-6. Even though in a real-life application the "checking out" of an online customer is probably more involved, this figure expresses the basic idea of the scenario, using the classes defined during analysis.

Note that the System object of Figure 9-5 is replaced in Figure 9-6 by a set of analysis-level objects. These objects, introduced as a result of use case analysis, collaborate to provide the same functionality that the single System object did before. The objects, representing boundaries, controllers, and entities, begin to segregate the functionality of the system into classes and collaborations of classes that will eventually be transformed into design-level objects.

So far, the discussions of the activities of analysis could have been equally applied to nearly every object-oriented system, regardless of architecture. When the architecture is known, as is probably the case during this stage of analysis, a different view can be made on the controller and boundary objects. Later, during design, these boundary objects have a tendency to map to HTML pages in the system; the controllers, to the server-side activities of dynamic Web pages. To the analyst, this means that the functionality assigned to boundary objects can—and should be—light; that is, each boundary object should remain focused on a singular task.

When the system is distributed, these boundary objects are delivered as HTML Web pages, so overloading a single boundary object to perform a number of tasks will make that page difficult to build and perhaps even unrenderable by basic client browsers. During classical client/server user interface design, a single user interface can offer a tremendous amount of functionality and use sophisticated user interface controls, such as tabs and multiple panes, to organize a large amount of information. With Web pages, especially those targeted for basic HTML 3.2–compatible browsers, this level of sophistication can be risky.

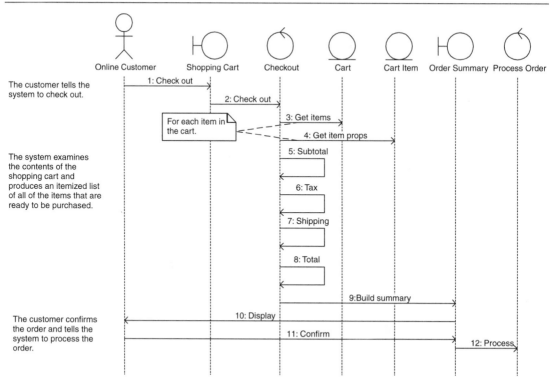

FIGURE 9-6   Sequence diagram elaborated during analysis

If the target architecture involves the use of scripted pages, as with Java Server Pages, Active Server Pages and Cold Fusion pages, much of the controller objects' functionality is executed in Web pages. Scripted pages have a tendency to act as controllers of server-side object activity. In the typical scripted-page Web application, these controllers, like the boundary objects, should be designed with singular functionality. Overloading a server-side scripted Web page can be complex and even lead to performance problems. There-fore, the analyst should design controllers to be "mean and lean." The golden rule for designing objects in general: "An object should do one thing and do it well." Controllers too should be focused on orchestrating a single task in the flow of a use case.

Collaboration Diagrams

Collaboration diagrams are essentially the same as sequence diagrams; in fact, the Ratio-nal Rose CASE tool even automates the conversion of sequence and collaboration diagrams. Even though semantically, they say the same thing, each type of diagram expresses the information with a different view. Sequence diagram focus on the time dimension: Every-thing is rigidly placed along the time axis. In collaboration diagrams, the focus is on ob-ject instances. Objects in a collaboration diagram can be placed anywhere in the diagram, with a single line representing all messages from one object to another. Each message is numbered—to preserve the time dimension—and lumped together on the one association between each object. Figure 9-7 shows the sequence diagram of Figure 9-6 converted to a collaboration diagram.

Activity Diagrams

A third type of diagram useful in the analysis model is the activity diagram. Activity diagrams are useful for expressing workflow. By definition, they show the flow of activities, which in turn result in actions. Activity diagrams, which do not directly use the objects and classes of the analysis model, tend to express the dynamic behavior at a higher level than sequence and collaboration diagrams do.

On the other hand, activity diagrams can be used to model the activities of a specific operation (see, for example, Figure 9-8). When used in this manner, they are similar to flowcharts. A properly designed activity diagram has the potential of real code generation and reverse engineering, since the level of detail necessary for coding an operation is all expressed in the diagram. To my knowledge, no CASE tool has yet to build such low-level code generation, but I expect the next generation or so of tools to begin including these capabilities.

In all but the most trivial system, analysis is carried out by a team. Each member of the team usually works on a package or set of packages independently and simultaneously. Early on, team members get together frequently to discuss and to negotiate the public interfaces of their packages. As the model becomes more refined and the interfaces more stable, these meetings are not needed as often; however, it is still important to have regular gettogethers and reviews to ensure that everyone is still marching in the same direction.

At some point, a package is considered to be completed and ready for design. This milestone is usually identified by having all of the use cases and scenarios—both main and alternative flows—accounted for. The package should be reviewed before proceeding onto design.

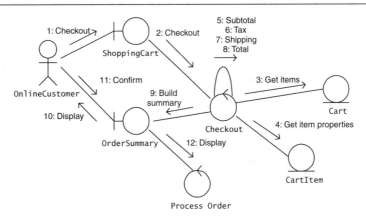

FIGURE 9-7 Collaboration diagram

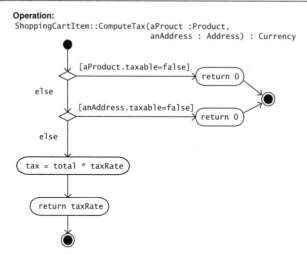

FIGURE 9-8   Activity diagram of ComputeTax operation

Chapter Summary

❑ The activities of analysis and design help transform the requirements of the
   system into a design that can be realized in software.

❑ The analysis model is made up of classes and collaborations of classes that
   exhibit the dynamic behaviors detailed in the use cases and the requirements.

❑ Analysis-level classes represent objects in the business domain.

❑ Analysis focuses on the functional requirements of the system, ignoring, for the
   moment, the architectural constraints of the system.

❑ When creating the top-level analysis model packages, it is often useful to copy
   the use case model top-level packages. At the lower levels, however, the
   structure of the package hierarchy is often different.

❑ Analysis begins with the analysis team's examining the use case model, the use
   cases and their scenarios, and the system functional requirements that are not
   included in the use cases.

❑ The analysis team identifies objects and classes of objects that can collaborate
   to perform the required behavior of the system.

❑ Expressing the dynamic interactions between collaborations of classes is an
   important part of analysis. These interactions follow the flow of events expressed
   in the use cases.

❑ Boundary and controller classes should be defined with singular purposes, since
   they will eventually be transformed into HTML and scripted Web pages.

Chapter 10
Design

Design is where the abstraction of the business takes its first step into the reality of software. Anything can be expressed in requirements and analysis models. (I've even got a technical manual on the inner workings of the starship *Enterprise's* Transporter System.[1]) Yet even these well thought out requirements and specifications are not likely to be implemented any time soon (what a shame!). Design can be a humbling experience.

Design starts with the analysis model and architecture as the major inputs. The principal activity of design is to refine the analysis model such that it can be implemented with the components of the architecture. Even though this sounds straightforward, it can be the most complex phase of a development project, especially when significant advances in software technology are happening so frequently.

As with analysis, design activities revolve around the class and interaction diagrams. Classes become more defined, with fully qualified properties (name and type) and operations (complete signatures). Additional classes, mostly helper and implementation classes, are often added during design. In the end, the resulting Design Model is something that can be mapped directly into code. This is the link between the abstractions of the business and the realities of software.

During analysis, we were content to work with only class diagrams and interaction diagrams. During design, a new diagram—in fact, a new view of the model: the component view—is introduced. This view of the model expresses the physical—if anything in software can be considered "physical"—modules and executables that will be distributed as the system.

---

1. Rick Sternbach and Michael Okuda, *Star Trek: The Next Generation Technical Manual*, Reissue Edition (Pocket Books, 1991).

A component typically maps to executable files, Java class files, static libraries, or dynamic link libraries (DLL). A component is something that realizes a set of interfaces. An interface is the bridge between the logical view of the system and the physical view. Simply put, interfaces are public functions that can be called by outside components. An interface defines the name of the function, its parameters and their data types, whether they are optional, whether they are input or output, and the function's return-value type. A component can realize multiple interfaces.

The realization of a component is done with the classes and collaborations expressed in the logical view. Every class in the logical view is implemented by at least one component; abstract classes defining interfaces may be implemented by many components.

Component diagrams visualize components, interfaces, and their interrelationships. Components are rendered in a diagram with a set of rectangles (see Figure 10-1). Interfaces are rendered with a "lollypop," or a circle on a stick. Dependencies are shown expressed with dashed lines and arrowheads.

Class icons can be represented in component diagrams to express dependencies and realizations. Components realize classes, and this relationship is shown with a dashed line and arrowhead. Figure 10-2 shows that the Shopping Cart component realizes the ShoppingCart and ShoppingCartItem classes.

During analysis, we were content to leave the interface between the actor and the system—as expressed in the interaction diagrams—as System. During design, the interface needs to be elaborated into a set of specific interfaces capable of handling the communication between the actors and the system, as well as support for the flow of activity of business processes. In addition to elaborating the classes and collaborations, design activities include

- Partitioning objects into tiers, such as client, server, and so on
- Separating and defining user interfaces, or Web pages

When we partition objects into their tiers, we need to know what tiers are available for objects. This depends on the specifics of the architecture. For example, a Web application that uses only the Thin Web Client architectural pattern is not capable of supporting user-defined objects on the client. Therefore, all objects will need to exist somewhere in the server's tier— depending, of course, on the complexity of the system that may exist in many different "tiers" behind the Web server.

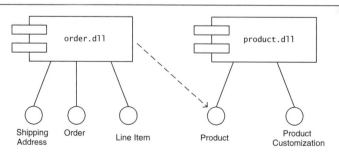

FIGURE 10-1 Component diagram

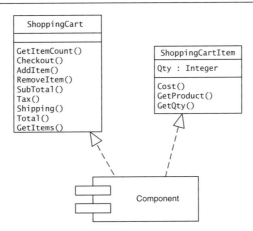

FIGURE 10-2 Shopping Cart component realizes ShoppingCart classes

The basic architectural patterns of Web applications all involve the use of Web pages. Web pages act as generalized user interface containers; and they are the glue that connects the browser with the rest of the system. Since one of the greatest uses of modeling is capturing all of the elements of a software system and their collaborations so that they answer questions about the system, it is vital to capture Web pages as first-class elements in the model and to represent them alongside the classes and components that make up the rest of the model.

Representing Web pages in the model, however, is not as straightforward as we would like. It should be clear that Web pages are objects, just like any other user interface in a system. The modeling problem occurs when you consider a Web page that has scripts to be executed on the server. This type of Web page interacts with server-side resources before being sent to the client as a completed user interface. To further complicate matters, this same page can contain a separate set of scripts that execute on the client as well. Psychologically speaking, this Web page is schizophrenic! When processed by the server, the same page does one thing; when processed by the client, it does a completely different thing.

The building blocks of UML—as they come out of the box—are just not sufficient to express the necessary subtleties of scripted Web pages as objects in a class diagram. Yet since they perform important business operations and act as real objects of the system, they need to coexist with the classes and objects of the system. The only solution is to modify the UML itself.

Modifying the UML may seem like a drastic solution; however, the creators of UML have built in a way to extend the language in a controllable way. They knew that in order for the UML to last, it would have in an orderly manner to adapt to the rapid pace of technology change. They also understood that there will always be unique situations, especially in vertical markets, where tools right out of the box might not be appropriate. To accommodate this need for flexibility, the creators of the UML have defined an extension mechanism for UML.

The following section presents an extension to UML for Web applications. This extension enables us to represent Web pages and other architecturally significant elements in the model alongside the "normal" classes of the model. Only by doing this can we accurately express the entirety of the system in a model and maintain its traceability and integrity.

UML Extension for Web Applications

An extension to UML is expressed in terms of stereotypes, tagged values, and constraints. Combined, these mechanisms enable us to create new types of building blocks that we can use in the model.

- *Stereotype*, an extension to the vocabulary of the language. A stereotype allows us to attach a new semantic meaning to a model element. Stereotypes can be applied to nearly every model element and are usually represented as a string between a pair of guillements « ». However, they can also be rendered by a new icon.
- *Tagged value*, an extension to a property of a model element. Most model elements have properties associated with them. Classes, for instance, have names, visibility, persistence, and other attributes associated with them. A tagged value is the definition of a new property that can be associated with a model element. A tagged value is rendered on a diagram as a string enclosed by brackets.
- *Constrain*, an extension to the semantics of the language. A constraint is a rule that defines how the model can be put together. A constraint specifies the conditions under which the model can be considered "well formed." Constraints are rendered as strings between a pair of braces { }.

An extension to the UML begins with a brief description and then lists and describes all of the stereotypes, tagged values, and constraints of the extension. In addition to these elements, an extension contains a set of well-formedness rules. These rules are used to determine whether a mode is semantically consistent with itself. Appendix A contains the full specification for the extension.

Designing Web Applications

Two major activities of designing Web applications are significantly different from designing other systems: partitioning of objects onto the client or server and defining Web page user interfaces. The Web Application Extension for UML has defined for us a notation we can use to express the Web technology components of the system with the rest of the model.

Proper partitioning of the business objects in a Web application is critical and depends very much on the architecture. Objects may reside exclusively on the server, the client, or both. In a sophisticated Web application, it is likely that input field validation objects and specialized user interface widgets will run on the client, whereas container objects, such as Customer List or Product Catalog, will exist only on the server. Some objects, such as Invoice, may have lives in both. For example, a customer invoice object could exist on the server, where its life cycle and persistence are managed. This object could be sent in the form of an XML document to the client. The XML document could be used as Invoice's state and bring to life a client-side Invoice object. That object would have some of the same interfaces as the one on the server. Sophisticated behaviors like this are what really make modeling invaluable.

When the job is at hand, partitioning objects is straightforward. Thin Web Client–patterned applications place all objects behind the server: either running on the Web server or another tier associated with the server. Thick Web Client applications allow some objects to execute on the client. There are, however, strict rules governing the use of objects on the client. Web Delivery applications have the most freedom in the placement of objects, since they are essentially distributed object systems that just happen to use a browser.

Partitioning Objects for Thick Web Client Web Applications

When designing Thick Web Client Web applications, you can easily partition, in the first pass, a large number of the objects discovered during analysis. For the most part, persistent objects, container objects, shared objects, and complex objects all belong on the server. Objects with associations to such server resources as databases and legacy systems also belong in the server tier. Objects that maintain static associations or dependencies with any of these objects also must exist on the server.

It is easier to identify which objects *can* exist on the client than to identify those that *can't* on the server. If an object has no associations or dependencies with objects on the server and has associations and dependencies only with other client resources, such as browsers and Java applets, it can exist on the client. Candidate objects for the partitioning on the client are field-validation objects, user interface controls, and navigation-assisting controls.

When we first think of objects on the client, there is no stipulation on how they are to be implemented. They are simply objects that are invoked during the browser's processing of the Web page. Client objects can be implemented with JavaScript, JavaBeans, applets, ActiveX (COM), or even plug-ins. During analysis, these objects simply represent a mechanism to implement a requirement or use case scenario. During design, however, they need to be given an architectural underpinning. They need to be realizable.

Partitioning Objects for Web Delivery Web Applications

The Web Delivery architectural pattern is essentially a distributed object system that is based on a Web site. This type of application uses client and server communication protocols other than HTTP. Real objects can execute in the context of the client or the browser and hence have access to its resources. These objects can also communicate directly with objects on the server or even other browsers!

Partitioning objects for this type of architecture is dependent mostly on the nature of the individual objects. One of the primary reasons for distributing objects to the client is to take some of the load off the server. It is also natural to place objects where they will be most effective in the system. Putting a date-validation object on the server, for example, doesn't seem like the brightest idea a designer might have. A date-validation object is most useful on the client, where it can notify the user of an invalid date immediately, avoiding all of the communication overhead of a server trip.

As a general rule, I like to place objects where they have the easiest access to the data and collaborations they require to perform their responsibilities. If an object can exist on the client and most, if not all, of its associations are on client objects, it is a likely candidate for placement on the client.

Elaborating the Design with Sequence Diagrams

While the objects are being partitioned, Web pages too are being defined. This activity involves the discovery of Web pages and their relationships with one another and with the objects of the system. This step too depends heavily on the architectural pattern of the application. For instance, it is entirely possible for a Web Delivery type of application to use only one Web page! This particular page would most certainly be loaded with complex objects and applets, yet for some situations, it would be the best solution. The remainder of this section, however, assumes that there will be more than one Web page in the application and will introduce some techniques for discovering Web pages and modeling their interactions with actors and the rest of the system with sequence diagrams.

In this activity, the System objects in the sequence diagrams created during analysis evolve into objects and Web pages, the principal user interface for the Web application.

Thin Web Client Design

The Thin Web Client architectural pattern places the most severe restrictions on the use of Web pages. It stipulates that each page contain only those architectural elements specified by the current version of HTML (version 4.0 at the time of this writing).

Since this is a design activity, we'll need to get a little more specific about the technology for the example. This example uses Microsoft's Active Server Pages as the principal «server page» mechanism. The Active Server Pages (ASP) environment also provides some server-side objects that are very useful, most notably the Session object, a dictionary-like object that stores values and objects in a dictionary keyed by a string. The remarkable thing about this dictionary is that is able to maintain its state across multiple client page requests. It offers the designer a mechanism to capture client state on the server.

The Active Server's Session works by placing on the browser a cookie that persists for some length of time. Its value is a unique key into the application's collection of all Session instances. Other Web application development environments use similar techniques to maintain client state on the server, and their mechanism can also be expressed in the diagrams.

It is often easiest to begin design by directly transforming the analysis model.[2] This activity can begin only when the architecture has been decided on and is well understood

---

2. In the Rational Unified Process (RUP), the analysis and design models are the same, so in this process, the design always begins by directly transforming the analysis model.

by the design team. In Thin Web Client applications, actors interact *only* with client pages, and server pages *only* interact with server resources. Therefore, we'll need to put a client and server page in the sequence diagram. The easiest thing to do is to directly transform boundary objects from the analysis model into client pages and transform controller objects into server pages.

The analysis model sequence diagram in Figure 9-6 describes the scenario of the Checkout use case. We begin modifying the sequence diagram by replacing the boundary and controller classes with client and server pages. Figure 10-3 shows the elaborated sequence diagram. The sequence diagram begins with the actor sending a message to the ShoppingCart client page. This message is essentially a command to request the Checkout page and most likely is implemented with the anchor tag (`<a href="Checkout.asp">`) in the client page ShoppingCart.

The server page Checkout is loaded by the Web server and, since it's a «server page», gets processed by the appropriate scripting engine (in this case, Active Server Pages). The logic in the page gets the actor's Cart instance and sends it the Checkout message. All of the business or domain logic involved with checking out a shopping cart is encapsulated in

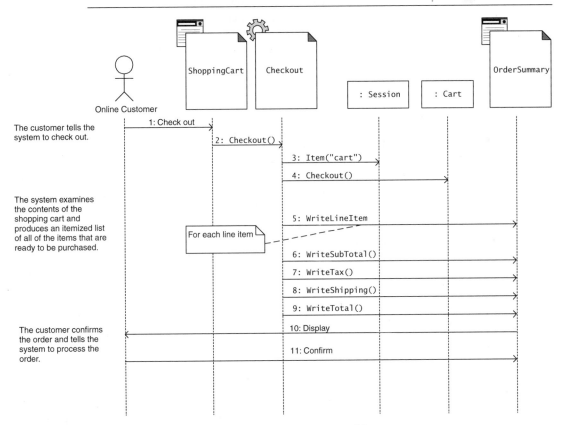

FIGURE 10-3 Sequence diagram for Thin Web Client

the Cart object. This is where it should be. Much of the detailed activity of the checkout process is not shown in the diagram of Figure 10-3 but can be expressed in additional diagrams. This type of activity might include the creation of transactions, or intermediate objects, necessary to check out a shopping cart. Server pages, even though they *can* implement this type of business logic, are often not the best place to put such logic, since their reuse is limited to the processing of pages. By putting this type of logic in compiled server components, they can be reused by non-Web application systems as well.

Even in Thin Web Client applications, server pages are often overloaded in responsibility. They are responsible for coordinating the activities of the server-side business objects and building a user interface to send back to the client. Keeping the details of the domain out of the server pages lessens their responsibilities and makes them easier to maintain.

The responsibilities of server pages can be lessened even further by separating the business logic coordination from user interface building. This can be done by introducing another page: BuildOrderSummary. The only job of this page is to build a summary page (OrderSummary) with the contents of the shopping cart, the totals, tax, and shipping costs. The Checkout server page delegates the user interface building to this page with a *redirection*. The revised sequence diagram is shown in Figure 10-4. By delegating the business logic to separate components and pulling out the user interface, making it into a separate page, the remaining page is now more objectlike and has a more singular purpose.

The remaining parts of this simple scenario start with the new client page, OrderSummary, since it has replaced the Checkout page in the client's browser. In the scenario, the actor confirms the checkout process by sending a message to the OrderSummary page, since this is the page now available to the actor. This message too is most likely a hyperlink to another server page.

The logical view of these new "page" objects is shown in Figure 10-5.

Figure 10-5 shows a very important diagram, one that is at the heart of this book. Together in the same diagram are conceptual Web pages and business objects. The Web pages are objectlike, logically having a single purpose and relations with other objects. In this diagram, they coexist with business classes (and system-provided classes) and, most important, have their relationships expressed in the diagram. The traceability in the model now extends from requirement to use case to business object to Web page.

Ultimately, these conceptual Web pages (server and client) need to find themselves in a component of the system. Figure 10-6 shows three components, each representing a Web page (ShoppingCart.asp, Checkout.asp, and BuildOrderSummary.asp) that will be delivered with the final system.

Once the Web pages, major collaborations, and responsibilities have been identified, it's time to start designing the individual pages themselves. For Thin Web Client architectures, this activity is limited to the operations and attributes of the server pages.

Server Pages

As much as we try to make Active Server Pages into objects, they are, sadly, inherently procedural. The engine processes a page by reading it from beginning to end. The first

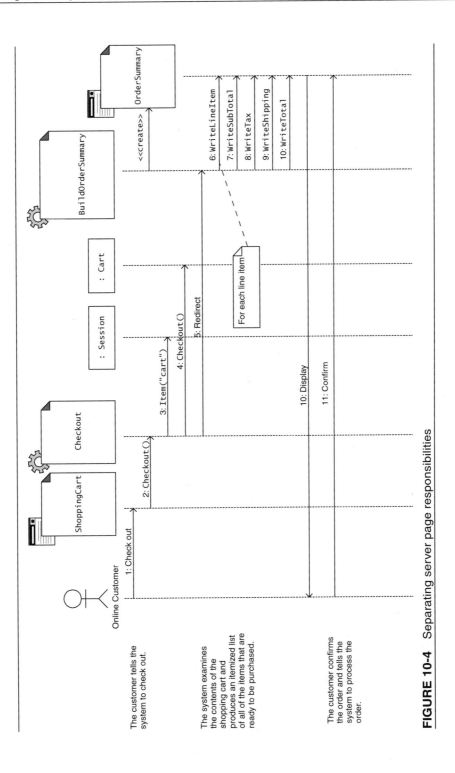

FIGURE 10-4 Separating server page responsibilities

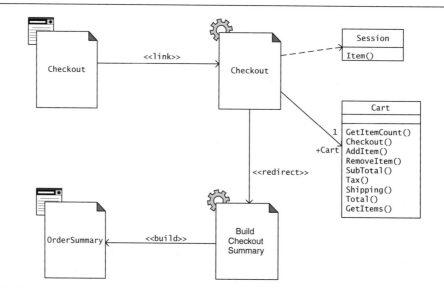

FIGURE 10-5 Logical–view classes related to checking out a shopping cart

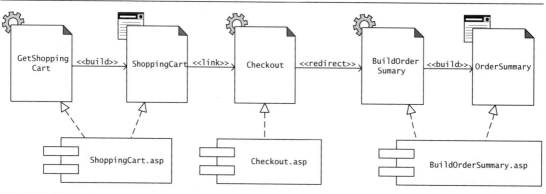

FIGURE 10-6 Component realizations of Checkout pages

executable statement it stumbles on gets executed, even if it is not part of a function! In a way, this makes the entire page a main()[3] function. Thus, any attribute defined for the «server page» class is going to mapped to a variable defined at the beginning of the page. This variable has page scope and is accessible by all of the functions defined in the page. Operations defined for the server page map to functions in the ASP file. Any code outside

---

3. In the C/C++ language, every executable program begins with a function called main.

of the functions in the ASP file is considered part of the page's entry function (the `main()` function). ISAPI, NSAPI, and Java Servlets, on the other hand, offer a more objectlike interface for server pages.

Already, the association to a Cart object implies a page variable that references a `Cart` instance. Most of the functionality of the `Checkout` server page has been rightly delegated to the Cart object; however, in a realistic application, several validation checks would be involved. For example, it is possible that the actor delayed so long in responding (or the network was temporarily down) that the actor's Session object on the server—the server's mechanism for managing client state—timed out and released itself back to the operating system, a very necessary feature for an Internet application. When this happens, there is no `Cart` instance in the session, since a new `Session` instance was assigned to the actor. Only the page is in a position to handle this error condition. This might prompt a need for a page operation called `ValidateShoppingCart()`. This function checks the `Session` and `Cart` instances before attempting to check out. If the `Cart` instance is invalid or doesn't exist, the function redirects further processing to another page. Figure 10-7 shows the structure for handling this error condition. Note that URL parameters are used to specify the details of the error condition.

The server page `ProcessError` is a generic error-handling page that accepts as a parameter an error number and an extended description, if available. The names of these parameters are captured in the model with tagged values on the «`redirect`» association and are identified by a note in the diagram.

Some server pages in the system may be even more complex, especially those that build complex client pages. The server page that creates the checkout summary page, `BuildOrderSummary`, is likely to have several attributes and operations. In Figure 10-8, this page is shown with a single attribute—the `Cart` instance—and several operations that break up the creation of the summary.

The summary is basically an order, with line items for all of the products selected and a subtotal, shipping cost, tax, and the final total. The `BuildLineItems` operation iterates through all of the items in the shopping cart, calling the `WriteLineItem` operation with a `ShoppingCartItem` parameter. Each product in a line item of the summary is hyperlinked to its the page in the catalog. The creation of this hyperlink (anchor tag) is delegated to the `CreateProductLink` operation, which accepts a `Product` reference and returns an anchor tag string. Once the line items have been written to the output—soon to be a client page— the `WriteTaxTotal` operation is called to write out the remaining items in the summary.

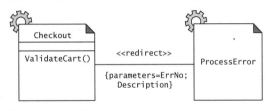

FIGURE 10-7   Redirection with parameters

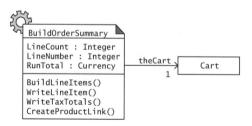

FIGURE 10-8   `BuildOrderSummary` server page

Links

Link relationships among pages can be expressed in a couple of ways. When it hyperlinks to another page, a client page is essentially linking to the Web page component, not to the client or server page abstraction. Therefore, the link from a client page to another client page and the link from a client page to the server page that «`builds`» the client page are essentially the same. Figure 10-9 shows two equivalent relationships, since `BuildDailySpecial` and `DailySpecial` are realized by the same component.

Being able to express links to either the client or the server page is very convenient when organizing diagrams. Diagrams intended to express the structural relationship of Web pages that support a particular flow through the application can contain only client pages—and hence links to only client pages—even though most of the pages are dynamic and built by server pages. Figure 10-10 shows a set of client pages, all of which are built by server pages, yet no server page appears in the diagram. The intent of the diagram is to show the structural relationships of a personal Web desktop. Note the bidirectional «`link`» relationships, which indicate that the actor can navigate back and forth between these pages.

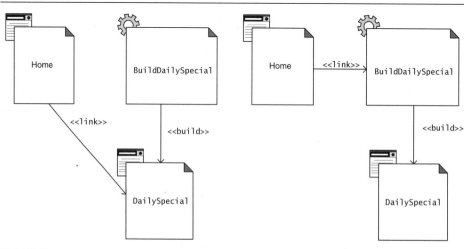

FIGURE 10-9   Equivalent link relationships

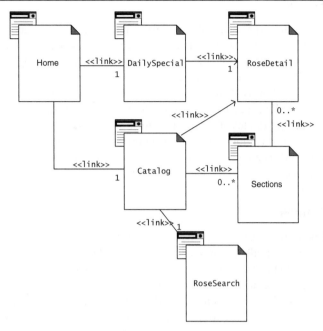

FIGURE 10-10   A client page–centric view of Web pages

In Figure 10-11, the intent is to show the server activity for building a RoseDetail page. In this partial diagram, the BuildRoseDetail page and relevant business objects are shown collaborating on the construction of a RoseDetail page.

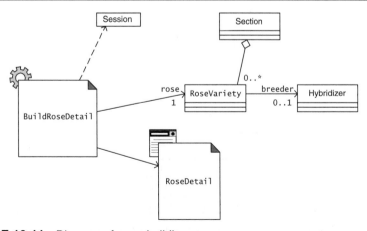

FIGURE 10-11   Diagram of page building

Forms

Forms are expressed in the model as an aggregate of a client page. A «form» object exists only in the context of a client page. This object is a collection of standard input elements that accept input from the user and submit it to a server page for processing. Figure 10-12 shows a simple form that collects basic customer information (name, e-mail, and postal address). Forms always submit their information to a server page, which, of course, could be an ASP page, a CGI script, or ISAPI/NSAPI DLL.

The attributes of the form are its input fields. In the diagram, their stereotype is shown; however, it is more practical to suppress the stereotype from the display to make it more readable. The tagged values of the stereotyped attributes include the additional information necessary to fully specify the HTML form's tags.

Frames

One of the most difficult Web elements to model is the frame. Frames enable the Web designer to divide a browser window into subrectangular areas, each with a different Web page. On the Internet, frames are commonly used to divide the window into a navigational pane and a content pane. The navigational pane, or index window, displays an index of all of the site's pages. Each item in the index is a hyperlink to a page. When the user clicks on one of these links, another pane is filled with the page. This type of link, a targeted link, requests Web pages for another pane or even another browser window instead of its own.

A frameset is a special type of Web page that divides its viewing area into multiple panes, each containing its own Web page. A frameset can define any number of rows and columns with which to divide its display area. Each of the panes is a target. A target in a frameset is a named frame that other client pages can request Web pages for.

The most common use of frames on the Internet is for implementing a book outline metaphor. An index frame, or table of contents, occupies the left or top frame, with the

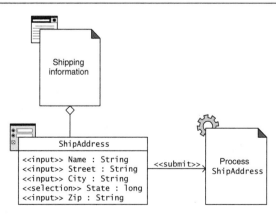

FIGURE 10-12   A shipping address collection form

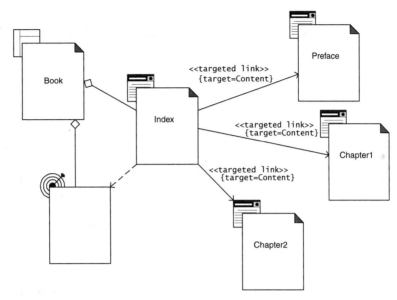

FIGURE 10-13   Expressing frames

main content displayed in the remaining space. This is similar to the Windows Explorer interface. The user clicks on links in the index pane, and the requested pages are loaded in the content pane. Using the Web application extensions for UML, this arrangement of pages is as shown in Figure 10-13.

The Book page is a frameset. Its tagged values define the size and shape of the frames. A frameset aggregates client pages and targets. When the content of a frame remains a single page, as an index page might, there is no need to define a target for this frame, since it will never be used in a targeted link relationship. The content frame, however, is loaded with any number of pages and hence requires a target to identify it. Since the index page has knowledge of the target Content, a dependency relationship is drawn. The Index page has links that load the Web pages into the content frame. These relationships are expressed with a «targeted link», and their tagged value for Target is set to Content to indicate where they are going to be rendered. In the diagram, the tagged value is expressed with a note icon.

Thick Web Client Design

Designing Web applications that have dynamic client pages requires careful attention to the partitioning of the objects. In Thin Web Client applications, there was no temptation to draw associations between client objects and server objects, since there are essentially no user-definable client objects to begin with! Thick Web Client applications, however can have all sorts of objects and activity occurring on the client.

Client-Side Scripting

Design of Thick Web Client systems begins with the sequence diagrams produced with the use cases. One of these scenarios describes the ability for the online customer to view the shopping cart, to change item quantities, and to have the totals be recomputed without having to go back to the server for processing. With a Thick Web Client system, this type of functionality can be placed on the client with JavaScript functions.

The sequence diagram in Figure 10-14 shows a client page (ShoppingCart) execut-ing operations on itself. The operations are JavaScript functions in the page. JavaScript functions are executed in response to certain events sent by the browser. These events are defined in the Document Object Model (DOM) and can be such things as the document loading but mostly are user-initiated events such as mouse movement and form element usage. In this example, the event is the button-clicked event on the Recalculate button.

An alternative way to diagram this scenario is by placing the <<form>> class in the sequence diagram and having the actor send the click message directly to the Recalculate button. The form then reacts by invoking the appropriate event handler in the client page (Figure 10-15).

Client Objects

Functionality can be supplied not only by scripting but also with objects such as ActiveX controls, Java applets, and JavaBeans. These types of components, often used when truly sophisticated functionality on the client is required, enable the designer to provide com-plex functionality in much the same way that classical client/server user interface systems can.

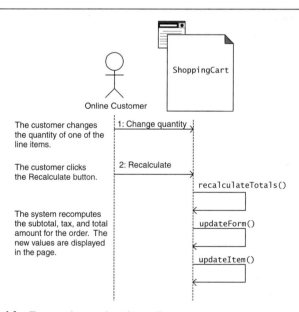

FIGURE 10-14   Expressing scripts in a client page

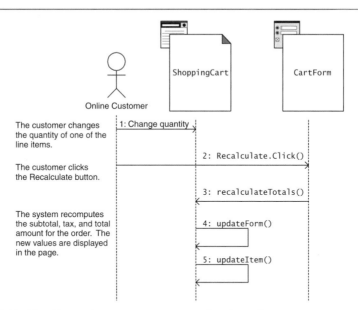

FIGURE 10-15   Alternative way to express scripts in a client page

When these types of components are used on the client, the actor or the page can interact with them directly (invoke operations on them). Figure 10-16 shows a class diagram that contains a frameset and a client page that contains two components—both ActiveX, in this particular case. The two controls are represented in the diagram with classes or interfaces, indicating that the object instance is known to the page only through that particular interface. The user selects a date with the calendar object. A date change event handler then updates the content of the target by linking to the page SeasonDescr (a dynamic page) and passes it the selected date as a parameter. The SeasonDescr page returns with the appropriate text for the selected date, which is displayed in the target Description. If a movie is available, it is instructed to fetch the stream and begin displaying it to the user.

It should be noted that this diagram expresses the required business logic functionality—the selection of growing-season information and the displaying of its contents—not any detailed user interface design. Figure 10-16 does not even specify the positioning of the frames or their sizes, although this could be expressed with tagged values in the aggregation relationship. The graphic artist responsible for managing the site's look and feel will take this design and apply the appropriate UI details for the final product. The focus of our modeling efforts at this point remains with delivering the business logic expressed in the use cases. The ActiveX controls in this example could have been a Java applet; in fact, the scenario and the class diagram would look identical, except for the object's stereotype.

Scripts and objects on the client can interact with the browser (see Figure 10-17). When it is necessary to model these interactions, the browser instance can be added to the sequence diagrams (and class diagrams, if necessary). The object and the methods available through the browser are defined by the W3C Document Object Model (DOM) standard.

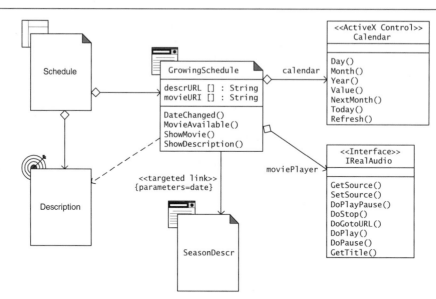

FIGURE 10-16   Class diagram with client page that uses ActiveX components

This standard defines an interface that browser manufacturers should implement to allow Web page designers access to the browser and document content. Dynamic HTML (DHTML) is an implementation of the DOM. DHTML includes all of the features of the DOM and also provides an event model, which, surprisingly, is missing in the current version of the DOM.

Web Delivery Design

For maximum flexibility, Web applications can use real distributed objects. Browser manufacturers make it very easy to deploy ActiveX and JavaBean objects with browsers. In part, this is due to the ongoing wars for technological dominance. Whichever company succeeds in having its technology be preeminent on the Internet is going to be in a very strong business position. As a result of this competition, we, the Web application designers, have a wide variety of technologies to choose from. Ultimately, the decision of when to use Java applets and Beans, RMI/IIOP, ActiveX, or DCOM depends on the application's needs and the development team's level of experience with these technologies. Typically, the need to use these technologies is driven by the inability of the other Web architectures to meet the functional or performance requirements. Direct communications between client and server objects is typically more efficient, especially when the nature of the communication is like a dialogue, that is, interaction with remote monitoring equipment.

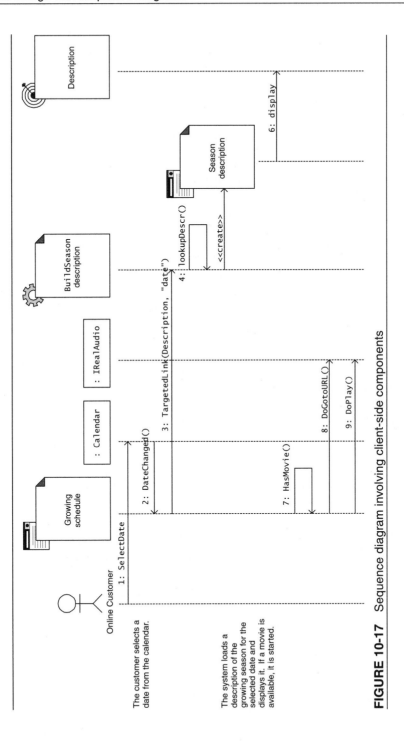

FIGURE 10-17   Sequence diagram involving client-side components

DCOM

Distributed COM is the Microsoft way for distributed objects to communicate with one another. DCOM is essentially an ORB (object request broker), like what you would find in an implementation of CORBA. Unlike CORBA ORBs, however, DCOM is part of the operating system. Formally introduced with Windows NT 4.0, DCOM is now shipped with Windows 98 and is expected to be part of the forthcoming Windows 2000. A freely available add-on gives Windows 95 DCOM functionality.

In order for any computer to use a COM (or ActiveX) object, it must be registered in the Windows registry, which contains the information about the component's actual location, either on the local machine or on a remote server. The server component could reside on any machine connected to the network. Even if the component is located on a remote machine, there is still a module particular to that remote object installed on the client machine. This object is a stub for the remote object and is responsible for marshalling the messages back and forth between the objects or components. It is during the setup of the component, or stub, that the identity of the server machine is needed.

Typically in application modeling, the issues involved during the setup of the client machines are either modeled separately or dealt with in a separate document—possibly, the deployment view of the software architecture document. Therefore, the class diagrams and the sequence diagrams involving the use of the client-side and server-side objects are restricted to their runtime use.

With this said, the modeling of DCOM-enabled Web applications is straightforward. Objects on the client can interact with and send messages to other objects on the client (and similarly for server objects), but communication between client and server objects represents something architecturally significant. Because of this importance, associations between objects executing on the client and objects executing on the server are stereotyped «DCOM», assuming that it is the mechanism for communication. Figure 10-18 shows an example of a distributed object in a class diagram.

Figure 10-19 shows a sequence diagram using the objects in the previous class diagram executing the Product Maintenance use case. The Product Maintenance client page contains an ActiveX control that acts like a data grid, enabling the actor to scroll through and edit database records. The control, DataGrid, is contained by the client page. When the client page is first loaded, the control connects to a server-side component that represents

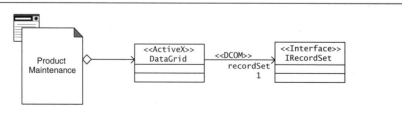

FIGURE 10-18   Class diagram with distributed objects

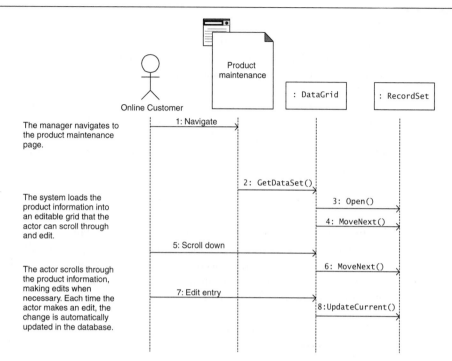

The manager navigates to the product maintenance page.

The system loads the product information into an editable grid that the actor can scroll through and edit.

The actor scrolls through the product information, making edits when necessary. Each time the actor makes an edit, the change is automatically updated in the database.

FIGURE 10-19 Sequence diagram of Product Entry use case

a database recordset via DCOM. While this page remains open in the browser, the ActiveX control maintains an open connection to the recordset object.[4] The actor scrolls through the list, making changes as necessary. The moment a change is made, the ActiveX component communicates it with the server component, which immediately updates the database recordset.

Modeling DCOM activity in a Web application is straightforward. Of course, the biggest drawback of using DCOM in a Web application is not in modeling but rather in the loss of platform independence. If, however, the application is an intranet in an organization in which all of the clients and servers are Windows based (Windows NT 4, Windows 95 and 98, and Windows 2000 only), DCOM is a very attractive option, especially since being a part of the operating system, it is a freebie.

---

4. For most applications, this is not the brightest idea a designer might have come up with. Keeping database connections open for long periods of time, especially if they have locks, is not good design practice. This example does illustrate, however, how to model DCOM communications between client and server objects.

RMI/IIOP

Despite the fact that RMI and IIOP seem to do the same thing, they actually complement each other. IIOP is a protocol, a specification of how distributed objects can communicate with one another. RMI is more than a specification; it is a concrete product. RMI is a high-level programming interface that makes the location of the server transparent to the client. Moreover, RMI is a Java-to-Java product, specifying how two Java components can communicate with each other. If Java components on the client need to interact with C++, COBOL, or Ada components on the server, using IIOP is the solution. If only Java components will provide the public interface to client components, RMI is a good candidate. Apart from some subtleties in their implementations and ability across languages, they are modeled and designed in essentially the same way.

In sequence and class diagrams, relationships between objects on the client and on the server are stereotyped with the communication mechanism (IIOP or RMI). This distinction is important, since only these protocols can maintain an open connection between a client and a server object. In the other two architectural patterns, all communication between client and server object was through a server page and HTTP.

As an example of RMI usage in an application, we can look at an online sporting event monitoring application. Figure 10-20 shows the sequence diagram of an applet that is used

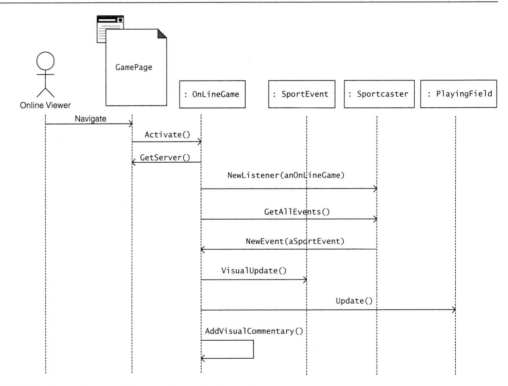

FIGURE 10-20   An online sporting event monitoring system

to monitor a sporting event in real time; the example is simplified to make it easier to understand. In this diagram the actor loads a page that starts an applet. Not shown in this diagram is all of the system activity that occurs to load the necessary components (OnLineGame applet and PlayingField class). Figure 10-20 is meant to express the exchange of messages between the logical components of the system over time, so the deployment details are left out. The deployment view of the architecture document, however, should cover those activities completely.

The OnLineGame applet begins by asking the client page for the name of the server it should contact. This information was embedded in the client page to facilitate load balancing. The applet then establishes a connection to the server's Sportscaster object which is responsible for forwarding all sporting event information to the OnLineGame. Information is exchanged in the form of SportingEvent, the object containing the details of the event that just happened in the real-life game. The applet queries SportingEvent and, if necessary, updates the PlayingField visual display. A textual description of the event is also displayed in the applet.

The structural view of these components is shown in Figure 10-21. Note the stereotypes for Java applet and IIOP. An association stereotyped «RMI» indicates that this relationship *may* be between a client and server object. The dependencies on the SportingEvent instance, however, do not represent a connection between client and server. These relationships just indicate that the OnlineGame and SportsCaster classes have knowledge of and depend on the public interface SportingEvent.

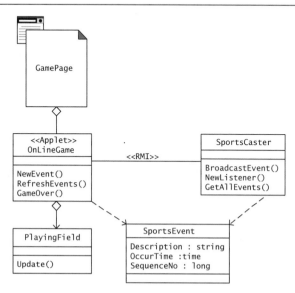

FIGURE 10-21 Logical view of sports event monitoring application

Guidelines for Web Application Design

The art of design, regardless of how we strive to automate it, will always contain situations that require the designer to make decisions on the basis of "gut" feelings. These decisions may have compelling arguments for every possible choice. In the end, it is the choices that are made that separate good designs from bad ones.

Here are a few guidelines that may help the designer when making these types of decisions.

- Be wary of using the latest capabilities of browsers. The browser wars continue, and it is difficult to predict which features will eventually become standard. The W3C has finalized a Document Object Model (DOM) standard that will, ideally, standardize the object interface of the browser. The standard is limited and missing some key elements, most notably an event model, and it is likely that each browser vendor will continue to have slightly different implementations. Just because it can be done doesn't mean it should be.

- Think about how the page is going to be tested. Don't use visual cues to let the actor know when the page is safe to interact with unless these same cues are accessible by an automated testing tool. I have seen sophisticated client pages use all sorts of dynamic HTML functions to prepare a page for use in response to the load event. It took several seconds to complete, and only a few visual cues let the actor know it was safe to begin using the page. Unfortunately, there was no event that an automated testing tool could easily use to know when it was safe to begin the test script. Until this page was redesigned, all testing had to be done manually.

- Avoid the temptation to use multiple browser windows simultaneously. Although this is a useful feature for some applications, designing and maintaining two client interfaces is more than just double the effort. Try to keep client-side complexity low, since the client is typically the component over which the development team has the least control.

- Keep consistent naming conventions when naming pages. If server pages are consistently separated to process input and build client pages, prefix all processing pages with `Process` and building pages with `Build` or something else suitable. When you are scanning the Web directory months later, trying to get a feel for what is going on, this consistently will pay off.

Chapter Summary

❑ Design is where the abstraction of the business takes its first step into the reality of software.

❑ Design starts with the analysis model and architecture as the major inputs.

❑ Design activities revolve around the class and interaction diagrams.

❑ The design model is something that can be mapped directly into code.

❑ The component view expresses the physical modules and executable that will be distributed as the system.

❑ Component diagrams visualize components, interfaces, and their interelationships.

❑ Mapping Web application–specific components, such as pages, to plain-vanilla UML is difficult.

❑ An extension to UML is an ordered way to add new semantics to UML notation.

❑ The UML extension mechanism defines stereotypes, tagged values, and constraints as a way to extend UML's semantics.

❑ The Web Application Extension for UML is a set of stereotypes, tagged values, and constraints that allows Web applications to be fully modeled with UML.

❑ Proper partitioning of the business objects in a Web application is critical and depends very much on the architecture.

❑ In Thin Web Client applications, actors interact *only* with client pages; server pages interact *only* with server resources.

❑ A server page is a stereotyped class that represents the Web page as it is processed on the server.

❑ A client page is a stereotyped class that represents the Web page as it is processed on the client.

❑ In Thick Web Client applications, the client can execute business logic with scripts, applets, or ActiveX controls, so interaction diagrams can include significant activity with client-side resources.

❑ In Web Delivery applications, objects on the client can engage in independent communication with objects on object servers.

Chapter 11
Implementation

The use cases have been completed, the problem has been analyzed, and a suitable design for the architecture has been defined. It is time for implementation. The activities of implementation include

- Mapping the design into code and components
- Unit testing
- Reverse engineering

The principal responsibility and activity of the implementer is to map the artifacts of design into executable code. The implementer, of course, uses more than just the artifacts modified by design. A thorough knowledge of the use cases is required to ensure that the meaning and the goals are not lost. The implementer's QA activities are continually validating the implementation decisions against the use cases and the requirements specification as a whole.

Every implementer is responsible for unit testing his or her own work. Some organizations may pair up implementers, and unit testing might be done by a partner; however, the goal is to have every artifact, or executable, unit tested before it is used by any other member of the team.

The final step in the sequence is reverse engineering any code changes that affect the artifacts in the model. This is important because the model is a view not only of the system to be built but also of the system *being* built and of the system that *was* built. Once the actual system and the model get out of sync, the model's ability to answer questions about the system is limited. Reverse engineering can be as simple as the developer or designer reviewing the code and manually updating the model. More sophisticated CASE tools have reverse-engineering capabilities built in and make this task much easier.

Since it is typical that most nontrivial Web applications will have a development staff of more than one, an important part of the development environment is to publish, as early as possible, interfaces between packages being worked on. This allows implementers to work asynchronously even when their own code is dependent on others'. Each developer will stub out his or her own public interface. In the case of Web page development, a suitable interface prototype can be created by implementing just the pages—in their correct directory—and their hyperlinks. For many CASE tools, this can be done automatically, with some scripts running against the design model.

This implementation of the public interface is also used by the testing team as it gets ready to write test scripts against the pages. The goal of this effort is to establish a concrete interface between fellow implementers and with the testing team. The graphic arts team can also use these pages—although they would have to make a personal copy—to begin implementing the look and feel of the user interface. With the look and feel in place, it is a small step to start using these pages for storyboarding and eliciting feedback from some of the more knowledgeable domain experts.

For the most part, the implementation of all of the server-side components—business objects, persistence layer, transaction components—is done exactly the same way as in any client/server system. The only difference, and the focus of this chapter, is in the construction of the Web-specific components, most notably the Web pages. Reiterating one of the main themes of this book: Web pages are architecturally significant components. They exist in the model and in the executable system. There is a direct mapping from Web page model elements to the actual Web page code. This chapter describes that mapping.

Web pages in a Web application can be implemented with scripted Web page files (ASP, JSP) or with compiled components (CGI, Java servlet, ISAPI, NSAPI). In either case, the logical separation of client-side and server-side activity is the same. Implementing the client pages in the model is essentially the same, regardless of which server-enabling technology is used.

The main differences encountered during implementation are with the server pages. The two strategies, scripted pages and compiled pages, break down to components differently. Compiled components often perform the role of multiple server pages. For example, one ISAPI DLL could be used to generate catalog pages with product information, to handle searches in the catalog, and to manage and process the shopping cart. One ISAPI DLL could be used to implement all of the dynamic Web pages. The design of this component will, obviously, be more complex than the design of any single server page in the system. The trick to implementing these types of designs is to pass appropriate parameters with the Web page request to indicate to the component which server page role it is to perform.

Scripted pages create one component per server page. That is, for every server page in the design model, there is a corresponding ASP or JSP file. It is possible for scripted pages to implement multiple client pages, assuming that the server page that it realizes also «builds» multiple client pages, although I tend to shy away from those kinds of designs.

The shopping cart section of the hypothetical Roses Alive! example is implemented with Microsoft's Active Server Pages. Figure 11-1 shows a screen shot of what the shopping cart looks like before the graphic arts team has a chance to "pretty it up."

The design model is shown in Figure 11-2. The stereotype icons are not shown in this particular diagram, since its main purpose is to provide a view for the implementer. The

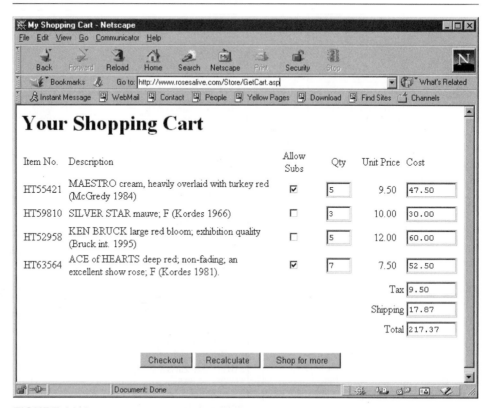

FIGURE 11-1 A rendered version of GetCart.asp

icons are great for getting an overall feel of the diagram, but when the individual attributes and operations need to be studied, the icons tend to get in the way. Again, the use of specialized stereotype icons is purely a personal matter.

The component view of the model begins with two packages: Server Components and Web Pages (Figure 11-3).[1] Server Components contains the server-side business components and can be implemented in any COM-able language. The attributes and operations in this model have been designed for Visual Basic implementation.[2] To keep things simple, there is only one server-side component, OnLineStore, and it is owned by the Server Components package. This component realizes the ShoppingCart, OrderLineItem and Product classes of the diagram in Figure 11-2.

Even though this is a simplistic example, the server-side components were separated from the Web page components because some semantics associated with the Web Pages

---

1. This is not the complete component view of the system, just the server component and pages necessary to implement the shopping cart page.

2. Let's face it, until COM+ comes out, it's much easier to read COM code written in Visual Basic than its equivalent in C++.

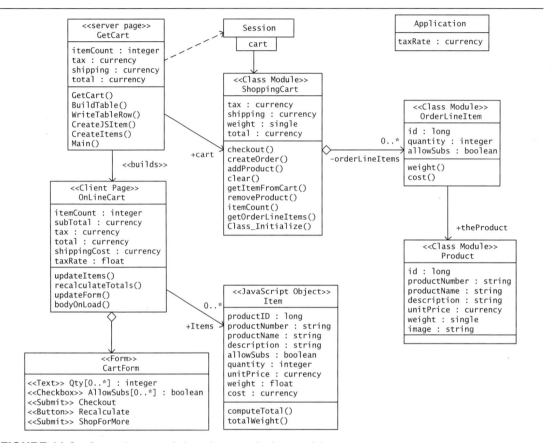

FIGURE 11-2 Class diagram of shopping cart design model

package are not appropriate for the server component. A Web Pages component package can be used to identify a directory location for the Web pages it owns. Web pages are distributed throughout the Web server's (and in particular the Web application's) home directory. They may be placed anywhere in the file system's hierarchy. A Web Pages package makes for a good abstraction of a Web server directory. All of the pages immediately owned by the page reside in the directory that the package represents. The actual values of the directory (its name and location) are assigned to a tagged value of the package. The tagged value *path* holds the name and location of a directory of the Web server. If the *path* tagged value is set to /store, the valid URLs in the application become

```
http://www.RosesAlive.com/store/StoreCatalog.asp
http://www.RosesAlive.com/store/OnLineCart.asp
http://www.RosesAlive.com/store/UpdateCart.asp
http://www.RosesAlive.com/store/CheckoutCart.asp
```

(At the time of this writing, the domain RosesAlive.com was not taken.)

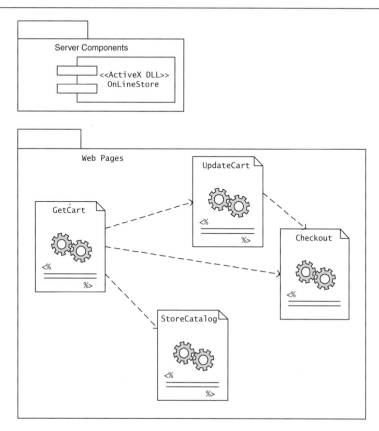

FIGURE 11-3   Component view

This, of course, assumes that each of these components realizes a server page. If the component realizes only a client page, the page can be implemented as an HTML file. Figure 11-4 shows the realizations of some of the Web Pages package's components[3]. Note that CheckoutCart and UpdateCart don't realize client pages. The reason is that they are pages that do only server-side processing. Once the processing is completed, they redirect to another page. This technique of separating responsibilities in pages helps make individual pages more reusable and further separates presentation from business logic.

The logical separation of client and server pages made during design also benefits the implementation. It is entirely possible for different team members to be responsible for the client page and the server page that builds it. The skill set of the client page implementer is JavaScript and a healthy knowledge of user interface design. The server page implementer

---

3. In this particular diagram, the icon form of the components is not used, to avoid any confusion with logical-view modeling elements.

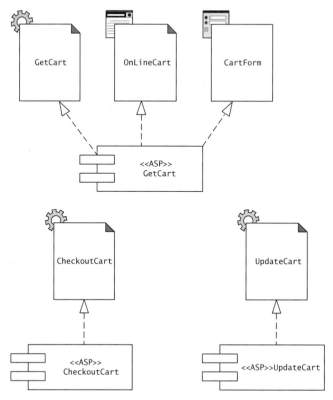

FIGURE 11-4   Web Pages component realizations

must be skilled in the use of the middle-tier components, persistence, and transaction systems. Additionally, the programming languages available on the server are limited only by
the available compilers.

Server Pages

Implementing server pages with Microsoft's Active Server Pages technology involves the
creation of scripted ASP files. These files, when requested by a client, are processed by
the Active Server Pages filter. Even though the extensions mentioned in the UML Extension for Web Applications document specify only «Page» as a possible component stereotype, when an enabling technology, such as ASP is selected, it is often useful to use a more
specific component stereotype. For ASP applications, I like to stereotype the component
«ASP». Should the architecture include the use of ISAPI DLLs in addition to ASP, there
would be «ISAPI» stereotyped elements in the component view. Specific stereotypes like
these help sort out the enabling technologies in mixed architectures.

The file name and location in the Web file system hierarchy are important pieces of information. These are captured as the *path* tagged value of the «Page» (or in this case «ASP») stereotyped component. The *path* tagged value specifies a complete path and file name for the ASP file. If this value is not set, it can be derived from the component's name and the package that owns it. If the package does not define its *path* tagged value, it too can be derived from the names in the package hierarchy. As a general rule, I define package paths and let the component's path be derived.

Figure 11-5 shows just the components involved with the GetCart server page. In this example, two ASP-specific singleton objects participate in the collaboration: the objects Session and Application. Session is a general-purpose dictionary object that maintains client state information on the server. There is one Session instance for each current client of the system. Application too is a dictionary object, maintaining general state information for the entire application (one Application object is shared by all clients).

The implementation of the GetCart server page begins by creating ASP code regions in the file and placing the necessary scripting language token at the beginning. The language used in this example is VBScript. Since ASP pages can be written in multiple languages, the tagged value Scripting language of a server page object specifies the language for the page. VBScript, like JavaScript, is not strictly typed. All variables in VBScript are variants and do not have to be declared before they are used. It is, however, nice to include them at the beginning of the file and to include a comment with a brief description of what they represent. All of this information is available from the GetCart class in the model.

Associations to server objects are implemented as variables. In this situation, it is up to the implementer to understand that the instance of ShoppingCart is obtained from the

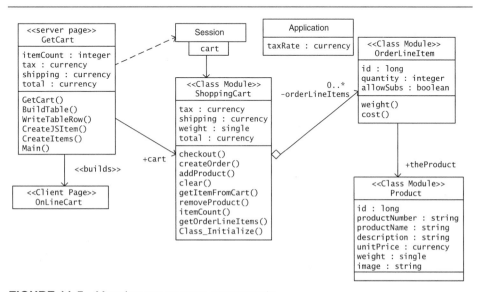

FIGURE 11-5 Mapping server page components

Session object. The structural information in the class diagram is insufficient to unambiguously produce the correct code to instantiate the correct ShoppingCart instance.

The shells of all of the functions and subroutines corresponding to the classes' operations are placed following the page's variables. Atop each function or subroutine is the operation's documentation as a comment. The following code represents the shell of the server page part of the GetCart ASP file.

```
<% language="VBSCRIPT">
<%
' <insert appropriate copyright information here>
' <insert appropriate version control information here>
' File: GetCart.asp
' Server Page: GetCart
'
' Description:
' The GetCart server page assembles the current user's shopping
' cart with the items that the user has selected over the
' course of the current session.

Dim cart  ' the user's server side shopping cart instance
Dim itemCount ' the number of items in the shopping cart
Dim tax  ' the total value of taxes for the items in this cart
Dim shipping  ' the total value of shipping charges for the items
              ' in this cart
Dim total ' the total cost for the items in this cart, including
          ' tax and shipping charges


'======================================================================
' Sub: GetCart
' Description:
' GetCart gets the current shopping cart instance from the session object
' and initializes the page's variables.
Sub GetCart

End Sub



'======================================================================
' Sub: BuildTable
' Description:
' BuildTable walks through each of the order line items to
' build a table containing all of the items currently in
' the user's shopping cart.
'
Sub BuildTable

End Sub

'======================================================================
' Sub: WriteTableRow
' Description:
' BuildTable walks through each of the order line items to
' build a table containing all of the items currently in
' the user's shopping cart.
```

```
'
' Parameters:
'   aLineItem - the OrderLineItem instance that represents one item
'   in a shopping cart.
'
'   i - the line item number.  This index is used to postfix the form
'   control names, so that they can be uniquely identified.
'
Sub WriteTableRow( aLineItem, i )

End Sub


'========================================================================
' Sub: CreateJSItem
' Description:
' Creates the JavaScript code that instantiates a specific JavaScript
' Item object instance.  Basically it just calls the Item's
' constructor (prototype).  This function does NOT define the
' JavaScript object (that is the job of the client page).
'
' Parameters:
'   aLineItem - the OrderLineItem instance that represents one item
'   in a shopping cart.
'
'   i - the line item number.  This index is used to index into the
'   array of Item JavaSctipt object.
'
Function CreateJSItem( lineItem, i )

End Function


'========================================================================
' Sub: CreateItems
' Description:
' Creates the JavaScript block that creates all of the JavaScript Item
' instances for the client.  This sub walks through each of the order
' line items in the current shopping cart and creates an Item instance
' in the resulting HTML page.
'
Sub CreateItems

End Sub


'========================================================================
' Sub: Main
' Description:
' The main VBScript function of the page.  The call to this
' VBScript sub is the only inline executable statement of this
' ASP file.
'
Sub Main

End Sub

%>
```

The semantics of the UML class diagram prevent the generation of any code inside the subroutines and functions of the page, so they are left blank. The preceding code can be automatically generated directly from the elements in the model.

The job of the implementer is to provide implementations to each of these functions and subroutines. The implementer uses additional documentation in the model, such as sequence diagrams, state diagrams, and activity diagrams, and examines the use cases to determine the appropriate dynamic behaviors for each class operation.

The easiest function to implement is the main function. In this page, main subroutine is simply a call to GetCart, which initializes the page's state. The GetCart implementation uses the Session object instance—a singleton in the context of an ASP page—to get the current cart and to initialize the page's variables. The cart variable is a reference to a ShoppingCart instance, which is implemented in a Visual Basic ActiveX DLL. Its interface supports calls to itemCount, tax, shipping, and total. The FormatNumber function converts the value to a string suitable for representing currency values.

```
Sub GetCart
  Set cart = Session("Cart")
  itemCount = cart.itemCount
  tax = FormatNumber(cart.tax,2)
  shipping = FormatNumber(cart.shipping,2)
  total = FormatNumber(cart.total,2)
End Sub
```

The BuildTable subroutine simply gets the order line items from the shopping cart as a variant array and walks through them, calling another subroutine to write out the appropriate HTML tags and values for a line item in the shopping cart.

```
Sub BuildTable
  Dim i
  Dim lineItems

  lineItems = cart.getOrderLineItems
  if isEmpty(lineItems) then
    ' empty cart
  else
    for i = 0 to ubound(lineItems)
      WriteTableRow lineItems(i), (i+1)
    next
  end if
End Sub
```

The WriteTableRow subroutine contains a significant amount of HTML and can be a little confusing to read. This function uses the ASP Response singleton, which is the object interface of the outgoing page, which is currently under construction. Its write method accepts a string and appends to the HTML stream that ultimately will be sent back to the client browser. The aLineItem parameter is an OrderLineItem instance. The parameter i is the index of the line item in the cart. The subroutine first gets the line item information and places it in easy-to-use and understand variables, then goes on to write out the HTML table row tags. The columns of the table contain the product's name, number, unit cost, and so on. Some of the columns contain form input elements, which let the user change the *quantity* and *allow substitutions* properties of the shopping cart item.

It must be noted that the total-cost column is also implemented as a form input field. The reason is that the client page will dynamically update these values when the user changes quantities and clicks the Recalculate button. Since the requirements of this application include the need to run on Netscape and IE browsers, the use of IE's DHTML capabilities to change the page's content can't be used here. The only way for a Netscape browser to update a displayed value is through the use of an input element in a form.

To help make the following code readable for non-VBScript coders, the VBScript double quote is used as an escape character. To embed a double quote in a string constant, a pair of double quotes must be used. For example, the string constant Roses Alive! "new" collection of live cut roses would require the VBScript string constant "Roses Alive! ""new"" collection of live cut roses". The line-continuation character in VBScript is the underscore (_). The vbCrLf string constant is used to force new lines in the resulting HTML page. In most cases, new lines do not affect the rendering of the HTML page and are done only to make the HTML output more readable, which is especially useful during implementation and debugging.

```
Sub WriteTableRow( aLineItem, i )
  Dim ProductNumber
  Dim ProductName
  Dim Description
  Dim AllowSubs
  Dim Qty
  Dim Weight
  Dim UnitPrice
  Dim ProductDescription

  ProductNumber = aLineItem.theProduct.ProductNumber
  ProductName = aLineItem.theProduct.ProductName
  Description = aLineItem.theProduct.Description
  ProductDescription = ProductName & " " & Description
  AllowSubs = aLineItem.allowSubs
  Qty = aLineItem.Quantity
  Weight = aLineItem.theProduct.Weight
  UnitPrice = FormatNumber(aLineItem.theProduct.UnitPrice,2)
  Cost = FormatNumber(aLineItem.Cost,2)

  response.write("<tr>" & vbCrLf)
  response.write("    <td width=""10%"">" & ProductNumber & "</td>" &  vbCrLf)
  response.write("    <td width=""50%"">" & ProductDescription & "</td>" &
    vbCrLf)
  if AllowSubs then
    response.write("    <td width=""10%"" align=""center""><input
      type=""checkbox"" name=""AllowSubs" & i & """ value=""AllowSubs""
      CHECKED></td>" & vbCrLf)
  else
    response.write("    <td width=""10%"" align=""center""><input
      type=""checkbox"" name=""AllowSubs" & i & """ value=""NotAllowSubs"" >
      </td>" & vbCrLf)
```

```
      end if
      response.write("    <td width=""10%"" align=""center""><input type=""text""
        name=""Qty" & i & """ size=""3""  value=""" & Qty & """></td>" & vbCrLf)
      response.write("    <td width=""10%"" align=""right"">" & UnitPrice & "
          </td>" & vbCrLf)
      response.write("    <td width=""10%"" align=""right""><input type=""text""
        name=""Cost" & i & """ size=""8"" value=""" & cost & """></td>" & vbCrLf)
      response.write("</tr>"& vbCrLf)

End Sub
```

This function illustrates one of the places in the implementation process where the presentation is meshed with the business logic. Normally, the relative sizes of the columns, and perhaps even their display styles, would be determined by the graphic artist and UI designer, yet it is the server page implementer who is in control of that here. Despite our best attempts at separating presentation from the business logic, it can't easily be separated in an ASP environment, and we just have to be careful when working with it. It is up to the process—and in particular the configuration and change management workflow—to facilitate the UI and business changes that will occur with this component.

The remaining function and subroutine create and initialize JavaScript Item objects. The subroutine must first write out the necessary tags and comments to define a script region in the HTML. The subroutine next initializes the client page's variables. Next, the Item instances are written out for each order line item in the shopping cart. Finally, the closing tags and comments of the script block are written out.

```
Sub CreateItems
  Dim i
  Dim lineItems

  response.write("<script language=""JavaScript""><!--" & vbCrLf)
  response.write("itemCount = " & cart.ItemCount & ";" & vbCrLf)
  response.write("taxRate = " & Application("TaxRate") & ";" & vbCrLf)
  response.write("tax = " & cart.Tax & ";" & vbCrLf)
  response.write("shipping = " & cart.Shipping & ";" & vbCrLf)
  response.write("total = " & cart.Total & ";" & vbCrLf)
  response.write("var items = new Array(itemCount);" & ";" & vbCrLf)


  ' for each item in the cart create a JS instance
  lineItems = cart.getOrderLineItems
  if isEmpty(lineItems) then
    ' empty cart
  else
    for i = 0 to ubound(lineItems)-1
      response.write( CreateJSItem( lineItems(i), i ) )
    next
  end if

  response.write("// --></script>" & vbCrLf)


End Sub
```

The CreateJSItem function returns a string that represents an executable JavaScript line of code that creates and instantiates an Item instance. To instantiate a custom JavaScript object, its prototype is called. The creation of JavaScript objects is discussed in more detail next.

```
Function CreateJSItem( lineItem, i )
  Dim str

  str = "items[" & i & "] = new "
  str = str & "Item( " & lineItem.theProduct.id & ", "
  str = str & """" & lineItem.theProduct.productNumber & """, "
  str = str & """" & lineItem.theProduct.productName & """, "
  str = str & """" & lineItem.theProduct.description & """, "
  str = str & lcase(lineItem.AllowSubs) & ", "
  str = str & lineItem.Quantity & ", "
  str = str & lineItem.theProduct.UnitPrice & ", "
  str = str & lineItem.theProduct.Weight & ", "
  str = str & lineItem.Cost & ");"
  str = str & vbCrLf

  CreateJSItem = str
End Function
```

The resulting JavaScript output[4] of CreateItems and CreateJSItem used in the Figure 11-1 screen shot is

```
<script language="JavaScript"><!--
itemCount = 4;
taxRate = 0.05;
tax = 9.50;
shipping = 17.87;
total = 217.37;
var items = new Array(itemCount);;
items[0] = new Item( 178, "HT55421", "MAESTRO", "cream, heavily overlaid with
  turkey red (McGredy 1984)", true, 5, 9.5, 1.6, 47.5);
items[1] = new Item( 283, "HT59810", "SILVER STAR", "mauve; F (Kordes 1966)",
  false, 3, 10, 1.7, 30);
items[2] = new Item( 148, "HT52958", "KEN BRUCK", "large red bloom; exhibition
  quality (Bruck int. 1995)", false, 5, 12, 1.3, 60);
items[3] = new Item( 2, "HT63564", "ACE of HEARTS", "deep red; non-fading; an
  excellent show rose; F (Kordes 1981).", true, 7, 7.5, 1.3, 52.5);
// --></script>
```

One other server page–related element that can be implemented—but not in the shopping cart example—is the «redirects» association. The concept of redirection is partly structural and partly dynamic. Structurally, the redirection captures the page to redirect to. The semantics of the class diagrams, however, do not capture when and under what conditions a redirection is made. Therefore, the VBScript Response.Redirect command cannot be

---

4. The exact format has been altered to make it a little more readable in this text.

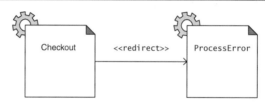

FIGURE 11- 6   Implementing redirection

automatically put in server-side code. ASP code generators could either identify possible redirections in comments or instead supply a subroutine that could be called for each redirection. For example, the redirection between the two server pages in Figure 11-6 would be implemented, via CASE tool code generation, as a subroutine in the checkout page called RedirectToProcessError.

```
Sub RedirectToProcessError
  Response.Redirect "ProcessError.asp"
End Sub
```

Of course, the URL specified in the operation Redirect would be determined by getting the URL from the ProcessError server page. Any page's URL must be obtained from the component that realizes it. The full URL is the determined by the *path* tagged value of the component and, it its absence, the *path* tagged value of its owning package.

Client Pages

The mappings between client page model elements and code are essentially the same for all server-side enabling technologies. Unless VBScript is used as the client-side scripting language, all client page code is implemented as JavaScript. This, of course, doesn't mean that objects in a Web Delivery architecture have to be coded with JavaScript; just the operations and attributes of the «client page» do.

In the shopping cart example, only the server page elements were mapped to the GetCart.asp file. The rest of the ASP file comes from the realizations of the OnLineCart client page and the CartForm form. Figure 11-7 shows the relevant model elements for this page.

The mapping of the client page element begins with the standard HTML headers and tags:

```
<html>
<head>
<meta HTTP-EQUIV="Content-Type" content="text/html; charset=iso-8859-1">
<title>My Shopping Cart</title>
</head>
```

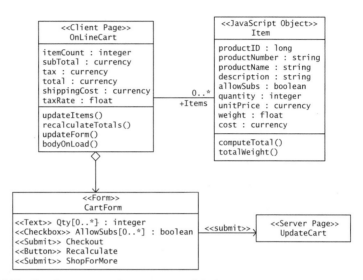

FIGURE 11-7 GetCart.asp client page model elements

The value for the title tag comes from the Title tagged value of the client page class. In Rational Rose, tagged values are captured as properties of tools. In Rose, it is possible to define your own tools and to capture custom tagged values.

Figure 11-8 shows a screen shot of the ASP tool I created to capture the Web Application Extension's tagged values. The first tagged value in the list is Title. Most UML-compliant CASE tools should have a mechanism for capturing custom tagged values. The Rose scripts to create the ASP tool and its tagged values are given in Appendix E.

After the required HTML headers come the client page's scripts. For each operation specified in the client page class, a JavaScript function is created. The script block begins with the following:

```
<script language="JavaScript"><!--
// <insert appropriate copyright information here>
// <insert appropriate version control information here>
// File: GetCart.asp
// Client Page: OnLineCart
//
// Description:
// The OnLineCart contains the list of all the items the user
// has selected to include in the shopping cart. This page
// allows the user to update the quantities and change the allow
// subsititutions property for each cart item.  If the user clicks
// the Recalculate button, the totals on the page are recomputed
// locally on the client with JavaScript functions.  The new values
// are updated in the fields.
//
```

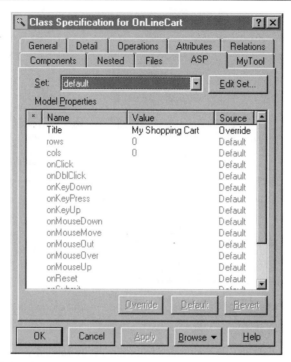

FIGURE 11-8   Custom ASP tool in Rational Rose

```
var itemCount;  // the number of items in the cart
var subTotal;  // the total value of just the items
var tax;  // the value of the tax charges applied to this order
var total;  // the total cost to the customer
var shippingCost; // the cost of the shipping charges
var taxRate;  // the tax rate applied to the computation of the taxes

//=====================================================================
// function: updateItems
// Description:
// Updates the state of the Item instances with the values that the
// user may have changed.
//
function updateItems() {

}


//=====================================================================
// function: recalculateTotals
// Description:
// Recalculates the current values of the line item totals
// and of the cart totals.  Once the values have been updated
// the visual form is updated.
//
```

```
function recalculateTotals() {

}

//========================================================================
// function: updateForm
// Description:
// Updates the visual display of the form with the current values in
// the Item instances.
//
function updateForm() {

}

//========================================================================
// function: asCurrency
// Description:
// Utility function to format a currency value with two decimals
// and at least one leading digit.  The return is formatted as a string.
//
// Parameters:
//    val - a currency value
//
function asCurrency(val)
{

}

//========================================================================
// function: bodyOnLoad
// Description:
// Event handler for the on load event from body tag.  This is the main
// client side function for the page.  It calls update form, to ensure
// that the correct information is displayed.
//
function bodyOnLoad(){

}

// --></script>
```

As with the VBScript code generation, the preceding shell can be automatically generated from the model. One thing to consider when documenting client page functions is that all of the comments used to help explain the JavaScript are open to the public. Any intelligent user, and potential competitors with access to the system, will be able to read this code and its comments. There are certain security implementations when referencing and describing client side-objects with database schema information. In this example, I have made the comments as clear and as concise as possible for readability.

If proprietary information or algorithms are needed on the client, it is best to package them up in a Java applet or an ActiveX control. Any comments made in these components cannot be reversed engineered by unscrupulous competitors.

Much of the implementation of the JavaScript Item object can be generated from the model. The Item object represents a line item in the shopping cart and contains information about the selected product and the quantity and substitution value the user has selected. The prototype and functions for the Item object are placed in the same code block as the client page.

```
//=====================================================================
// prototype: Item
// Description:
// Defines and instantiates an instance of an Item JavaScript object.
//
// Parameters:
//   productID - The internal unique ID (DB primary key) of the product.
//   productNumber - The public number of the product (carryover of
//        legacy system).
//   productName - The name of the product
//   description - a one line description of the project
//   allowSubs - A true value means the customer allows the Roses Alive!
//        substitute rose varieties with similar ones, if the exact
//        variety is not available.
//   quantity - The number of products
//   unitPrice - The cost per unit of the product
//   weight - The unit weight of the product
//   cost - The cost of this line item (quantity * unitPrice)
//
function Item(productID, productNumber, productName, description, allowSubs,
quantity, unitPrice, weight, cost) {
  this.productID = productID;
  this.productNumber = productNumber;
  this.productName = productName;
  this.description = description;
  this.allowSubs = allowSubs;
  this.quantity= quantity;
  this.unitPrice = unitPrice;
  this.weight = weight;
  this.cost = cost;
  this.computeTotal = computeTotal;
  this.totalWeight = totalWeight;
}


//=====================================================================
// Item member function: computeTotal
// Description:
// Computes the total cost for this line item.
//
function computeTotal() {

}


//=====================================================================
// Item member function: totalWeight
// Description:
// Computes the total weight for this line item.
//
function totalWeight() {

}
```

It is possible for code generators to automate the generation of the prototype function body, given the convention that all of the parameters represent properties of the object. Additionally, the model contains the necessary information to associate the two functions with the object. The function bodies of the two functions—computeTotal and totalWeight—however, must be implemented manually.

The shells of these scripts can all be forward engineered directly from the model. As with the server-side scripts, the implementer must provide implementations of all of the functions specified in the script. And again, the implementer looks to the other design artifacts—sequence, state, and activity diagrams—and to the use cases to provide the proper code for these functions. The following script block represents the implemented functions, which is appended to the existing GetCart.asp.

```javascript
<script language="JavaScript"><!--
// <insert appropriate copyright information here>
// <insert appropriate version control information here>
// File: GetCart.asp
// Client Page: OnLineCart
//
// Description:
// The OnLineCart contains the list of all the items the user
// has selected to include in the shopping cart. This page
// allows the user to update the quantities and change the allow
// subsititutions property for each cart item.  If the user clicks
// the Recalculate button, the totals on the page are recomputed
// locally on the client with JavaScript functions.  The new values
// are updated in the fields.
//
var itemCount;  // the number of items in the cart
var subTotal;  // the total value of just the items
var tax;  // the value of the tax charges applied to this order
var total;  // the total cost to the customer
var shippingCost; // the cost of the shipping charges
var taxRate;  // the tax rate applied to the computation of the taxes


//===================================================================
// function: updateItems
// Description:
// Updates the state of the Item instances with the values that the
// user may have changed.
//
function updateItems() {
  var i; // index into items;
  var key; // name of form field

  // update objects and the display
  for (i = 0; i < itemCount; i++ ){
    key = 'AllowSubs' + (i + 1);
    items[i].allowSubs = document.forms[0].elements[key].checked;
    key = 'Qty' + (i + 1);
    items[i].quantity = document.forms[0].elements[key].value;
  }
}
```

```
//========================================================================
// function: recalculateTotals
// Description:
// Recalculates the current values of the line item totals
// and of the cart totals.  Once the values have been updated
// the visual form is updated.
//
function recalculateTotals() {
  var i; // index into items;
  var shipWeight = 0;

  subTotal = 0;
  tax = 0;
  shipping = 0;

  updateItems();

  for (i = 0; i < itemCount; i++ ){
    items[i].computeTotal();
    subTotal = subTotal + items[i].cost;
    tax = tax + taxRate * subTotal;
    shipWeight = shipWeight + items[i].totalWeight();
  }

  if ( shipWeight < 75 ) {
    shipping = 15 + shipWeight * 0.10;
  }
  else {
    shipping = 15 + shipWeight * 0.15;
  }

  updateForm();
}

//========================================================================
// function: updateForm
// Description:
// Updates the visual display of the form with the current values in
// the Item instances.
//
function updateForm() {
  var i; // index into items;
  var key; // name of form field
  var itemCost;

  total = 0;

  // update objects and the display
  for (i = 0; i < itemCount; i++ ){
    key = 'AllowSubs' + (i + 1);
    document.forms[0].elements[key].checked = items[i].allowSubs;
    key = 'Qty' + (i + 1);
    document.forms[0].elements[key].value = items[i].quantity;
    key = 'Cost' + (i + 1);
    itemCost = items[i].cost;
    document.forms[0].elements[key].value = asCurrency(itemCost);
```

```
    total = total + itemCost;
  }

  document.forms[0].elements['Tax'].value = asCurrency(tax);
  document.forms[0].elements['Shipping'].value = asCurrency(shipping);
  document.forms[0].elements['Total'].value = asCurrency(total);

}

//=====================================================================
// prototype: Item
// Description:
// Defines and instantiates an instance of an Item JavaScript object.
//
// Parameters:
//   productID - The internal unique ID (DB primary key) of the product.
//   productNumber - The public number of the product (carryover of
//         legacy system).
//   productName - The name of the product
//   description - a one line description of the project
//   allowSubs - A true value means the customer allows the Roses Alive!
//         substitute rose varieties with similar ones, if the exact
//         variety is not available.
//   quantity - The number of products
//   unitPrice - The cost per unit of the product
//   weight - The unit weight of the product
//   cost - The cost of this line item (quantity * unitPrice)
//
function Item(productID, productNumber, productName, description, allowSubs,
quantity, unitPrice, weight, cost) {
  this.productID = productID;
  this.productNumber = productNumber
  this.productName = productName;
  this.description = description;
  this.allowSubs = allowSubs;
  this.quantity= quantity;
  this.unitPrice = unitPrice;
  this.weight = weight;
  this.cost = cost;
  this.computeTotal = computeTotal;
  this.totalWeight = totalWeight;
}

//=====================================================================
// Item member function: computeTotal
// Description:
// Computes the total cost for this line item.
//
function computeTotal() {

  if ( this.quantity > 0 ) {
    this.cost = this.unitPrice * this.quantity;
  }
  else {
    this.cost  = 0;
  }

}
```

```
//======================================================================
// Item member function: totalWeight
// Description:
// Computes the total weight for this line item.
//
function totalWeight() {
  return this.quantity * this.weight;
}


//======================================================================
// function: asCurrency
// Description:
// Utility function to format a currency value with two decimals
// and at least one leading digit.  The return is formatted as a string.
//
// Parameters:
//    val - a currency value
//
function asCurrency(val)
{
    var dp;
  var intgr;
  var dec;
    var beg;
    var end;
    var str;

    str = val.toString();
    dp = str.indexOf(".");
    if (dp > 0 ) {
        intgr = str.substr(0,dp);
        dec = str.substr(dp+1,str.length);
    }
    else {
    if ( dp == 0 ){
        intgr = str.substr(1,str.length-1);
        dec = '0';
    }
    else {
      if ( dp == -1 ){ // must be whole number
        dec = '0';
        intgr = str;
      }
      else { // invalid value
        intgr = "invalid value"
        return intgr;
      }
    }
  }

  // now that we have the parts, let's reassemble them
  // into a currency form

  // round decimal portion
  if ( dec.length >= 2 ){
    d = dec.substr(2,1);
```

```
     if ( d >= 5 ) { // round up
       v = dec.substr(1,1) - 0;
       dec = dec.substr(0,1) + (v + 1);
     }
     else {
       dec = dec.substr(0,2);
     }
   }

   // now make sure that the decimal is always 2 digits
   switch (dec.length) {
     case 0:
       dec = '00';
       break;
     case 1:
       dec = dec + '0';
       break;
   }

   return (intgr + '.' + dec);
}

//========================================================================
// function: bodyOnLoad
// Description:
// Event handler for the on load event from body tag.  This is the main
// client side function for the page.  It calls update form, to ensure
// that the correct information is displayed.
//
function bodyOnLoad(){
  updateForm();
}

// --></script>
```

The client page attributes and operations are only half of the model elements that need to be implemented. The remainder of the page is coded in HTML. The main body of the HTML page begins with the <body> tag. There is only one such tag per HTML page. It turns out that the client page onLoad tagged value is set to the value bodyOnLoad(). This means that the on-load event of the body tag should be directed to the client page function bodyOnLoad(). Figure 11-9 shows the same Rose specifications dialog and ASP tool settings (only this time scrolled down), showing the onLoad event tagged value setting. This tagged value is used in the <body> tag for the page.

The client page OnLineCart has a form class: CartForm. The form is mapped directly to <form> tags in HTML. The construction of forms is one of those Web elements that is half presentation and half business. There is relatively little presentation information in the structural model of the system, so the ability to generate HTML form code is limited to the following;

```
<body onLoad="bodyOnLoad()">

<form name="CartForm" method="POST" action="UpdateCart.asp">
```

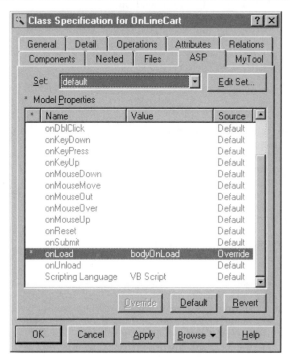

FIGURE 11-9   The Rose class specification dialog, showing the `onLoad` tagged value of the `OnLineCart` client page

```
        <!--
        Insert array of form elements
        <input type="checkbox" name="AllowSubs[0..*]">
        <input type="text" name="Qty[0..*]" size="3">
        <input type="text" name="Cost[0..*]" size="8">
        -->

  <input type="text" name="Tax" size="8">
  <input type="text" name="Shipping" size="8">
  <input type="text" name="Total" size="8">
  <input type="submit" name="Checkout" value="Checkout">
  <input type="button" name="Recalculate" value="Recalculate"
         onClick="recalculateTotals()">
  <input type="submit" name="shopForMore" value="Shop for more" >

</form>

</body>
</html>
```

The name of the form is the name of the «form» stereotyped class. The method POST is determined from the tagged value SubmitMethod of the «submit» association between the form and processing server page. The value of the action parameter is the URL of the server page that processes the form. Remember, the URL comes from the component that realizes the server page; in this case, the component and the server page are both named UpdateCart.asp.

Variable-length arrays of form input elements just can't be automatically generated from the model. In these situations, the best that can be done is a comment placed in the form. If the form element multiplicity is exactly 1 or if the array of elements is fixed, code generation can place these tags in the form.

The stereotype of the «form» attribute determines which tag should be used (<input>, <selection>, <textarea>) and, if necessary, what the type of the <input> element is. Each form element specified in the form class makes use of a different set of attribute tagged values. Text box elements use the name of the attribute for the tag's name. The size tagged value is used to set the field's size value. For buttons, the value tagged value is accessed; if it is not set in the model, it is defaulted to the button's name.

Form elements can react to a large number of events. Event handlers are assigned with attribute tagged values. The only event that is handled in this situation is the clicking of the Recalculate button. The on click event is handled by the recalculateTotals() client function. In the model, the attribute tagged value onClick is set to recalculateTotals() (see Figure 11-10).

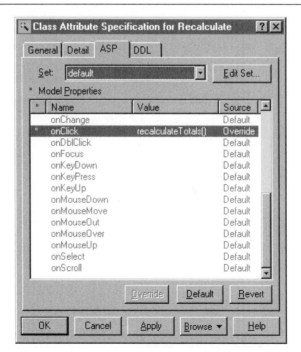

FIGURE 11-10 Tagged values for Recalculate form button

The results of code generation from the model are pretty slim but offer a good structured start. If we were to look at the generated page, there would be only a few fields and buttons showing (Figure 11-11).

The implementer must modify or insert the necessary HTML to implement a functional (if not pretty) version of the shopping cart. Making the user interface pretty is the job of the graphic artist; the job of the implementer is to make it functional. At this stage, a combination of server-side and client-side function usage is required. This is where the server page meets the client page, and plenty of care must be taken by the implementer.

First, the implementer puts in the necessary call to the server page's main subroutine. This does not happen automatically, since the proper dynamics are not captured in the mostly static model. This is very easily accomplished by just putting the call to `main` at the very end of the VBScript block. The VBScript interpreter will read and parse all of the server-side scripts and at last see the call to the `main` function and execute it, before any of the client page parts of the ASP file are seen.

The next subtle part to be coded is the instantiation of the JavaScript Item objects. The code for the instantiation of these objects is produced by sever-side VBScript code. They are therefore separate from the code-generated client JavaScripts and are placed in their own `<script>` block. Since they are executed as in-line JavaScript, they must be placed after the `main` JavaScript code block. This is done with a call to the VBScript function `CreateItems`.

The rest of the HTML code is in a `<table>` tag. The table is defined, and tentative column headings are inserted. The implementer sees the comments regarding the variable-length line item input fields and replaces it with a call to the VBScript server function `BuildTable`. This function outputs table rows, each containing a shopping cart item. The implementer also takes the liberty of defining column widths and alignments to the table

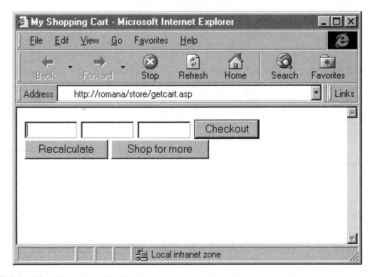

FIGURE 11- 11   Results of initial code generation

cells. The final result is a fully functional ASP page that calls server-side objects to create a shopping cart page, which allows the user to locally adjust quantities and substitution values without requiring a separate server trip.

```asp
<%@ LANGUAGE="VBSCRIPT" %>
<%

' <insert appropriate copyright information here>
' <insert appropriate version control information here>
' File: GetCart.asp
' Server Page: GetCart
'
' Description:
' The GetCart server page assembles the current user's shopping cart
' with the items that the user has selected over the course of the
' current session.

Dim cart  ' the user's server side shopping cart instance
Dim itemCount ' the number of items in the shopping cart
Dim tax  ' the total value of taxes for the items in this cart
Dim shipping  ' the total value of shipping charges for the items in this cart
Dim total ' the total cost for the items in this cart, including tax and
            ' shipping charges

'=======================================================================
' Sub: GetCart
' Description:
' GetCart gets the current shopping cart instance from the session object
' and initializes the page's variables.
'
Sub GetCart
  Set cart = Session("Cart")
  itemCount = cart.itemCount
  tax = FormatNumber(cart.tax,2)
  shipping = FormatNumber(cart.shipping,2)
  total = FormatNumber(cart.total,2)
End Sub


'=======================================================================
' Sub: BuildTable
' Description:
' BuildTable walks through each of the order line items to
' build a table containing all of the items currently in
' the user's shopping cart.
'
Sub BuildTable
  Dim i
  Dim lineItems

  lineItems = cart.getOrderLineItems
  if isEmpty(lineItems) then
    ' empty cart
  else
    for i = 0 to ubound(lineItems)-1
      WriteTableRow lineItems(i), (i+1)
```

```
        next
    end if

End Sub

'=======================================================================
' Sub: WriteTableRow
' Description:
' WriteTableRow writes a single table row for a line item.
'
' Parameters:
'   aLineItem - the OrderLineItem instance that represents one item
'   in a shopping cart.
'
'   i - the line item number.  This index is used to postfix the form
'   control names, so that they can be uniquely identified.
'
Sub WriteTableRow( aLineItem, i )
    Dim ProductNumber
    Dim ProductName
    Dim Description
    Dim AllowSubs
    Dim Qty
    Dim Weight
    Dim UnitPrice
    Dim ProductDescription

    ProductNumber = aLineItem.theProduct.ProductNumber
    ProductName = aLineItem.theProduct.ProductName
    Description = aLineItem.theProduct.Description
    ProductDescription = ProductName & " " & Description
    AllowSubs = aLineItem.allowSubs
    Qty = aLineItem.Quantity
    Weight = aLineItem.theProduct.Weight
    UnitPrice = FormatNumber(aLineItem.theProduct.UnitPrice,2)
    Cost = FormatNumber(aLineItem.Cost,2)

    response.write("<tr>" & vbCrLf)
    response.write("    <td width=""10%"">" & ProductNumber &_
        "</td>" &  vbCrLf)
      response.write("    <td width=""50%"">" & ProductDescription &_
        "</td>" & vbCrLf)
      if AllowSubs then
        response.write("    <td width=""10%"" align=""center"">" &_
            "<input type=""checkbox"" name=""AllowSubs" & i &_
            """ value=""AllowSubs"" CHECKED></td>" & vbCrLf)
      else
        response.write("    <td width=""10%"" align=""center"">" &_
            "<input type=""checkbox"" name=""AllowSubs" & i &_
            """ value=""NotAllowSubs"" ></td>" & vbCrLf)
      end if
      response.write("    <td width=""10%"" align=""center"">" &_
        "<input type=""text"" name=""Qty" & i &_
        """ size=""3""  value=""" & Qty & """></td>" & vbCrLf)
      response.write("    <td width=""10%"" align=""right"">" &_
        UnitPrice & "   </td>" & vbCrLf)
```

```
    response.write("    <td width="""10%""" align="""right""">" &_
       <input type="""text""" name="""Cost" & i &_
       """ size="""8""" value=""" & cost & """></td>" & vbCrLf)
    response.write("</tr>"& vbCrLf)

End Sub

'========================================================================
' Sub: CreateJSItem
' Description:
' Creates the JavaScript code that instantiates a specific JavaScript
' Item object instance.  Basically it just calls the Item's
' constructor (prototype).  This function does NOT define the
' JavaScript object (that is the job of the client page).
'
' Parameters:
'   aLineItem - the OrderLineItem instance that represents one item
'   in a shopping cart.
'
'   i - the line item number.  This index is used to index into the
'   array of Item JavaSctipt object.
'
Function CreateJSItem( lineItem, i )
  Dim str

  str = "items[" & i & "] = new "
  str = str & "Item( " & lineItem.theProduct.id & ", "
  str = str & """" & lineItem.theProduct.productNumber & """, "
  str = str & """" & lineItem.theProduct.productName & """, "
  str = str & """" & lineItem.theProduct.description & """, "
  str = str & lcase(lineItem.AllowSubs) & ", "
  str = str & lineItem.Quantity & ", "
  str = str & lineItem.theProduct.UnitPrice & ", "
  str = str & lineItem.theProduct.Weight & ", "
  str = str & lineItem.Cost & ");"
  str = str & vbCrLf

  CreateJSItem = str
End Function

'========================================================================
' Sub: CreateItems
' Description:
' Creates the JavaScript block that creates all of the JavaScript Item
' instances for the client.  This sub walks through each of the order
' line items in the current shopping cart and creates an Item instance
' in the resulting HTML page.
'
Sub CreateItems
  Dim i
  Dim lineItems

  response.write("<script language="""JavaScript"""><!--" & vbCrLf)
  response.write("itemCount = " & itemCount & ";" & vbCrLf)
  response.write("taxRate = " & Application("TaxRate") & ";" & vbCrLf)
  response.write("tax = " & tax & ";" & vbCrLf)
```

```
      response.write("shipping = " & shipping & ";" & vbCrLf)
      response.write("total = " & total & ";" & vbCrLf)
      response.write("var items = new Array(itemCount);" & ";" & vbCrLf)

      ' for each item in the cart create a JS instance
      lineItems = cart.getOrderLineItems
      if isEmpty(lineItems) then
        ' empty cart
      else
        for i = 0 to ubound(lineItems)-1
          response.write( CreateJSItem( lineItems(i), i ) )
        next
      end if

      response.write("// --></script>" & vbCrLf)


End Sub


'=======================================================================
' Sub: Main
' Description:
' The main VBScript function of the page.  The call to this
' VBScript sub is the only inline executable statement of this
' ASP file.
'
Sub Main

  GetCart

End Sub

Main
%>

<html>
<head>

<title>My Shopping Cart</title>
</head>

<script language="JavaScript"><!--
// <insert appropriate copyright information here>
// <insert appropriate version control information here>
// File: GetCart.asp
// Client Page: OnLineCart
//
// Description:
// The OnLineCart contains the list of all the items the user
// has selected to include in the shopping cart. This page
// allows the user to update the quantities and change the allow
// substitutions property for each cart item.  If the user clicks
// the Recalculate button, the totals on the page are recomputed
// locally on the client with JavaScript functions.  The new values
// are updated in the fields.
//
```

```
var itemCount;  // the number of items in the cart
var subTotal;  // the total value of just the items
var tax;  // the value of the tax charges applied to this order
var total;  // the total cost to the customer
var shippingCost; // the cost of the shipping charges
var taxRate;  // the tax rate applied to the computation of the taxes


//========================================================================
// function: updateItems
// Description:
// Updates the state of the Item instances with the values that the
// user may have changed.
//
function updateItems() {
  var i; // index into items;
  var key; // name of form field

  // update objects and the display
  for (i = 0; i < itemCount; i++ ){
    key = 'AllowSubs' + (i + 1);
    items[i].allowSubs = document.forms[0].elements[key].checked;
    key = 'Qty' + (i + 1);
    items[i].quantity = document.forms[0].elements[key].value;
  }
}


//========================================================================
// function: recalculateTotals
// Description:
// Recalculates the current values of the line item totals
// and of the cart totals.  Once the values have been updated
// the visual form is updated.
//
function recalculateTotals() {
  var i; // index into items;
  var shipWeight = 0;

  subTotal = 0;
  tax = 0;
  shipping = 0;

  updateItems();

  for (i = 0; i < itemCount; i++ ){
    items[i].computeTotal();
    subTotal = subTotal + items[i].cost;
    tax = tax + taxRate * items[i].cost;
    shipWeight = shipWeight + items[i].totalWeight();
  }

  if ( shipWeight < 75 ) {
    shipping = 15 + shipWeight * 0.10;
  }
  else {
    shipping = 15 + shipWeight * 0.15;
  }
```

```
  updateForm();
}

//=======================================================================
// function: updateForm
// Description:
// Updates the visual display of the form with the current values in
// the Item instances.
//
function updateForm() {
  var i; // index into items;
  var key; // name of form field
  var itemCost;

  total = 0;

  // update objects and the display
  for (i = 0; i < itemCount; i++ ){
    key = 'AllowSubs' + (i + 1);
    document.forms[0].elements[key].checked = items[i].allowSubs;
    key = 'Qty' + (i + 1);
    document.forms[0].elements[key].value = items[i].quantity;
    key = 'Cost' + (i + 1);
    itemCost = items[i].cost;
    document.forms[0].elements[key].value = asCurrency(itemCost);
    total = total + itemCost;
  }

  total = total + tax + shipping;

  document.forms[0].elements['Tax'].value = asCurrency(tax);
  document.forms[0].elements['Shipping'].value = asCurrency(shipping);
  document.forms[0].elements['Total'].value = asCurrency(total);

}

//=======================================================================
// prototype: Item
// Description:
// Defines and instantiates an instance of an Item JavaScript object.
//
// Parameters:
//   productID - The interal unique ID (DB primary key) of the product.
//   productNumber - The public number of the product (carry over of
//        legacy system).
//   productName - The name of the product
//   description - a one line description of the project
//   allowSubs - A true value means the customer allows the Roses Alive!
//         substitute rose varieties with similar ones, if the exact
//         variety is not available.
//   quantity - The number of products
//   unitPrice - The cost per unit of the product
//   weight - The unit weight of the product
//   cost - The cost of this line item (quantity * unitPrice)
//
function Item(productID, productNumber, productName, description, allowSubs,
quantity, unitPrice, weight, cost) {
```

```
        this.productID = productID;
        this.productNumber = productNumber
        this.productName = productName;
        this.description = description;
        this.allowSubs = allowSubs;
        this.quantity= quantity;
        this.unitPrice = unitPrice;
        this.weight = weight;
        this.cost = cost;
        this.computeTotal = computeTotal;
        this.totalWeight = totalWeight;
}


//=================================================================
// Item member function: computeTotal
// Description:
// Computes the total cost for this line item.
//
function computeTotal() {
  if ( this.quantity > 0 ) {
    this.cost = this.unitPrice * this.quantity;
  }
  else {
    this.cost  = 0;
  }
}


//=================================================================
// Item member function: totalWeight
// Description:
// Computes the total weight for this line item.
//
function totalWeight() {
  return this.quantity * this.weight;
}



//=================================================================
// function: asCurrency
// Description:
// Utility function to format a currency value with two decimals
// and at least one leading digit.  The return is formatted as a string.
//
// Parameters:
//    val - a currency value
//
function asCurrency(val)
{
    var dp;
    var intgr;
    var dec;
    var beg;
    var end;
    var str;

    str = val.toString();
    dp = str.indexOf(".");
```

```
    if (dp > 0 ) {
        intgr = str.substr(0,dp);
        dec = str.substr(dp+1,str.length);
    }
    else {
    if ( dp == 0 ){
        intgr = str.substr(1,str.length-1);
        dec = '0';
    }
    else {
      if ( dp == -1 ){ // must be whole number
        dec = '0';
        intgr = str;
      }
      else { // invalid value
        intgr = "invalid value"
        return intgr;
      }
    }
  }


// now that we have the parts, let's reassemble them
// into a currency form

// round decimal portion
if ( dec.length >= 2 ){
  d = dec.substr(2,1);
  if ( d >= 5 ) { // round up
    v = dec.substr(1,1) - 0;
    dec = dec.substr(0,1) + (v + 1);
  }
  else {
    dec = dec.substr(0,2);
  }
}

// now make sure that the decimal is always 2 digits
switch (dec.length) {
  case 0:
    dec = '00';
    break;
  case 1:
    dec = dec + '0';
    break;
}

  return (intgr + '.' + dec);
}


//========================================================================
// function: bodyOnLoad
// Description:
// Event handler for the on load event from body tag.  This is the main
// client side function for the page.  It calls update form, to ensure
// that the correct information is displayed.
//
```

```
function bodyOnLoad(){
  updateForm();
}

// --></script>

<%   CreateItems %>

<body onLoad="bodyOnLoad()">

<h1>Your shopping Cart</h1>

<form name="CartForm" method="POST" action="updatecart.asp">
  <table border="0" width="100%">
    <tr>
      <td width="10%">Item No.</td>
      <td width="50%">Description</td>
      <td width="10%" align="center">Allow Subs</td>
      <td width="10%" align="center">Qty</td>
      <td width="10%">Unit Price</td>
      <td width="10%">Cost</td>
    </tr>

<%  BuildTable %>

    <tr>
      <td width="90%" colspan="5" align="right">Tax</td>
      <td width="10%" align="right">
        <input type="text" name="Tax" size="8" value="<%=Tax%>">
      </td>
    </tr>
    <tr>
      <td width="90%" colspan="5" align="right">Shipping</td>
      <td width="10%" align="right">
        <input type="text" name="Shipping" size="8" value="<%=Shipping%>">
      </td>
    </tr>
    <tr>
      <td width="90%" colspan="5" align="right">Total</td>
      <td width="10%" align="right">
        <input type="text" name="Total" size="8" value="<%=Total%>">
      </td>
    </tr>
  </table>
  <div align="center"><p>
    <input type="submit" value="Checkout" name="checkout">
    <input type="button" value="Recalculate" name="recalculate"
                 onClick="recalculateTotals()">
    <input type="submit" value="Shop for more" name="shopForMore">
  </p></div>
</form>

</body>
</html>
```

Links

This shopping cart is a good example of how to implement forms, but it does not have an example of the more common «links» association. The Roses Alive! Web site, like most sites, has a home page, which acts as a welcome page to the site's visitors. Home pages typically introduce the company and provide some links to specific parts of the site. The Roses Alive! home page has links to several other pages in the site. In addition, the home page allows the user to browse the store's catalog. Figure 11-12 shows the site's home page and some of its links.

Most of these pages are client pages that are not built by a server page. This means that they can be implemented as HTML files instead of the less efficient ASP files. Even though no server page processing is occurring with these pages, it doesn't mean that they don't belong in the model or that they can't be code generated from the model. The fact that they are architecturally significant to the application makes them part of the model.

The code generation of the home page is very simple. Each link association is mapped to an anchor tag (<a>). The visual display of the hyperlink is initialized with the client or server page name that the link points to. If a role has been specified on the association, its value is assigned to the name attribute of the anchor tag, as with the Catalog page association. In the Catalog page link, a target of _top has been specified—by a tagged value in the association—to prevent the catalog page frameset from being embedded inside another frameset by accident. The following is the model-generated home page as an HTML file, since there is no "builds" relationship with a server page.

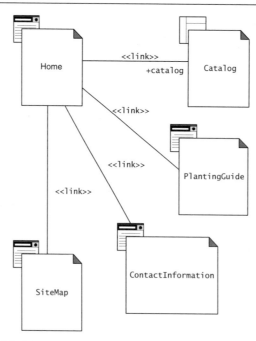

FIGURE 11-12   Model around site's home page

```
<HTML>
<HEAD>
<TITLE>Roses Alive! Home Page</TITLE>
</HEAD>
<BODY>

<a href="Catalog.htm" name="catalog" target="_top">Catalog</a>
<a href="PlantingGuide.htm">PlantingGuide</a>
<a href="ContactInformation.htm">ContactInformation</a>
<a href="SiteMap.htm">SiteMap</a>

</BODY>
</HTML>
```

Valid parameter names can be specified in the model with the *parameters* tagged value on the «link» association. In Figure 11-13, the DailySpecial client page has a link back to its building server page. This link specifies a *parameter* tagged value of ShowYesterdaysSpecial. This is just the parameter name; its value and meaning are determined at runtime. In Figure 11-13, the tagged value is shown in braces. If additional parameters were applicable, they would be separated by semicolons.

The code generated for the DailySpecial page includes the server page code that builds it. The link of the client page portion is generated as

```
<a href="DailySpecial.asp?ShowYesterdaySpecial">DailySpecial</a>
```

The implementer is responsible for taking this anchor tag and augmenting it with the appropriate code to fill in the parameter value at runtime.

Frames

The site's catalog uses frames to simultaneously display the catalog's index, or sections, and specific pages in the catalog; see Figure 11-14. The frameset is implemented as an HTML page—again, because no server page builds it. Its tagged values indicate the number of columns and rows in the frameset, as well as the page's title (Figure 11-15).

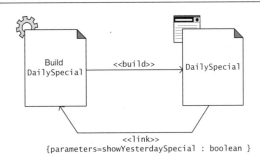

FIGURE 11-13 Using link parameters

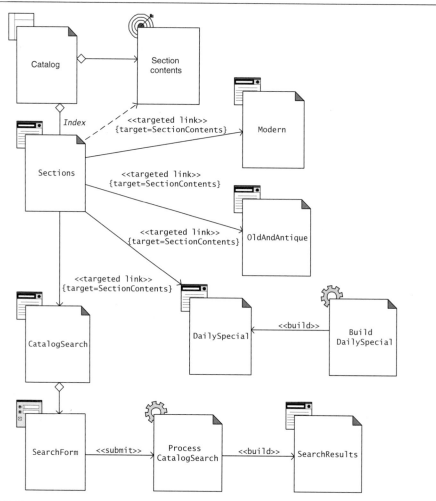

FIGURE 11-14 The catalog frameset design class diagram

The generated code for the Catalog frameset is simple:

```
<HTML>
<HEAD>
<TITLE>Roses Alive! Catalog</TITLE>
</HEAD>

<frameset cols="*,*">
    <frame src="Sections.htm">
    <frame name="SectionContents">
</frameset>

</HTML>
```

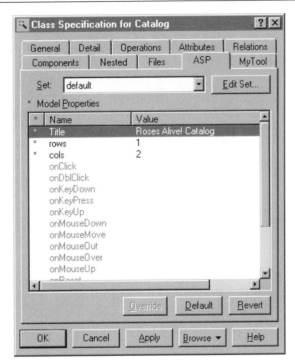

FIGURE 11-15 Catalog page tagged values in Rose model

The tagged values for rows and columns indicate that only one row and two columns make up the frameset. Since row and column sizing is more of a presentation issue, the code generator just uses * as the default. The Sections page is the *src* of the first frame, since aggregation association from the frameset to the page *(Index)* has tagged values indicating a row of 1 and a column of 1 (Figure 11-16). No target is specified as a tagged value in this association, since this particular frame's contents do not change; only the other frames' do. Since there are no other aggregation associations with the frameset, there is no *src* default for the second frame.[5]

The Sections client page has the targeted links of the remaining catalog pages. This page is implemented with the standard client page headers and an anchor tag for each «targeted link» association originating from the page. The values of the target are tagged values of the «targeted link» association, since the pages themselves may be used in other frames and targets. The generated code for this page is

```
<HTML>
<HEAD>
```

---

5. In most situations, there will be an initial *src* for every frame in a frameset. I chose to not model it here, since the diagram is complex enough, and the point has already been made with the Sections client page.

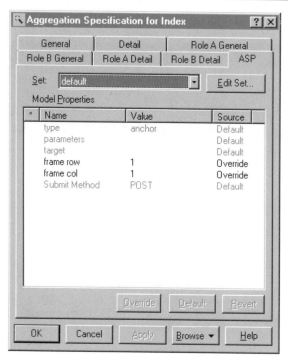

FIGURE 11-16 *Index* aggregation association tagged values

```
<TITLE>Roses Alive! Catalog Sections</TITLE>
</HEAD>
<BODY>

<p><a href="home.htm" target="_top">Home</a></p>

<p><a href="Modern.htm"
    target="SectionContents">Modern </a></p>
<p><a href="OldAnAntique.htm"
    target="SectionContents">OldAndAntique</a></p>
<p><a href="DailySpecial.asp"
    target="SectionContents">DailySpecial</a></p>
<p><a href="CatalogSearch.htm"
    target="SectionContents">CatalogSearch</a></p>

</BODY>
</HTML>
```

Note that the Daily Specials page is an ASP page because of the «builds» association from the BuildDailySpecial to the DailySpecial client page. Ultimately, both of
these pages are realized by the DailySpecial.asp component. All of the links from the
Sections page are targeted. The link to the home page, however, is targeted to _top, which

is a special HTML target indicating that the page should replace any and all framesets in the browser window.

Client-Side Objects

The HTML <object> tag is the preferred way to reference Java applets and ActiveX controls in an HTML page. In the design model, the client page may have an aggregation or regular association to «Java Applet» or «ActiveX» stereotyped class. In the class diagram of Figure 11-17, a frameset with two frames uses one to hold a client page with an ActiveX calendar control; the other is a dynamic page that contains the selected day's activities.

Figure 11-17 represents the design of a frames-based Web page that has a visual calendar in the top frame and a list of the selected day's activities in the bottom frame. When the user selects a date in the calendar, the page's scripts determine the selected date and make a targeted link call to the Activities page, passing with it the selected day, month, and year.

The tagged values associated with the «object» stereotyped aggregation and those of the ActiveX/applet class define the characteristics of the HTML <object> tag. The tags classid, codebase, codetype, and type values come from the class's tagged values. The data attribute comes from the «object» association. When an ActiveX or applet object is initialized in a page, it is possible to pass it parameters. This is done with a <param> tag for each parameter. Each tag contains the name and value of a parameter that is passed along to the object in the page. The parameters and their values, if known at design time, are captured in the «object» association with the single *object parameters* tagged value. The set of parameters must be recorded as a semicolon-delimited string of name/value pairs. For example, the list of parameters for the ActiveX calendar object of the example would be

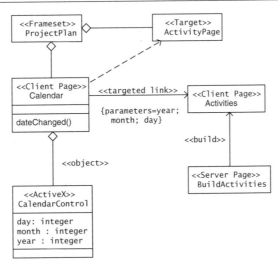

FIGURE 11-17 Using an ActiveX control

```
_Version=524288;_ExtentX=7620;_ExtentY=5080;_StockProps=1;
BackColor=-2147483633;DayLength=1;MonthLength=2;DayFontColor=0;FirstDay=1;
GridCellEffect=1;GridFontColor=10485760;GridLinesColor=-2147483632;
ShowDateSelectors=-1;ShowDays=-1;ShowHorizontalGrid=-1;
ShowTitle=-1;ShowVerticalGrid=-1;TitleFontColor=10485760;
ValueIsNull=0;
```

Since the event model for ActiveX controls is special to IE, the handling of the ActiveX control's events must be implemented manually in the client page's scripts. With the help of Microsoft's Visual Interdev, the Calendar client page's implementation is

```html
<HTML>
<script language="JavaScript"><!--

function dateChanged() {
  var day;  // the selected date
  var month; // the selected month
  var year; // the selected year
  var url; // the constructed url of the daily activities
           // page with parameters

  day = Calendar.Day;
  month = Calendar.Month;
  year = Calendar.Year;

  url = "Activities.asp?day=" + day + "&month=" +
           month + "&year=" + year;

  // now open the new page in the frame below
  parent.frames["ActivityPage"].location = url;

}

// --></script>

<HEAD>
<TITLE>Calandar Control Page</TITLE>
<SCRIPT LANGUAGE=javascript FOR=Calendar EVENT=Click>
<!--
 dateChanged()
//-->
</SCRIPT>

</HEAD>
<BODY>

<P>
<OBJECT classid="clsid:8E27C92B-1264-101C-8A2F-040224009C02"
  name="Calendar" style="LEFT: 0px; TOP: 0px">
  <PARAM NAME="_Version" VALUE="524288">
  <PARAM NAME="_ExtentX" VALUE="7620">
  <PARAM NAME="_ExtentY" VALUE="5080">
  <PARAM NAME="_StockProps" VALUE="1">
  <PARAM NAME="BackColor" VALUE="-2147483633">
  <PARAM NAME="DayLength" VALUE="1">
```

```
      <PARAM NAME="MonthLength" VALUE="2">
      <PARAM NAME="DayFontColor" VALUE="0">
      <PARAM NAME="FirstDay" VALUE="1">
      <PARAM NAME="GridCellEffect" VALUE="1">
      <PARAM NAME="GridFontColor" VALUE="10485760">
      <PARAM NAME="GridLinesColor" VALUE="-2147483632">
      <PARAM NAME="ShowDateSelectors" VALUE="-1">
      <PARAM NAME="ShowDays" VALUE="-1">
      <PARAM NAME="ShowHorizontalGrid" VALUE="-1">
      <PARAM NAME="ShowTitle" VALUE="-1">
      <PARAM NAME="ShowVerticalGrid" VALUE="-1">
      <PARAM NAME="TitleFontColor" VALUE="10485760">
      <PARAM NAME="ValueIsNull" VALUE="0"></OBJECT>
</P>

</BODY>
</HTML>
```

The browser view of the frameset and a minimal implementation of the other pages are shown in Figure 11-18.

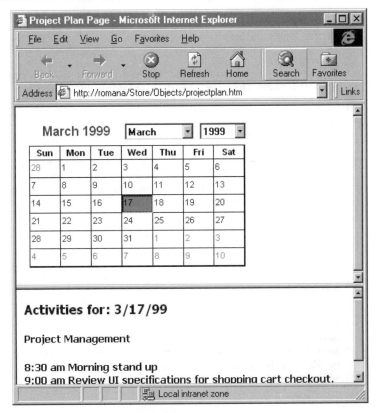

FIGURE 11-18   Sample use of ActiveX control on the client

Server Side Includes

Another option for ASP systems (and others) is to create a separate client page file and to use it as an include file. If the server-side include mechanism works so that the enabling technology filter processes the include as well, it is possible to physically separate the server page and the client page into distinct files. Doing this in ASP means adding the following server-side include statement at the end of all of the server page code:

```
<!--#INCLUDE FILE="GetCart.inc" -->
```

When separate files are used, it is convenient for the client page developer to include—in a set of comments at the top of the page—all of the server page variables and operations that may be called or used when working on the client page file. For example, if the shopping cart ASP page was implemented with two pages, the top of the included file would have the following comments:

```
<%
' Client Page include: GetCart

' <insert appropriate copyright information here>
' <insert appropriate version control information here>
' File: GetCart.asp
' Server Page: GetCart
'
' Description:
' The GetCart server page assembles the current user's shopping cart
' with the items that the user has selected over the course of the
' current session.
'
' Server Page Variables:
' cart - the user's server side shopping cart instance
' itemCount - the number of items in the shopping cart
' tax - the total value of taxes for the items in this cart
' shipping - the total value of shipping charges for the items in this cart
' total - the total cost for the items in this cart, including tax and
'          shipping charges
'
' Server Page Subs/Functions
'====================================================================
' Sub: GetCart
' Description:
' GetCart gets the current shopping cart instance from the session object
' and initializes the page's variables.
'
'
'====================================================================
' Sub: BuildTable
' Description:
' BuildTable walks through each of the order line items to
' build a table containing all of the items currently in
' the user's shopping cart.
'
```

```
'=========================================================================
' Sub: WriteTableRow
' Description:
' WriteTableRow writes a single table row for a line item.
'
' Parameters:
'   aLineItem - the OrderLineItem instance that represents one item
'   in a shopping cart.
'
'   i - the line item number.  This index is used to postfix the form
'   control names, so that they can be uniquely identified.
'
'=========================================================================
' Sub: CreateJSItem
' Description:
' Creates the JavaScript code that instantiates a specific JavaScript
' Item object instance.  Basically it just calls the Item's
' constructor (prototype).  This function does NOT define the
' JavaScript object (that is the job of the client page).
'
' Parameters:
'   aLineItem - the OrderLineItem instance that represents one item
'   in a shopping cart.
'
'   i - the line item number.  This index is used to index into the
'   array of Item JavaSctipt object.
'
'=========================================================================
' Sub: CreateItems
' Description:
' Creates the JavaScript block that creates all of the JavaScript Item
' instances for the client.  This sub walks through each of the order
' line items in the current shopping cart and creates an Item instance
' in the resulting HTML page.
'
'=========================================================================
' Sub: Main
' Description:
' The main VBScript function of the page.  The call to this
' VBScript sub is the only inline executable statement of this
' ASP file.
'
%>
```

Using include files in Web application design makes reuse easier in the same project. Include files are especially convenient for utility functions, such as the `asCurrency` JavaScript function, and JavaScript objects, such as the shopping cart `Item`.

Chapter Summary

❑ The activities of implementation include mapping the design into code and components, unit testing, and reverse engineering.

❑ Client-side and server-side programmers deal with the implementation of business logic. Graphic artists provide the implementation for the look and feel of the user interface.

❑ When the enabling technology is scripted pages (ASP, JSP), each server page maps to one map to one scripted page file (Page component).

❑ With the enabling technology, each Page component might realize multiple server pages. In this case, parameters are used to denote which server page role is to be performed.

❑ Use component stereotype names specific to the enabling technology, such as «ASP», «servlet», «JSP», «ISAPI», or «NSAPI». Doing so makes working in mixed architectures much easier.

❑ Packages can be used to denote Web site directories.

❑ Server pages are implemented with whatever enabling technology is used.

❑ Client pages are almost always implemented with JavaScript, applets, or ActiveX controls.

❑ A significant amount of structural code can be generated directly from the model.

Appendices

Appendix A
Web Application Extension for UML

Description

This extension to the UML defines a set of stereotypes, tagged values, and constraints that enable us to model Web applications. The stereotypes and constraints are applied to certain components that are particular to Web applications, allowing us to represent them in the same model and on the same diagrams that describe the rest of the system.

The principal element specific to Web applications is the Web page. Several stereotypes can be applied to a Web page, and additional stereotypes are assigned to other HTML elements that represent architecturally significant components of the system, such as frames, targets, and forms.

Many of the tagged values mentioned in this extension may be considered presentational rather than structural. This extension has erred on the side of too much information rather than omitting valuable tagged value specifications. It is expected that as code generators are developed, additional tagged values will be added to the extension.

Prerequisite Extensions

No other extension to the language is required for the definition of this extension.

Stereotypes

Server Page

Metamodel class	Class
Description	A server page represents a Web page that has scripts executed by the server. These scripts interact with server resources such as databases, business logic, and external systems. The object's operations represent the functions in the script, and its attributes represent the variables that are visible in the page's scope (accessible by all functions in the page).
Icon	
Constraints	Server pages can have relationships only with objects on the server.
Tagged values	Scripting engine: Either the language or the engine that should be used to execute or interpret this page (JavaScript, VBScript, PERL, and so on).

Client Page

Metamodel class	Class
Description	An instance of a client page is an HTML-formatted Web page and is a mix of data, presentation, and even logic. Client pages are rendered by client browsers and may contain scripts that are interpreted by the browser. Client page functions map to functions in script tags in the page. Client page attributes map to variables declared in the page's script tags that are accessible by any function in the page (page scoped). Client pages can have associations with other client or server pages.
Icon	
Constraints	None
Tagged values	• TitleTag: The title of the page as displayed by the browser.
	• BaseTag: The base URL for dereferencing relative URLs.
	• BodyTag: The set of attributes for the <body> tag, which sets background and default text attributes.

Form

Metamodel class   Class

Description   A class stereotyped as a «form» is a collection of input fields that are part of a client page. A form class maps directly to the HTML «form» tag. The attributes of this class represent the HTML form's input fields (input boxes, text areas, radio buttons, check boxes, and hidden fields).

A «form» has no operations, since they can't be encapsulated in a form. Any operations that interact with the form are the property of the page that contains the form.

Icon

Constraints   None

Tagged values   The method—either GET or POST—used to submit data to the action URL.

Frameset

Metamodel class   Class

Description   A frameset is a container of multiple Web pages. The rectangular viewing area is divided into smaller rectangular frames. Each frame may be associated with a single named «target», although not necessarily.

The contents of a frame may be a Web page or another frameset.

A frameset stereotyped class maps directly to a frameset Web page and the HTML frame tag.

Because a frameset is a «client page», it too can have operations and attributes, but these are activated only by browsers that do not render frames.

Icon

Constraints   None

Tagged values

- Rows: The value of the row's attribute of the HTML <frameset> tag. This is a string with comma-delimited row heights.
- Cols: The value of the cols attribute of the HTML <frameset> tag. This is a string with comma-delimited column widths.

Target

Metamodel class	Class
Description	A target is a named compartment in a browser window in which Web pages can be rendered. The name of the stereotyped class is the name of the target. Typically, a target is one frame in a window defined by a frameset; however, a target could be a completely new browser instance or window.
	«Targeted link» associations specify targets as the place where a new Web page is to be rendered.
Icon	
Constraints	A target's name must be unique for each client of the system. Therefore, only one instance of a target can exist on the same client.
Tagged values	None

JavaScript Object

Metamodel class	Class
Description	On a JavaScript-enabled browser, it is possible to simulate user-defined objects with JavaScript functions. «JavaScript Object» instances exist only in the context of client pages.
Icon	None
Constraints	None
Tagged values	None

ClientScript Object

Metamodel class	Class
Description	A ClientScript object is a separate collection of client-side scripts that exist in a separate file and are included by a separate request on the part of the client browser. These objects are often bundles of commonly used functions across an application or an enterprise. Some browsers are capable of caching these files, reducing overall download times for an application.
Icon	

Constraints   None

Tagged values   None

Link

Metamodel class   Association

Description   A link is a pointer from a client page to another «Page». In a class diagram, a link is an association between a «client page» and either another «client page» or a «server page». A link association maps directly to the HTML anchor tag.

Icon   None

Constraints   None

Tagged Values   Parameters: A list of parameter names that should be passed along with the request for the linked page.

Targeted Link

Metamodel class   Association

Description   Similar to a «link» association, a «targeted link» is a link whose associated page is rendered in another target. This association maps directly to the HTML anchor tag, with the target specified by the tag's target attribute.

Icon   None

Constraints   None

Tagged Values   • Parameters: A list of parameter names that should be passed along with the request for the linked page.

                     • Target Name: The name of the «target» that the page this link points to should be rendered in.

Frame Content

Metamodel class   Association

Description   A frame content association is an aggregation association that expresses a frame's containment of another page or target.

                     A frame content association can also point to another frameset, indicating nested frames.

Icon   None

Constraints   None

Tagged values   • Row: An integer indicating the specific row of the frame in the frameset that the associated page or target belongs in.

                     • Col: An integer indicating the specific column of the frame in the frameset that the associated page or target belongs in.

Submit

Metamodel class	Association
Description	A «submit» association is always between a «form» and a «server page». Forms *submit* their field values to the server through «server pages» for processing. The Web server processes the «server page», which accepts and uses the information in the submitted form.
	This relationship indicates which page (or pages) can process the form and which forms a «server page» has some knowledge about.
Icon	None
Constraints	None
Tagged Values	Parameters: A list of parameter names that should be passed along with the request for the linked page.

Builds

Metamodel class	Association
Description	The «builds» relationship is a special relationship that bridges the gap between client and server pages. Server pages exist only on the server. They are used to *build* client pages.
	The «builds» association identifies which server page is responsible for the creation of a client page. This is a directional relationship, since the client page contains no knowledge of how it came into existence.
	A server page can build multiple client pages, but a client page can be built by only one server page.
Icon	None
Constraints	None
Tagged values	None

Redirect

Metamodel class	Association
Description	A «redirect» relationship, a unidirectional association with another Web page, can be directed both from and to client and server pages.
	If the relationship originates from a «server page», the processing of the page request may continue on with the other page. This does not indicate that the destination page always participates in the building of a client page, just that it could. This particular relationship is not completely structural, since the invocation of a redirection operation must be done programmatically in the code of the originating page.
	If the relationship originates from a «client page», this indicates that the destination page will automatically be requested by the browser, without user input. A time-delay value can be set that specifies a delay,

in seconds, before the second page is requested. This use of redirection corresponds to the «META» tag and HTTP-EQUIV value of "Refresh".

Icon	None
Constraints	None
Tagged Values	Delay: The amount of time a client page should wait before redirecting to the next page. This value corresponds to the Content attribute of the «META» tag.

IIOP

Metamodel class	Association
Description	IIOP (Internet Inter-ORB Protocol) is a special type of relationship between objects on the client and objects on the server. IIOP represents a mechanism other than HTTP for client/server communications.

Typically, this relationship is between JavaBeans on the client and Enterprise JavaBeans on the server. |
Icon	None
Constraints	None
Tagged values	None

RMI

Metamodel class	Association
Description	RMI (Remote Method Invocation) is a mechanism for Java applets and JavaBeans to send messages to other JavaBeans on different machines.

Typically, this relationship is between JavaBeans or applets on the client and Enterprise JavaBeans on the server. |
Icon	None
Constraints	None
Tagged values	None

Input Element

Metamodel class	Attribute
Description	An input element, an attribute of a «Form» object, maps directly to the <input> tag in an HTML form. This attribute is used to input a single word or line of text.

The tagged values associated with this stereotyped attribute correspond to the <input> tag's attributes.

To complete the required values for the HTML tag, the attribute name is used as the <input> tag's *name*, and the attribute's initial value is the tag's *value*. |

Icon	None
Constraints	None
Tagged values	• Type: The type of input control to be used: text, number, password, checkbox, radio, submit, or reset. • Size: Specifies how large an area to allocate on screen, in characters. • Maxlength: The maximum number of characters the user can input.

Select Element

Metamodel class	Attribute
Description	An input control used in forms. This control allows the user to select one or more items from a list. Most browsers render this control as a combo or list box.
Icon	None
Constraints	None
Tagged values	• Size: Specifies how many items should be displayed at the same time. • Multiple: A Boolean indicating whether multiple items may be selected from the list.

Text Area Element

Metamodel class	Attribute
Description	An input control, used in forms, that allows multiple-line input.
Icon	None
Constraints	None
Tagged values	• Rows: The number of visible text lines. • Cols: The visible width of the control in average character widths.

Web Page

Metamodel class	Component
Description	A page component is a Web page. It can be requested by name by a browser. A page component may or may not contain client or server scripts. Typically, page components are text files accessible by the Web server, but they can also be compiled modules that are loaded and invoked by the Web server. Ultimately, when accessed by the Web server as either a file or an executable, a page produces an HTML-formatted document that is sent in response to a browser's request.

Icon

Constraints   None

Tagged values   Path: The path required to specify the Web page on the Web server. This value should be relative to the Web application's (site's) root directory.

ASP Page

Metamodel class   Component

Description   Web pages that implement ASP server-side code. This stereotype is applicable only in Microsoft's Active Server Pages–based application environment.

Icon

Constraints   None

Tagged values   Same as Web page

JSP Page

Metamodel class   Component

Description   Web pages that implement JSP server-side code. This stereotype is applicable only in Web application development environments that use Java Server Pages.

Icon

Constraints   None

Tagged values   Same as Web page

Servlet

Metamodel class   . Component

Description   A Java servlet component. This stereotype is applicable only in Web application development environments that support Sun's servlets.

Icon	

| Constraints | None |
| Tagged values | Same as Web page |

Script Library

| Metamodel class | Component |
| Description | The component that provides a library of subroutines or functions that can be included by other Web page components. |

Icon	

| Constraints | None |
| Tagged values | Same as Web page |

Well-Formedness Rules

- *Component Realization:* In general, Web page components can realize «server page», «client page», «form», «JavaScript Object», «ClientScript object», «frameset», and «target» stereotyped classes. When a specific development environment, such as ASP or JSP is used, Web pages cannot realize «server page» stereotyped classes.

- *Generalization:* All of the modeling elements in a generalization must be of the same stereotype.

- *Association:* Client pages can have at most one «builds» relationship with a server page, yet a server page can have multiple «builds» relationships with different client pages. Apart from standard UML combinations, the combinations in Table A-1 are allowed for each stereotype.

TABLE A-1   Valid Association Stereotype Combinations

To: From:	Client Page	Server Page	Frameset	Target	Form
Client Page	Link Targeted Link Redirect	Link Targeted Link Redirect	Link Targeted Link Redirect	Dependency	Aggregation
Server Page	Builds Redirect	Redirect	Redirect Builds		
Frameset	Frame Content		Frame Content	Frame Content	
Target	—	—	—	—	—
Form	Aggregated By	Submit			

Comments

- To maintain some visual sense of consistency, all "page" icons have a little "dog ear" in the upper-right corner to convey the notion that they represent an entire Web page—as seen either by the client browser or by the Web server.
- Code generators are expected to specify additional tagged values for class and association stereotypes. The tagged values specified in this specification are important enough to be considered either logically or structurally significant.

Appendix B

An E-Commerce Use Case Example— Use Case Specification: Browse Catalog

1. Browse Catalog

1.1 Goal

The online customer wishes to examine the varieties of roses in the RosesAlive! catalog.

1.2 Brief Description

Anonymous customers with access to the Internet and a forms-capable browser have the ability to search the RosesAlive! online catalog. There are no identity restrictions for use of the catalog. Even though not purchasing anything from RosesAlive!, the visitor is still considered an online customer.

The customer can browse the catalog by either navigating the variety hierarchy or performing a search of the product database. The hierarchy groups rose varieties, allowing the customer to view similar varieties of roses. The search allows the customer to search variety names and descriptions for keywords. Customers with specific roses in mind are expected to use the searching functions, with the other customers expected to navigate the variety hierarchy and to generally "browse" RosesAlive! offerings.

The information about each rose variety includes name, brief description, breeder name, year introduced, cost, and, if available, a picture of the rose in bloom. When the customer finds a rose variety to buy, this use case is extended by the use case Add Item To Shopping Cart. When the customer decides to purchase the items in the shopping cart, this use case is extended by the use case Checkout Shopping Cart.

2. Flow of Events

2.1 Basic Flow

The online customer uses a standard HTML 3.2–capable Web browser to load the RosesAlive! home page on the Internet. The customer decides to examine the store's product selection.

The customer selects the Search Catalog link on the main RosesAlive! Web page. The system returns with a search form and instructions on how the search process works.

The customer reviews the instructions and enters in search criteria, which include keyword searches in variety names and descriptions. The customer also has the option of limiting the number of search results returned. The default number of returned items is ten. The customer enters in the search criteria and submits the query to the system.

The system searches all of the products for varieties that match the criteria entered. The system collects these matches and presents the first ten (or whatever the customer set as the maximum number of results to return) to the customer. Each result includes the variety's name, description, breeder, introduction date, and unit cost. If a picture is available, it is included with the description as well.

If the number of matching varieties is greater than the limit set by the customer, the customer is presented with options to move forward in the result set or backward, if appropriate. The customer can browse the returned matches in any order.

The customer can at any time return to the search page, or home page, and revise the search criteria to perform a new search or can browse the catalog by navigating the hierarchy.

The customer can at any time select a rose to add to the shopping cart (Add to Shopping Cart use case).

The customer can at any time decide to check out, and to purchase all of the items in the shopping cart (Checkout Shopping Cart use case).

This use case ends when the customer stops navigating the RosesAlive! Web site, which can happen at any time, either by choice or by equipment failure.

2.2 Alternative Flows

2.2.1 Browse by Variety Hierarchy

The customer decides to browse the catalog by navigating the variety hierarchy. The customer tells the system to display the overview of the product catalog.

The system displays a hierarchical map of rose varieties. The customer selects one of these categories.

The system returns with the list of rose varieties for that category. At the beginning of the list is a brief description of this category. The description contains all of the common features and, perhaps, history of this particular category of varieties. Hyperlinks from this description can lead to more detailed descriptions.

The customer scrolls through the list. If the list is longer than a predetermined amount (configurable by the system administrator and, typically, 20 roses per page), the customer is presented with options to move forward in the result set or backward, if appropriate.

The customer can at any time select a rose to add to the shopping cart (Add to Shopping Cart use case).

The customer can at any time decide to check out and to purchase all of the items in the shopping cart (Checkout Shopping Cart use case).

3. Preconditions

3.1 Internet Access

The customer must have access to the Internet. In particular, the customer must be able to request Web pages from port 80 of the RosesAlive! Web server.

3.2 HTML 3.2–Compliant Browser

The customer's Web browser must be capable of accepting and submitting forms. Ideally, the customer's browser should be HTML 3.2 compliant.

4. Extension Points

Extension points of the use case.

4.1 Add Item to Shopping Cart

If the customer decides to purchase a RosesAlive! product, it can be added to a virtual shopping cart. This cart hold references to products with a quantity.

4.2 Checkout Shopping Cart

The customer decides to purchase the items collected in the shopping cart.

Appendix C

Glossary ASP Application Sample Model

Vision Statement

The Glossary Application provides an online version of a software development project's glossary of terms. This application gives software development team members access to a database of glossary entries/terms for a particular project, using a common Web browser. Team members may also update, add, and remove entries from the database, using the same browser interface.

This application is to leverage the existing project intranet, which all team members have access to. Any team member can browse, search, and update entries in the glossary.

The Glossary Application is intended to be a simple ASP-based application that demonstrates the most basic features of the Web Application Extension for UML. Despite its simplicity, it is a practical application that can be built on and used in real-life software development projects.

Top-Level Use Case View

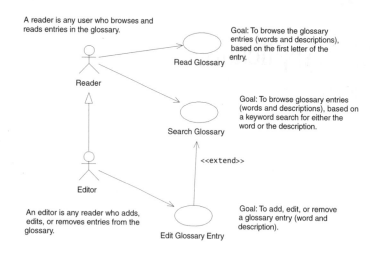

A reader is any user who browses and reads entries in the glossary.

Reader

Read Glossary

Goal: To browse the glossary entries (words and descriptions), based on the first letter of the entry.

Search Glossary

Goal: To browse glossary entries (words and descriptions), based on a keyword search for either the word or the description.

<<extend>>

Editor

An editor is any reader who adds, edits, or removes entries from the glossary.

Edit Glossary Entry

Goal: To add, edit, or remove a glossary entry (word and description).

Analysis Model: Main Diagram

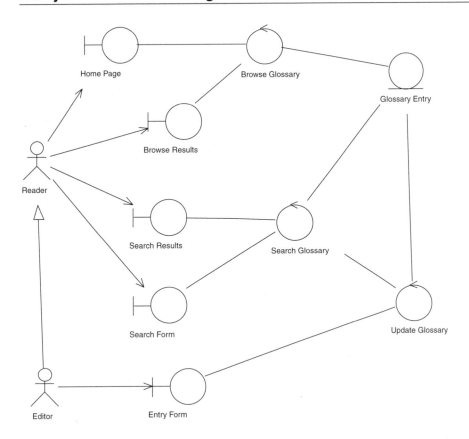

Analysis Model: Use Case Sequence Diagrams

Browse Glossary Main Sequence Diagram

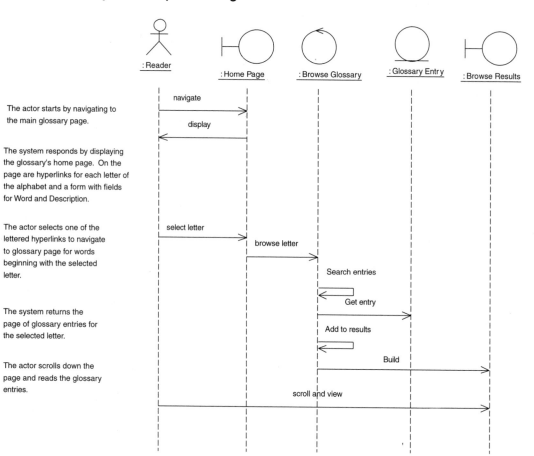

Search Glossary Main Sequence Diagram

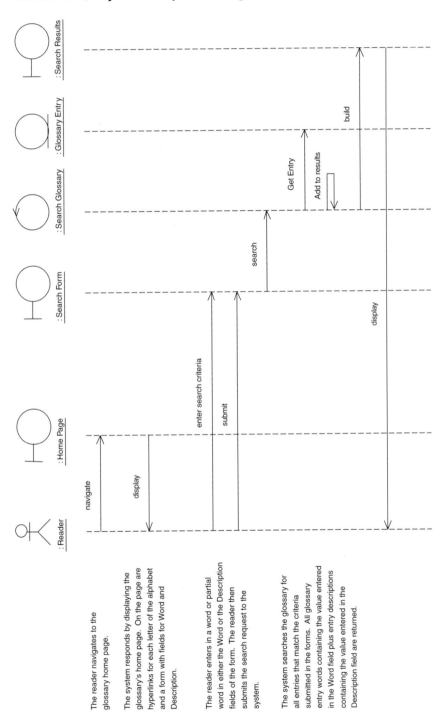

The reader navigates to the glossary home page.

The system responds by displaying the glossary's home page. On the page are hyperlinks for each letter of the alphabet and a form with fields for Word and Description.

The reader enters in a word or partial word in either the Word or the Description fields of the form. The reader then submits the search request to the system.

The system searches the glossary for all entries that match the criteria submitted in the forms. All glossary entry words containing the value entered in the Word field plus entry descriptions containing the value entered in the Description field are returned.

Edit Glossary Sequence Diagram for Entry Use Case

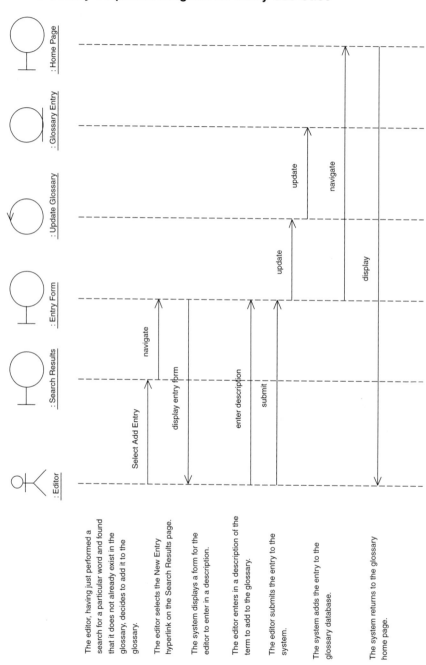

Design Model

Top-Level Class Diagram

File: Glossary.mdl
Date: 12-May-1999
Author: Jim Conallen, jim@conallen.com

Description:

This model is a simple example of the use of the UML Extension for
Web Applications. It uses only the most basic elements of the
extension and is intended as an introductory example of modeling
page-based Web applications.

This model is a complete design model for a Microsoft Active Server
Page–based Web application. The server-side component was
implemented with Visual Basic.

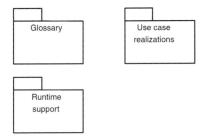

Use Case Realizations

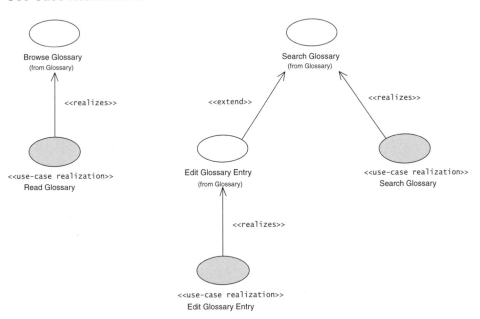

Sequence Diagram for Browse Glossary Use Case Realization

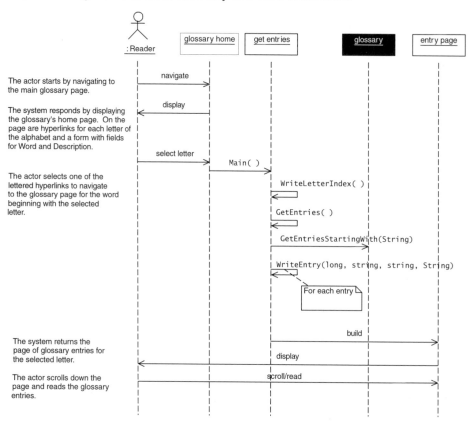

The actor starts by navigating to the main glossary page.

The system responds by displaying the glossary's home page. On the page are hyperlinks for each letter of the alphabet and a form with fields for Word and Description.

The actor selects one of the lettered hyperlinks to navigate to the glossary page for the word beginning with the selected letter.

The system returns the page of glossary entries for the selected letter.

The actor scrolls down the page and reads the glossary entries.

Sequence Diagram for Search Glossary Use Case Realization

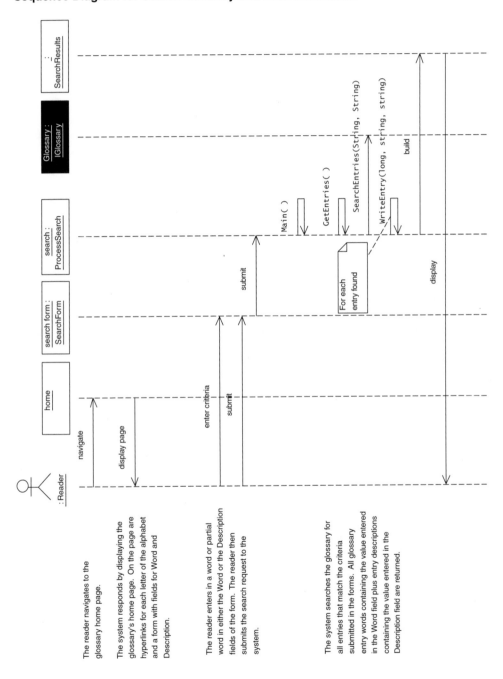

The reader navigates to the glossary home page.

The system responds by displaying the glossary's home page. On the page are hyperlinks for each letter of the alphabet and a form with fields for Word and Description.

The reader enters in a word or partial word in either the Word or the Description fields of the form. The reader then submits the search request to the system.

The system searches the glossary for all entries that match the criteria submitted in the forms. All glossary entry words containing the value entered in the Word field plus entry descriptions containing the value entered in the Description field are returned.

Top-Level Logical View

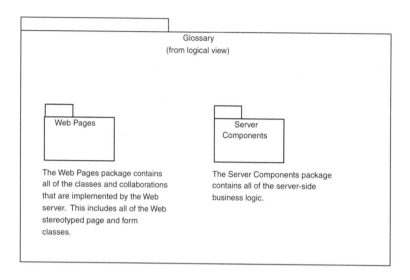

Glossary
(from logical view)

Web Pages

The Web Pages package contains
all of the classes and collaborations
that are implemented by the Web
server. This includes all of the Web
stereotyped page and form
classes.

Server
Components

The Server Components package
contains all of the server-side
business logic.

Server Components Package: <u>Main</u> Class Diagram

| <<Interface>> |
| IGlossary |
| 🔑 mdsn : String |
| 🔷 GetEntriesStartingWith() |
| 🔷 SearchEntries() |
| 🔷 NewEntry() |
| 🔷 UpdateEntry() |
| 🔷 RemoveEntry() |
| 🔷 <<Let>> dsn() |
| 🔒 MassageText() |

The IGlossary interface is the
main API for all glossary functions
on the server. All access to the
glossary is made through
instances of this interface.

Web Pages Package

Browsing Overview Class Diagram

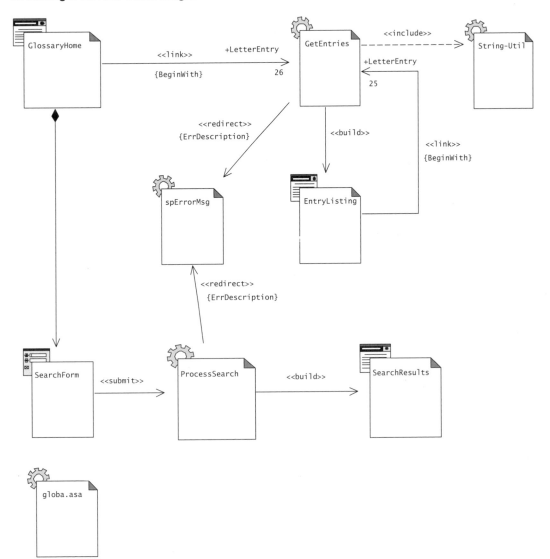

Browsing Detail Class Diagram

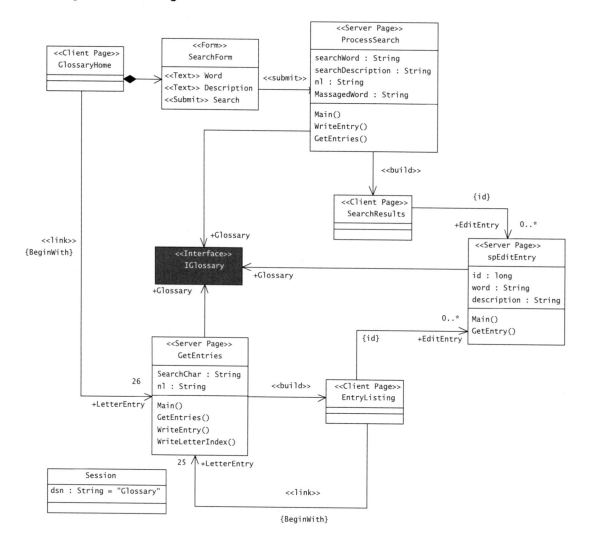

Edit Entry Overview Class Diagram

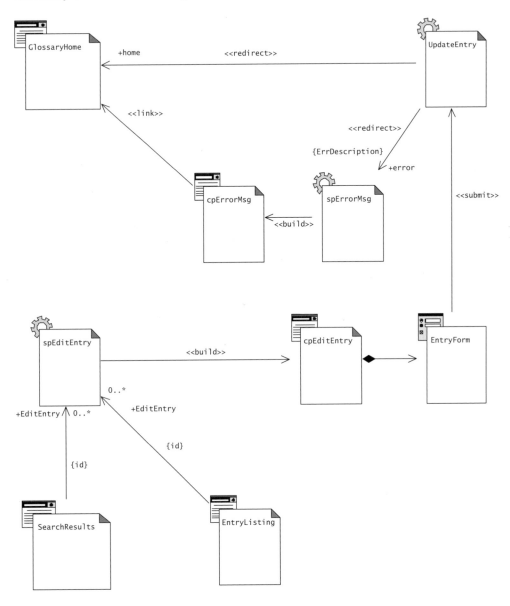

Edit Entry Detail Class Diagram

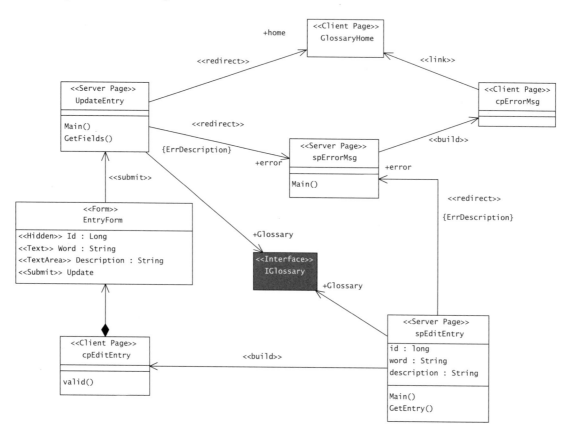

Component View

Main Component Diagram for Server Components

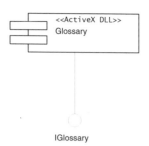

Main Component Diagram for Web Pages

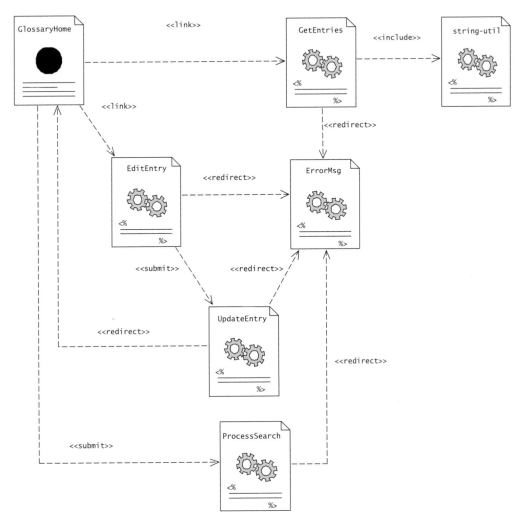

Source Code (after Implementation)

GlossaryHome.htm

```
<html>
<head>
<title>Project Glossary</title>
</head>

<!--
Copyright (C) 1999  jim conallen
This program is free software; you can redistribute it and/or
modify it under the terms of the GNU General Public License
as published by the Free Software Foundation; either version 2
of the License or (at your option) any later version.
This program is distributed in the hope that it will be useful,
but WITHOUT ANY WARRANTY; without even the implied warranty of
MERCHANTABILITY or FITNESS FOR A PARTICULAR PURPOSE.  See the
GNU General Public License for more details.
You should have received a copy of the GNU General Public License
along with this program; if not, write to the Free Software
Foundation, Inc., 59 Temple Place - Suite 330, Boston, MA  02111-1307, USA.

 <insert appropriate version control information here>

File: GlossaryHome.htm
Client Page: GlossaryHome

Description:
    The home page for the application.  All use cases begin
    with this page.

-->

<body>
<H2>Project Glossary Home Page</H2>

<p>
<!-- 26 link to GetEntries
     <a href="GetEntries.asp">GetEntries</a>
-->
| <a href="GetEntries.asp?BeginWith=a">A</a>
| <a href="GetEntries.asp?BeginWith=b">B</a>
| <a href="GetEntries.asp?BeginWith=c">C</a>
| <a href="GetEntries.asp?BeginWith=d">D</a>
| <a href="GetEntries.asp?BeginWith=e">E</a>
| <a href="GetEntries.asp?BeginWith=f">F</a>
| <a href="GetEntries.asp?BeginWith=g">G</a>
| <a href="GetEntries.asp?BeginWith=h">H</a>
| <a href="GetEntries.asp?BeginWith=i">I</a>
| <a href="GetEntries.asp?BeginWith=j">J</a>
| <a href="GetEntries.asp?BeginWith=k">K</a>
| <a href="GetEntries.asp?BeginWith=l">L</a>
| <a href="GetEntries.asp?BeginWith=m">M</a>
| <a href="GetEntries.asp?BeginWith=n">N</a>
```

```
|   <a href="GetEntries.asp?BeginWith=o">O</a>
|   <a href="GetEntries.asp?BeginWith=p">P</a>
|   <a href="GetEntries.asp?BeginWith=q">Q</a>
|   <a href="GetEntries.asp?BeginWith=r">R</a>
|   <a href="GetEntries.asp?BeginWith=s">S</a>
|   <a href="GetEntries.asp?BeginWith=t">T</a>
|   <a href="GetEntries.asp?BeginWith=u">U</a>
|   <a href="GetEntries.asp?BeginWith=v">V</a>
|   <a href="GetEntries.asp?BeginWith=w">W</a>
|   <a href="GetEntries.asp?BeginWith=x">X</a>
|   <a href="GetEntries.asp?BeginWith=y">Y</a>
|   <a href="GetEntries.asp?BeginWith=z">Z</a>  |
</p>

<p>Or Search the Glossary for a keyword.</p>

<form name="SearchForm" method="POST" action="ProcessSearch.asp">
    <table>
        <tr>
            <td>Keyword in glossary entry:</td>
            <td><input name="Word" type="text" size="30"></td>
        </tr>
        <tr>
            <td>Keyword in description:</td>
            <td><input name="Description" type="text" size="30"></td>
        </tr>
        <tr>
            <td></td>
            <td><input name="Search" type="submit" value="Search"></td>
        </tr>
    </table>
</form>




</body>
</html>
```

GetEntries.asp

```
<% @Language="VBScript" %>
<!--#INCLUDE FILE="string-util.asp"-->
<%
' Copyright (C) 1999  jim conallen
' This program is free software; you can redistribute it and/or
' modify it under the terms of the GNU General Public License
' as published by the Free Software Foundation; either version 2
' of the License or (at your option) any later version.
' This program is distributed in the hope that it will be useful,
' but WITHOUT ANY WARRANTY; without even the implied warranty of
' MERCHANTABILITY or FITNESS FOR A PARTICULAR PURPOSE.  See the
' GNU General Public License for more details.
' You should have received a copy of the GNU General Public License
' along with this program; if not, write to the Free Software
' Foundation, Inc., 59 Temple Place - Suite 330, Boston, MA  02111-1307, USA.
'
```

```
' <insert appropriate version control information here>
'
' File: GetEntries.asp
' Server Page: GetEntries
'
' Description:
' Builds a listing of glossary entries by accessing the server
' side Glossary api.
'


Dim SearchChar  '(String) The character to search the
                ' glossary for.
                '
Dim Glossary '(IGlossary)
Dim nl '(string) a new line


Sub RedirectTospErrorMsg( ErrDescription )
    dim url ' as string
    url = "ErrorMsg.asp?ErrDescription=" & ErrDescription
    'redirect url
    Response.Write ("<h1>" & url & "</h1>" )
End Sub



'=======================================================================
' Sub: Main
' Description:
'   Main entry point for this page.
Sub Main
  nl = chr(13) & chr(10)
  Set Glossary = Server.CreateObject("Glossary.IGlossary")
  Glossary.dsn = Application("dsn")
  SearchChar = Request("BeginWith")
  if SearchChar = "" Then
    ' todo: make sure is an alpha char
    RedirectTospErrorMsg( "Unknown character")
  end if
  SearchChar = ucase(SearchChar)

End Sub


'=======================================================================
' Sub: GetEntries
' Description:
'   Uses the Glossary server API to find all entries in the
'   glossary beginning with the char. Each entry is written
'    out to an HTML table.
'
Sub GetEntries
    Dim entries ' as variant
    Dim id ' as long
    Dim word ' as string
    Dim description ' as string
    Dim bgColor ' as color
```

```
    Response.Write( "<table width=""80%"">" )
    Response.Write( "    <tr>" )
    Response.Write( "        <td><i>Word</i></td>")
    Response.Write( "        <td><i>Description</i></td>")
    Response.Write( "    </tr>" )

    entries = Glossary.GetEntriesStartingWith( cstr(SearchChar) )

    bgColor = "white"

    if Not IsEmpty(entries) then
        ' now loop through the entries
        for i = 0 to ubound(entries,2)
            id = entries(0,i)
            word = entries(1,i)
            description = entries(2,i)
            WriteEntry id, word, description, bgColor
            if bgColor = "white" then
                bgColor = "lightgrey"
            else
                bgColor = "white"
            end if
        next

    end if

    Response.Write( "</table>" )

End Sub

'=========================================================================
' Sub: WriteEntry
' Description:
'   Writes out an entry and table row to the output.
' Parameters:
'   id -
'   word -
'   description -
Sub WriteEntry( id, word, description, bgColor)

    Dim link 'as string

    link = "        <td><b><a href=""EditEntry.asp?id=" & id & """>" & _
        ForHTML(word) & "</a></b></td>"

    Response.Write( "    <tr bgcolor=""" & bgColor & """>" & nl)
    Response.Write( link & nl)
    Response.Write( "        <td>" & ForHTML(description) & "</td>" & nl )
    Response.Write( "    </tr>" & nl)

End Sub

'=========================================================================
' Sub: WriteLetterIndex
' Description:
'   Writes out the hyperlinks to the remaining letters of the
```

```
'     alphabet.
'
Sub WriteLetterIndex
    Dim i 'as index into alphabet
    Dim c 'as character
    Dim tag 'as string

    Response.Write("<p>")
    For i = 1 to 26  ' A thorugh Z
        c = chr( i + 64 )
        if c <> SearchChar then
            tag = "<a href=""GetEntries.asp?BeginWith=" & c & """>" & c & "</a>"
        Else
            tag = " " & c
        end if
        Response.Write( " | " & tag & nl )
    next
    Response.Write( " |</p>" & nl )

End Sub

Main

%>

<html>
<head>
<title>EntryListing</title>
</head>

<!--
<insert appropriate copyright information here>
<insert appropriate version control information here>
File: GetEntries.asp
Client Page: EntryListing

Description:
    The HTML listing of glossary entries that begin with a
    certain letter. This page also has links to the other
    letters in the alphabet.

-->

<body>
<!-- 25 link to GetEntries
     <a href="GetEntries.asp">GetEntries</a>
-->
<h3>Project Glossary</h3>

<% WriteLetterIndex %>

<p>To edit any of the entries click on its hyperlink.<p>

<% GetEntries %>

<hr>
<p><a href="GlossaryHome.htm">Home</a></p>
```

```
</body>
</html>
```

ProcessSearch.asp

```
<% @Language="VBScript" %>
<!--#INCLUDE FILE="string-util.asp"-->
<%
' Copyright (C) 1999  jim conallen
' This program is free software; you can redistribute it and/or
' modify it under the terms of the GNU General Public License
' as published by the Free Software Foundation; either version 2
' of the License or (at your option) any later version.
' This program is distributed in the hope that it will be useful,
' but WITHOUT ANY WARRANTY; without even the implied warranty of
' MERCHANTABILITY or FITNESS FOR A PARTICULAR PURPOSE.  See the
' GNU General Public License for more details.
' You should have received a copy of the GNU General Public License
' along with this program; if not, write to the Free Software
' Foundation, Inc., 59 Temple Place - Suite 330, Boston, MA  02111-1307, USA.
'
' <insert appropriate version control information here>
'
' File: ProcessSearch.asp
' Server Page: ProcessSearch
'
' Description:
' Uses the Glossary API to search the glossary for words (or
' descriptions) that match a string.
'

Dim Glossary  '(Glossary)
Dim searchWord '(String)
Dim searchDescription '(String)
Dim nl '(string) a new line
Dim massagedWord '(string) The word searched for, modified for use as a hyperlink parameter
Dim ExactMatchFound '(Boolean) True if the search was a success and a whole word was found.

Sub RedirectTospErrorMsg( ErrDescription )
    Response.Redirect "ErrorMsg.asp?ErrDescription=" & Replace(ErrDescription, " ", "%20" )
End Sub




'=====================================================================
' Sub: Main
' Description:
'
Sub Main
    Set Glossary = Server.CreateObject("Glossary.IGlossary")
    Glossary.dsn = Application("dsn")
    nl = chr(13) & chr(10)

    searchWord = Trim(Request.Form.Item("Word"))
    searchDescription = trim(Request.Form.Item("Description"))
```

```
    massagedWord = replace( searchWord, " ", "%20" )

End Sub


'=====================================================================
' Sub: GetEntries
' Description:
'    Uses the Glossary server API to find all entries in the
'    glossary that match the given criteria. Each entry is written
'     out to an HTML table.
'
Sub GetEntries
    Dim entries ' as variant
    Dim id ' as long
    Dim word ' as string
    Dim description ' as string
    Dim bgColor ' as color

    Response.Write( "<h1>" & word & "</h1>")

    entries = Glossary.SearchEntries( cstr(searchWord), cstr(searchDescription) )
    bgColor = "white"

    ExactMatchFound = false
    if Not IsEmpty(entries) then
        ' now loop through the entries
        for i = 0 to ubound(entries,2)
            id = entries(0,i)
            word = entries(1,i)
            description = entries(2,i)
            WriteEntry id, word, description, bgColor
            if bgColor = "white" then
                bgColor = "lightgrey"
            else
                bgColor = "white"
            end if
            If lcase(word) = lcase(searchWord) then ExactMatchFound = true
        next
    end if

End Sub


'=====================================================================
' Sub: WriteEntry
' Description:
'    Writes a single table row to output.  Each row contains the
'    word, description, and an edit hyperlink (with id as
'     parameter) to the editing page.
'
' Parameters:
'    id -
'    word -
'    description -
Sub WriteEntry( id, word, description, bgColor)
    Dim link 'as string
```

```
    link = "          <td><b><a href="""EditEntry.asp?id=" & id & """">" & _
        ForHTML(word) & "</a></b></td>"

    Response.Write( "    <tr bgcolor=""" & bgColor & """>" & nl)
    Response.Write( link & nl)
    Response.Write( "        <td>" & ForHTML(description) & "</td>" & nl )
    Response.Write( "    </tr>" & nl)

End Sub

Main

%>

<html>
<head>
<title>SearchResults</title>
</head>

<!--
<insert appropriate copyright information here>
<insert appropriate version control information here>
File: ProcessSearch.asp
Client Page: SearchResults

Description:
    The HTML listing of all the words that matched the criteria
    specified in the submitted form.

    Each entry in the listing has a hyperlink next to it to allow
    the user to edit the entry.

-->

<body>
<h2>Project Glossary Search Results</h2>

<table width="80%">
    <tr>
        <td><i>Word</i></td>
        <td><i>Description</i></td>
    </tr>

<% GetEntries %>

</table>

<%    if Not ExactMatchFound and searchWord<>"" then %>
<p><a href="EditEntry.asp?Word=<%=massagedWord%>">Create New Entry for
<i><%=searchWord%></i></a></p>
<%    end if %>

<hr>
<p><a href="GlossaryHome.htm">Home</a></p>
</body>
</html>
<!--#INCLUDE FILE="string-util.asp"-->
```

EditEntry.asp

```
<% @Language="VBScript" %>
<%
' Copyright (C) 1999  jim conallen
' This program is free software; you can redistribute it and/or
' modify it under the terms of the GNU General Public License
' as published by the Free Software Foundation; either version 2
' of the License or (at your option) any later version.
' This program is distributed in the hope that it will be useful,
' but WITHOUT ANY WARRANTY; without even the implied warranty of
' MERCHANTABILITY or FITNESS FOR A PARTICULAR PURPOSE.  See the
' GNU General Public License for more details.
' You should have received a copy of the GNU General Public License
' along with this program; if not, write to the Free Software
' Foundation, Inc., 59 Temple Place - Suite 330, Boston, MA  02111-1307, USA.
'
' <insert appropriate version control information here>
'
' File: EditEntry.asp
' Server Page: spEditEntry
'
' Description:
' Builds an edit page for a specific entry in the glossary.
' This page depends on a valid id of the word to edit.
'

Dim id  '(long)
Dim word  '(String)
Dim description  '(String)
Dim Glossary '(IGlossary)

Sub RedirectTospErrorMsg( ErrDescription )
    Dim descr ' as string
    descr = replace(ErrDescription, " ", "%20")
    redirect "ErrorMsg.asp?ErrDescription=" & ErrDescription
End Sub


'=======================================================================
' Sub: Main
' Description:
'    Page's main entry point.
'    If the parameter for new is equal
'    to "no", then an existing entry is used to predefine the
'    fields; otherwise a blank client page is built.
'
Sub Main
    Set Glossary = Server.CreateObject("Glossary.IGlossary")
    Glossary.dsn = Application("dsn")

    word = request("Word")

    id = request("id")
    if id = "" then
    ' report an error
```

```
          else
              GetEntry(id)
          end if

End Sub

'=================================================================
' Sub: GetEntry
' Description:
'    Sets the page's attributes given the id of a glossary entry.
'    If an error is encountered, then control is redirected to
'    the error page.
'
' Parameters:
'    id -
Sub GetEntry( id)
    Dim entry ' as variant array

    entry = Glossary.GetEntry( clng(id) )
    if IsEmpty( entry ) then
        ' report an error
    else
        ' take the first one in the array
        word = entry(1,0)
        description = entry(2,0)
    end if

End Sub

Main

%>

<html>
<script language="JavaScript"><!--

//////////////////////////////////////////////////////////////////////
// Function: valid
// Description:
// Returns a true if the word and description fields are not
// empty.  If either is empty, the user is alerted to the fact
// that both fields are required and  a false is returned
// (which will prevent the form from being submitted).
//
function valid(){
    var word;
    var descr;

    word = document.forms[0].item('Word');
    descr = document.forms[0].item('Description');

    if ( (word="") || (descr="") ) {
        alert( 'You must enter a word and a description to add an entry for the glossary.' );
        return false;
    }
```

```
    return true;

};

// --></script>
<head>
<title>cpEditEntry</title>
</head>

<!--
<insert appropriate copyright information here>
<insert appropriate version control information here>
File: EditEntry.asp
Client Page: cpEditEntry

Description:
    Allows a user to edit a glossary entry.
-->

<body>
<h3>Edit Glossary Entry</h3>

<form name="EntryForm" method="POST" action="UpdateEntry.asp" onSubmit="valid()">
<input name="id" type="hidden" value="<%=id%>">
<input name="Word" type="hidden" value="<%=word%>">
<p>Word:  <b><%=word%></b></p>
<p>Description:</p>
<p><textarea rows=5 cols=50 name="Description"><%=description%></textarea></p>
<input name="Update" type="submit" value="Update">
<% if id<>"" then %>
<input name="Remove" type="submit" value="Remove">
<% end if %>

</form>

<hr>
<p><a href="GlossaryHome.htm">Home</a></p>
</body>
</html>
```

UpdateEntry.asp

```
<% @Language="VBScript" %>
<%
' Copyright (C) 1999  jim conallen
' This program is free software; you can redistribute it and/or
' modify it under the terms of the GNU General Public License
' as published by the Free Software Foundation; either version 2
' of the License or (at your option) any later version.
' This program is distributed in the hope that it will be useful,
' but WITHOUT ANY WARRANTY; without even the implied warranty of
' MERCHANTABILITY or FITNESS FOR A PARTICULAR PURPOSE.  See the
' GNU General Public License for more details.
' You should have received a copy of the GNU General Public License
' along with this program; if not, write to the Free Software
' Foundation, Inc., 59 Temple Place - Suite 330, Boston, MA  02111-1307, USA.
'
```

```
' <insert appropriate version control information here>
'
' File: UpdateEntry.asp
' Server Page: UpdateEntry
'
' Description:
' Processes the submission of an edit entry form.  The word
' in the glossary is updated to the new meaning. If an error
' is encountered, then the output is redirected to an error
' display page; otherwise control is returned to the main
' home page (any use case ends).
'

Dim Glossary '(IGlossary)
Dim Word
Dim Description
Dim ID

Sub RedirectToGlossaryHome
    Response.Redirect CStr("GlossaryHome.htm")
End Sub

Sub RedirectTospErrorMsg( ErrDescription )
    Response.Redirect "ErrorMsg.asp?ErrDescription=" & Replace(ErrDescription, " ", "%20" )
End Sub


'===================================================================
' Sub: Main
' Description:
'   Main entry point for this page's processing.
Sub Main

    Set glossary = server.CreateObject("Glossary.IGlossary")
    Glossary.dsn = Application("dsn")

    GetFields

    If Request("Update") = "Update" then
        UpdateEntry
    else
        if Request("Remove") = "Remove" then
            RemoveEntry
        end if
    end if

    RedirectToGlossaryHome

End Sub


'===================================================================
' Sub: GetFields
' Description:
'     Get the values of the submitted form and check to make sure that
'     there is enough data to properly submit to the server.
'
```

```
Sub GetFields()
   Word = Request("Word")
   Description = Request("Description")
   ID = Request("ID")
   If Word = ""  or Description ="" then
      RedirectTospErrMsg( "Both a word and description are required to enter a glossary entry.")
   end if

End Sub


'===================================================================
' Sub: UpdateEntry
' Description:
'    Updates the glossary entry with the submitted data.  IF the id
'       is blank, then a new glossary entry is created.
'
Sub UpdateEntry
      ' determine if this is a new one or not
      if ID = "" then
         ' then we can just add the entry
         Glossary.NewEntry CStr(Word), CStr(Description)
      else
         Glossary.UpdateEntry Clng(id), CStr(Word), CStr(Description)
      end if
End Sub


'===================================================================
' Sub: RemoveEntry
' Description:
'    Updates the glossary by removing the selected entry.
'
Sub RemoveEntry
      ' determine if this is a new one or not
      if ID = "" then
         ' then we should have never have gotten here
         ' todo : error msg
      else
         Glossary.RemoveEntry Clng(id)
      end if
End Sub

Main
%>
```

string-util.asp

```
<% @Language="VBScript" %>
<%
' Copyright (C) 1999  jim conallen
' This program is free software; you can redistribute it and/or
' modify it under the terms of the GNU General Public License
' as published by the Free Software Foundation; either version 2
' of the License or (at your option) any later version.
' This program is distributed in the hope that it will be useful,
' but WITHOUT ANY WARRANTY; without even the implied warranty of
' MERCHANTABILITY or FITNESS FOR A PARTICULAR PURPOSE.  See the
```

```
' GNU General Public License for more details.
' You should have received a copy of the GNU General Public License
' along with this program; if not, write to the Free Software
' Foundation, Inc., 59 Temple Place - Suite 330, Boston, MA  02111-1307, USA.
'
' <insert appropriate version control information here>
'
' File: string-util.asp
' Server Page: string-util
'
' Description:
' Misc. string manipulation routines.
'


'=====================================================================
' Sub: ForHTML
' Description:
'    Massages a string for HTML use.
Function ForHTML( aString ) 'as String
    Dim str 'as string

    str = replace( aString, "<", "&lt" )
    str = replace( str, ">", "&gt" )

    ForHTML = str

End Function
%>
```

ErrorMsg.asp

```
<% @Language="VBScript" %>
<%
' Copyright (C) 1999  jim conallen
' This program is free software; you can redistribute it and/or
' modify it under the terms of the GNU General Public License
' as published by the Free Software Foundation; either version 2
' of the License or (at your option) any later version.
' This program is distributed in the hope that it will be useful,
' but WITHOUT ANY WARRANTY; without even the implied warranty of
' MERCHANTABILITY or FITNESS FOR A PARTICULAR PURPOSE.  See the
' GNU General Public License for more details.
' You should have received a copy of the GNU General Public License
' along with this program; if not, write to the Free Software
' Foundation, Inc., 59 Temple Place - Suite 330, Boston, MA  02111-1307, USA.
'
' <insert appropriate version control information here>
'
' File: ErrorMsg.asp
' Server Page: spErrorMsg
'
' Description:
' Builds an error message display page. This is only valid
'  for server side generated messages.
'
```

```
'=====================================================================
' Sub: Main
' Description:
'    Main entry point for this page.
Sub Main
   'TODO: insert your code here

End Sub

%>

<html>
<head>
<title>Project Glossary Error Message</title>
</head>

<!--
<insert appropriate copyright information here>
<insert appropriate version control information here>
File: ErrorMsg.asp
Client Page: cpErrorMsg

Description:
    Displays an error message encountered during some stage of
      server side processing.

-->

<body>

<h1>Glossary Error</h1>

<h3><%=Request("ErrDescription")%></h3>

<hr>
<p><a href="GlossaryHome.htm">Home</a></p>

</body>
</html>
```

global.asa

```
<SCRIPT LANGUAGE=VBScript RUNAT=Server>

'You can add special event handlers in this file that will get run
'automatically when special Active Server Pages events occur. To create
'these handlers, just create a subroutine with a name from the list
'below that corresponds to the event you want to use. For example,
'to create an event handler for Session_OnStart, you would put the
'following code into this file (without the comments):

'Sub Session_OnStart
'**Put your code here **
'End Sub
```

```
'EventName         Description
'Session_OnStart   Runs the first time a user runs any page in your application
'Session_OnEnd     Runs when a user's session times out or quits your
                   'application
'Application_OnStart Runs once when the first page of your application is run
                    'for the first time by any user
'Application_OnEnd   Runs once when the web server shuts down

Sub Application_OnStart
    Application("dsn") = "Glossary"
End Sub

</SCRIPT>
```

Appendix D
Roses Alive! Project Plan Outline

Roses Alive! is a hypothetical live cut rose wholesale and retail company. It has been decided that Roses Alive! needs to create an Internet presence to both maintain and create new market share. The project begins with an idea that is worked into a vision statement. From there, a project plan is created and executed. The ultimate outcome is a working e-commerce site for Roses Alive!

The outline presented here is just that, an outline. It is meant to convey an idea of a practical e-commerce project schedule. The goals of this particular project are minimal and will serve as a pilot for future Web applications at the company.

Iteration 1: Getting Started

Time: 2 weeks

Project management	• A vision statement and business case are commissioned.
	• The project plan is created.
	• The second iteration's plan is started.
	• The glossary is started.
	• Staffing decisions are made.
Architecture	• Architectural options are reviewed.
	• Prototypes are constructed.
Requirements	• A high-level use case package diagram is made.
	• Requirements documents are started, and very high-level, nonfunctional requirements are gathered.

Analysis	• Procedures are defined.
	• Tools are evaluated.
Design	• Procedures are defined.
	• Tools are evaluated.
Implementation	• Development environments and tools are evaluated.
	• Assistance with prototypes is given.
Test	• Testing procedures are defined.
	• Testing tools are evaluated and, if possible, they are run against existing prototypes.
Deployment	• Web-based deployment options are considered.
	• Work is begun on the logistics of hosting a Web server.
Configuration and change management	• Standards documents are gathered or, if needed, defined.
	• Change management process and procedures are communicated to the team, and necessary infrastructure is put in place.

Iteration 2: Elaboration of the Vision

Time: 2 weeks

Project management	• Vision statement and business case are presented and accepted.
	• The project plan and iteration plans are updated.
Architecture	• Architectural prototypes are examined, and others started, if necessary.
	• Software architecture document is started.
	• Persistence and transaction strategies are evaluated. Prototypes are made.
	• The decision is made to go with Microsoft's Active Server Pages enabling technology.
Requirements	• Requirements team divides up and tackles specific use case packages.
	• The Shopping Cart package, identified as having high risk, is tackled first. The team members working on this package include a domain expert, a client programmer, and a user interface expert.
	• Project manager, architect, and key domain experts (management, marketing, sales) begin specifying key nonfunctional requirements for the system. It is decided the minimal browser configuration is going to be Netscape 3, IE 3, and Opera 3.5.
	• Security issues are examined.

Analysis	• Analysis model is started.
	• The package hierarchy starts with initial use case packages.
	• Very high-level objects are defined.
	• External system interfaces are examined (these include billing, inventory, and the merchant account system).
Design	• Development libraries are collected and evaluated (these include security, database access, and special printing libraries).
Implementation	• Look and feel is defined by graphic artist. HTML mockups are constructed; storyboards are used, if available.
Test	• Test plans are updated.
	• Tests are made against prototypes.
Deployment	• Web and application server evaluations are made.
	• RAID and backup devices are evaluated.
Configuration and change management	• Internal intranet is set up to facilitate project communications.
	• Access to all system artifacts is made via the Web. The version control system is incorporated into the Web with third-party add-on to IIS.

Iteration 3: Realizing Use Cases

Time: 2 weeks

Project management	• The project plan and iteration plans are updated.
Architecture	• Software architecture document is completed.
	• Persistence and transaction strategies are outlined. MTS and SQL Server are used for persistence. MTS-style component design is communicated to design and implementation teams.
Requirements	• Shopping Cart use cases are completed.
	• Catalog use cases are the next critical area to focus on.
	• SSL 3–compliant systems are made a requirement.
	• Billing and inventory system requirements are defined.
Analysis	• Analysis model is elaborated.
	• Shopping Cart use case scenarios are completed.
	• Scenarios are tied to analysis objects.
Design	• Persistence and interface classes are defined.
	• Utility classes and components are started.

Implementation

Test
- Test scripts are created for Shopping Cart use cases.
- Web server stress and performance testing are performed. These are made part of system regression tests.

Deployment
- Contract established with major Internet vendor to offer backup services.
- Merchant account system interface is identified, and procedures for doing e-commerce are defined.

Configuration and change management

Iteration 4: First Real Executables

Time: 2 weeks

Project management
- The project plan and iteration plans are updated.

Architecture
- The decision was made to use the same architecture for back-office functions as with the storefront.

Requirements
- Back-office use cases for order processing and inventory management are defined.
- User and training manuals started for back-office functions.

Analysis
- Analysis model is elaborated with additional completed use cases.

Design
- Catalog components are designed.

Implementation
- First version of Shopping Cart components are coded. Full functionality is not available, however, since there are some dependencies on other systems.
- Coding continues with Catalog components.

Test
- Shopping Cart scripts are completed, and testing begins.

Deployment
- Deployment plans are started.

Configuration and change management

Iteration 5: The System Comes to Life

Time: 2 weeks

Project management
- The project plan and iteration plans are updated.

Architecture

Requirements	• Back-office use cases are completed.
Analysis	• Analysis model is elaborated with new use cases.
Design	• Back-office components are designed.
Implementation	• Catalog components are completed.
Test	• Catalog browsing scripts are completed and tested.
Deployment	• Deployment plans are elaborated.
Configuration and change management	

Iteration 5: The System Continues to Evolve

Time: 2 weeks

Project management	• The project plan and iteration plans are updated.
Architecture	
Requirements	• Use cases are refined as needed.
Analysis	• Analysis model is elaborated and adjusted.
Design	• Design model is refined.
Implementation	• Back-office components are built.
Test	• Integration and system testing begins.
Deployment	• Deployment plans are tested.
Configuration and change management	

Iteration 5–6: Beta Releases and Updates

Time: 2 weeks

Project management	• The project plan and iteration plans are updated.
Architecture	
Requirements	• Use cases are refined as needed.
Analysis	• Analysis model is elaborated and adjusted.
Design	• Design model is refined.
Implementation	• Back-office components are built.
Test	• Integration and system testing begins.
Deployment	• Deployment plans are tested.
Configuration and change management	

Iteration 7: Initial System Release

Time: 2 weeks

Project management	• The project plan and iteration plans are updated.
Architecture	
Requirements	• Use cases are refined as needed.
Analysis	• Defects discovered in beta are corrected.
Design	• Defects discovered in beta are corrected.
Implementation	• Defects discovered in beta are corrected.
Test	• Integration and system testing begins.
Deployment	• System is deployed.
Configuration and change management	

Appendix E
Sample Rational Rose Scripts

ASPTool

```
' ----------------------------------------------------------------
' File:   ASPTool.ebs
' Date: 12-May-1999
' Author: jim conallen, jim@conallen.com
'
' Description:
'    Creates a new tool, and set of properties as the basis for modeling
'    ASP applications using the UML Extension for Web Applications.
'
'    This not the most cleanly written software I've ever done,
'    but somehow it gets the job done.  If anyone feels like enhancing
'    it, let me know so I can update my own copy.
'
' Copyright (C) 1999  jim conallen
' This program is free software; you can redistribute it and/or
' modify it under the terms of the GNU General Public License
' as published by the Free Software Foundation; either version 2
' of the License or (at your option) any later version.
' This program is distributed in the hope that it will be useful,
' but WITHOUT ANY WARRANTY; without even the implied warranty of
' MERCHANTABILITY or FITNESS FOR A PARTICULAR PURPOSE.  See the
' GNU General Public License for more details.
' You should have received a copy of the GNU General Public License
' along with this program; if not, write to the Free Software
' Foundation, Inc., 59 Temple Place - Suite 330, Boston, MA  02111-1307, USA.
' ----------------------------------------------------------------

Dim modelProps As DefaultModelProperties
Dim ToolName As String
```

```
Sub DefineProperty( ElemType As String, PropType As String, PropName As String, value As String)

    If Not modelProps.AddDefaultProperty(ElemType, ToolName, "default", _
        PropName, PropType, value) Then
      msgbox "Couldn't add default property: " & PropName
      Exit Sub
    End If

End Sub

Sub DeleteProperty( ElemType As String, PropType As String, PropName As String, dummy As String)

    ok = modelProps.DeleteDefaultProperty (ElemType, ToolName, "default", PropName)

End Sub


Sub CreatePropertySet( ElemType As String )

    If Not ModelProps.createDefaultPropertySet( ElemType, ToolName, "default" ) Then
      MsgBox "Couldn't create property set"
      Exit Sub
    End If
End Sub

Sub Main
    ToolName = "ASP"
    Set modelProps = RoseApp.CurrentModel.DefaultProperties

    CreatePropertySet "Subsystem"
    DefineProperty "Subsystem", "String", "Web Location", ""
    DefineProperty "Subsystem", "String", "Project Directory", ""

    'DeleteProperty "Subsystem", "String", "Location", ""
    'DeleteProperty "Subsystem", "String", "Directory", ""


    CreatePropertySet "Class"
    DefineProperty "Class", "String", "Title", ""
    DefineProperty "Class", "Enumeration", "LanguageSet", "VB Script,JScript"
    DefineProperty "Class", "LanguageSet", "Scripting Language", "VB Script"
    DefineProperty "Class", "String", "rows", ""
    DefineProperty "Class", "String", "cols", ""

    ' event handlers
    DefineProperty "Class", "String", "onClick", ""
    DefineProperty "Class", "String", "onDblClick", ""
    DefineProperty "Class", "String", "onKeyDown", ""
    DefineProperty "Class", "String", "onKeyPress", ""
    DefineProperty "Class", "String", "onKeyUp", ""
    DefineProperty "Class", "String", "onMouseDown", ""
    DefineProperty "Class", "String", "onMouseMove", ""
    DefineProperty "Class", "String", "onMouseOut", ""
    DefineProperty "Class", "String", "onMouseOver", ""
    DefineProperty "Class", "String", "onMouseUp", ""
    DefineProperty "Class", "String", "onReset", ""
```

```
DefineProperty "Class", "String", "onSubmit", ""
DefineProperty "Class", "String", "onLoad", ""
DefineProperty "Class", "String", "onUnload", ""

CreatePropertySet "Attribute"
DefineProperty "Attribute", "Enumeration", "ButtonTypeSet", "button,submit,reset"
DefineProperty "Attribute", "ButtonTypeSet", "Button type", "submit"
DefineProperty "Attribute", "String", "value", ""
DefineProperty "Attribute", "String", "accesskey", ""
DefineProperty "Attribute", "String", "alt", ""
DefineProperty "Attribute", "String", "id", ""
DefineProperty "Attribute", "String", "maxlength", ""
DefineProperty "Attribute", "Boolean", "readonly", "false"
DefineProperty "Attribute", "String", "size", ""
DefineProperty "Attribute", "String", "src", ""
DefineProperty "Attribute", "Enumeration", "InputTypeSet", _
    "text,button,checkbox,file,hidden,image,password,radio,reset,submit"
DefineProperty "Attribute", "InputTypeSet", "Input type", "text"
DefineProperty "Attribute", "String", "cols", ""
DefineProperty "Attribute", "String", "rows", ""
DefineProperty "Attribute", "String", "style", ""
DefineProperty "Attribute", "Boolean", "multiple", "false"
DefineProperty "Attribute", "Boolean", "prototype param", "false"

' event handlers
DefineProperty "Attribute", "String", "onBlur", ""
DefineProperty "Attribute", "String", "onChange", ""
DefineProperty "Attribute", "String", "onClick", ""
DefineProperty "Attribute", "String", "onDblClick", ""
DefineProperty "Attribute", "String", "onFocus", ""
DefineProperty "Attribute", "String", "onKeyDown", ""
DefineProperty "Attribute", "String", "onKeyPress", ""
DefineProperty "Attribute", "String", "onKeyUp", ""
DefineProperty "Attribute", "String", "onMouseDown", ""
DefineProperty "Attribute", "String", "onMouseMove", ""
DefineProperty "Attribute", "String", "onMouseOut", ""
DefineProperty "Attribute", "String", "onMouseOver", ""
DefineProperty "Attribute", "String", "onMouseUp", ""
DefineProperty "Attribute", "String", "onSelect", ""
DefineProperty "Attribute", "String", "onScroll", ""

CreatePropertySet "Association"
DefineProperty "Association", "Enumeration", "TypeSet", "anchor,link"
DefineProperty "Association", "TypeSet", "type", "anchor"
DefineProperty "Association", "String", "parameters", ""
DefineProperty "Association", "Boolean", "relative URL", "true"
DefineProperty "Association", "String", "target", ""
DefineProperty "Association", "Integer", "frame row", ""
DefineProperty "Association", "Integer", "frame col", ""
DefineProperty "Association", "Enumeration", "SubmitSet", "POST, GET"
DefineProperty "Association", "SubmitSet", "Submit Method", "POST"

DefineProperty "Association", "String", "object parameters", ""
DefineProperty "Association", "String", "object name", ""
DefineProperty "Association", "String", "object type", ""
DefineProperty "Association", "String", "classid", ""
```

```
    CreatePropertySet "Module-Spec"
    DefineProperty "Module-Spec", "String", "Location", ""
    DefineProperty "Module-Spec", "String", "Filename", ""

End Sub
```

MakeASPComponents

```
' ----------------------------------------------------------------
' File:   MakeASPComponents.ebs
' Date: 12-May-1999
' Author: jim conallen, jim@conallen.com
'
' Description:
'   This script creates <<ASP Page>> and <<HTML Page>> components
'   for web extension classes in the logical view.  This assumes that
'   <<client page>>, <<server page>>, <<form>>, <<JavaScript>>, and
'   <<clientscript object>> stereotypes are used.
'
'   This script creates a mirror package hierarchy in the component view.
'   The general algorithm is, for every selected class, check its stereotype
'   and immediate associations to determine if it is an ASP page, HTML page
'   or JavaScript include file.  Then it creates that component in the
'   component view.  The component is placed in a package that corresponds to
'   a package of the same name as in the logical view.
'
'   The appropriate classes in the logical view are then assigned to the Web
'   page component.
'
'
' Copyright (C) 1999  jim conallen
' This program is free software; you can redistribute it and/or
' modify it under the terms of the GNU General Public License
' as published by the Free Software Foundation; either version 2
' of the License or (at your option) any later version.
' This program is distributed in the hope that it will be useful,
' but WITHOUT ANY WARRANTY; without even the implied warranty of
' MERCHANTABILITY or FITNESS FOR A PARTICULAR PURPOSE.  See the
' GNU General Public License for more details.
' You should have received a copy of the GNU General Public License
' along with this program; if not, write to the Free Software
' Foundation, Inc., 59 Temple Place - Suite 330, Boston, MA  02111-1307, USA.
' ----------------------------------------------------------------

Declare Sub CreateComponent( aClass As Class )
Declare Function GetPackage( aClass As Class ) As SubSystem
Declare Function GetBuilder( aClass As Class ) As Class
Declare Function GetServerPageClass( aRole As Role ) As Class
Declare Sub ExpandServerPageIntoComponent( aSP As Class, aMod As Module )
Declare Sub ExpandClientPageIntoComponent( aCP As Class, aMod As Module )
Declare Sub AddModuleDependencies( aMod As Module )
Declare Function GetModule( aClass As Class ) As Module
Declare Sub SetDependency(fromMod As Module, toMod As Module, _
            stereotype As String)
```

```
Declare Function HasVisibilityRelationship( fromMod As Module, _
              toMod As Module, stereotype As String ) As Boolean
Declare Sub SetPackageDependency( fromSubSystem As Subsystem, _
              toSubSystem As Subsystem )



Dim theModel As Model

Sub Main
    Dim aClass As Class
    Dim i As Integer
    Dim classes As ClassCollection
    Dim modules As ModuleCollection


    Set theModel = RoseApp.CurrentModel

    Set classes = theModel.GetSelectedClasses
    For i = 1 To classes.count
       Set aClass = classes.getat(i)
       CreateComponent aClass
    Next i

End Sub

Function GetPackage( aClass As Class ) As SubSystem
    ' first get the hierarchyt of the class' pkg
    Dim aCat As Category
    Dim childCat As Category
    Dim aSub As Subsystem
    Dim childSub As Subsystem
    Dim catHierarchy As New CategoryCollection
    Dim i As Integer
    Dim nCats As  Integer

    Set aCat = aClass.ParentCategory
    If aCat.GetUniqueID = theModel.RootCategory.GetUniqueID Then
       Set GetPackage = theModel.RootSubSystem
    Else

       Do While Not aCat Is Nothing
          catHierarchy.add aCat
          Set aCat = aCat.ParentCategory
       Loop

       ' now let's walk down the list and make sure that a mirror hierarchy
       ' exists in the component view
       nCats = catHierarchy.count

       Set aSub = theModel.RootSubsystem

       For i = (nCats-1) To 1 Step -1
          ' see if a child sub exists for this one
          Set aCat = catHierarchy.getAt(i)
          Set childSub = aSub.Subsystems.GetFirst( aCat.Name )
```

```
            If childSub Is Nothing Then
                Set aSub = aSub.AddSubsystem( aCat.Name )
            Else
                Set aSub = childSub
            End If
        Next i

        ' aSub is now the one we want!
        Set GetPackage = aSub
    End If

End Function




Sub CreateComponent( aClass As Class )
    Dim pkg As Subsystem
    Dim aMod As Module
    Dim mods As ModuleCollection
    Dim builder As Class

    ' if class is stereotyped <<server page>> then
    '   if not already realized then
    '      create a component for it - use <<sp>> name as component name
    '          make it also realize every <<cp>> it builds, and all forms/JSObjects
    '          that it owns.
    '
    ' if class is <<client page>> and its builder is not realized, then create
    ' component for the builder <<sp>>

    Set mods = aClass.GetAssignedModules
    ' only create a component if it doesn't already have one.
    If mods.Count <= 0 Then

        Select Case lcase(aClass.Stereotype)

            Case "server page"
                Set pkg = GetPackage( aClass )
                Set aMod = pkg.Modules.GetFirst( aClass.Name )
                If aMod Is Nothing Then
                    Set aMod = pkg.addModule( aClass.Name )
                    aMod.Stereotype = "ASP Page"
                End If
                MakeClassAssignment aClass, aMod
                ExpandServerPageIntoComponent aClass, aMod

            Case "client page"
                ' find the builder then call this again
                Set builder = GetBuilder(aClass)
                If builder Is Nothing Then
                    ' create a CP component
                    Set pkg = GetPackage( aClass )
                    ' make sure there isn't one there already
                    Set aMod = pkg.Modules.GetFirst( aClass.Name )
                    If aMod Is Nothing Then
                        Set aMod = pkg.addModule( aClass.Name )
```

```
                        aMod.Stereotype = "HTML Page"
                    End If
                    ExpandClientPageIntoComponent aClass, aMod
                    MakeClassAssignment aClass, aMod
                Else
                    CreateComponent builder
                End If

            Case "clientscript object"
                ' this becomes a .js file
                Set pkg = GetPackage( aClass )
                Set aMod = pkg.Modules.GetFirst( aClass.Name )
                If aMod Is Nothing Then
                    Set aMod = pkg.addModule( aClass.Name )
                    aMod.Stereotype = "Script Libary"
                End If
                MakeClassAssignment aClass, aMod

            Case Else

        End Select

        ' now check for dependencies
        If Not aMod Is Nothing Then
            AddModuleDependencies aMod
        End If

    End If


End Sub


Sub ExpandServerPageIntoComponent( aSP As Class, aMod As Module )
    Dim Roles As RoleCollection
    Dim aRole As Role
    Dim i As Integer

    Set Roles = aSP.GetAssociateRoles
    For i = 1 To Roles.count
        Set aRole = Roles.GetAt(i)
        If lcase(aRole.Association.Stereotype) = "builds" Or
lcase(aRole.Association.Stereotype) = "build" Then
            MakeClassAssignment aRole.Class, aMod
            ExpandClientPageIntoComponent aRole.Class, aMod
        End If
    Next i

End Sub

Sub ExpandClientPageIntoComponent( aCP As Class, aMod As Module )
    Dim Roles As RoleCollection
    Dim aRole As Role
    Dim otherRole As Role
    Dim anAss As Association
    Dim classes As New ClassCollection
    Dim i As Integer
```

```
    Set Roles = aCP.GetAssociateRoles
    For i = 1 To Roles.count
        Set aRole = Roles.GetAt(i)
        If lcase(aRole.Association.Stereotype) = "object"  Then
            MakeClassAssignment aRole.Class, aMod
        Else
            ' check to see if it's part of an aggregation
            Set anAss = aRole.Association
            If anAss.Role1.GetUniqueID = aRole.GetUniqueID Then
                Set otherRole = anAss.Role2
            Else
                Set otherRole = anAss.Role1
            End If
            If otherRole.Aggregate Then
                MakeClassAssignment aRole.Class, aMod
            End If
        End If
    Next i

End Sub

' returns a client page's builder server page (if it exists)
Function GetBuilder( aClass As Class ) As Class
    ' walk through all the associations looking for one stereotyped
    ' builder.  if the class on the other end is a SP then that is it
    Dim assCollection As AssociationCollection
    Dim anAss As Association
    Dim spClass As Class
    Dim aRole As Role
    Dim i As Integer

    Set assCollection = aClass.GetAssociations
    For i = 1 To assCollection.Count
        Set anAss = assCollection.GetAt(i)
        If lcase(anAss.stereotype) = "builds" Or lcase(anAss.Stereotype) = "build" Then
            Exit For
        End If
    Next i

    If anAss Is Nothing Then
        Set spClass = Nothing
    Else
        ' make sure the class on the other end is a <<sp>>
        Set spClass = GetServerPageClass( anAss.Role1 )
        If spClass Is Nothing Then ' one more try
            Set spClass = GetServerPageClass( anAss.Role2 )
        End If

    End If

    Set GetBuilder = spClass

End Function

Function GetServerPageClass( aRole As Role ) As Class
    If lcase(aRole.Class.stereotype) = "server page" Then
        Set GetServerPageClass = aRole.Class
```

```
      Else
         Set GetServerPageClass = Nothing
      End If
End Function

Sub MakeClassAssignment( aClass As Class, aMod As Module )
   ' remove all previous assignments.
   Dim i As Integer
   Dim mods As ModuleCollection
   Dim otherMod As Module

   Set mods = aClass.GetAssignedModules
   For i = 1 To mods.count
      Set otherMod = mods.Getat(i)
      aClass.RemoveAssignedModule otherMod
   Next i

   aClass.addAssignedModule aMod

End Sub


Sub AddModuleDependencies( aMod As Module )
   Dim classes As ClassCollection
   Dim aClass As Class
   Dim relatedRoles As RoleCollection
   Dim aRole As Role
   Dim otherRole As Role
   Dim relatedClass As Class
   Dim relatedMod As Module
   Dim i As Integer
   Dim j As Integer
   Dim st As String

   st = lcase(aMod.Stereotype)
   If st="html page" Or st = "asp page" Or st = "script library" Then
      Set classes = aMod.GetAssignedClasses ( )
      'walk through each of these and find which modules it is dependent on
      For i = 1 To classes.count
         Set aClass = classes.getat(i)
         ' now what is this puppy related to
         Set relatedRoles  = aClass.GetAssociateRoles
         For j = 1 To relatedRoles.Count
            Set aRole = relatedRoles.getat(j)
            st = lcase(aRole.Association.Stereotype)
            If st = "link" Or st = "submit" Or st = "redirect" Then
               If aRole.Navigable Then
                  Set relatedMod = GetModule(aRole.Class)
                  SetDependency aMod, relatedMod, st
               Else
                  ' then they must be dependent on this guy
                  Set otherRole = aRole.Association.GetCorrespondingRole(aRole.Class)
                  Set relatedMod = GetModule( otherRole.Class )
                  SetDependency relatedMod, aMod, st
               End If
            End If
```

```
        Next j
      Next i

   End If

End Sub

Sub SetDependency(fromMod As Module, toMod As Module, stereotype As String)
   Dim relationship As ModuleVisibilityRelationship

   If Not fromMod Is Nothing And Not toMod Is Nothing Then
      ' first make sure we don't already have one of these
      If Not HasVisibilityRelationship( fromMod, toMod, stereotype) Then

         ' first check to make sure the packages have the appropriate dependencies
         SetPackageDependency fromMod.ParentSubsystem, toMod.ParentSubsystem

         Set relationship = Nothing
         On Error Resume Next ' just in case have self dependency
         Set relationship = fromMod.AddVisibilityRelationship(toMod)
         On Error GoTo 0
         If Not relationship Is Nothing Then relationship.name = "<<" & stereotype & ">>"
      End If
   End If

End Sub

Sub SetPackageDependency( fromSubSystem As Subsystem, toSubSystem As Subsystem )
   Dim subsystems As SubSystemCollection
   Dim aSub As Subsystem
   Dim relationship As Object
   Dim i As Integer
   Dim obj As Object
   Dim obj2 As Object

   If fromSubsystem.GetUniqueID = toSubsystem.GetUniqueID Then
      Exit Sub  '************* EXIT POINT
   End If

   Set subsystems = fromSubSystem.GetVisibleSubsystems
   For i = 1 To subsystems.count
      Set aSub = subsystems.getat(i)
      If aSub.GetUniqueID = toSubSystem.GetUniqueID Then
         ' we already have one
         Exit Sub '************* Exit POINT
      End If
   Next i

   ' gotta do all this object stuff since it seems that the
   ' api is not available in RoseScript just in the REI.... go figure
   Set obj = toSubsystem.GetObject
   Set obj2 = fromSubsystem.GetObject
   Set relationship = obj2.AddSubsystemVisibilityRelation( obj )

End Sub
```

```
Function HasVisibilityRelationship( fromMod As Module, toMod As Module, _
                              stereotype As String ) As Boolean
    ' does mod1 one depend on mod two in a << stereotype >> way?
    Dim visibilities As  ModuleVisibilityRelationshipCollection
    Dim relationship As ModuleVisibilityRelationship
    Dim aMod As Module
    Dim i As Integer
    Dim hasit As Boolean

    hasit = false

    Set visibilities = fromMod.GetAllDependencies
    For i = 1 To visibilities.count
        Set relationship = visibilities.getat(i)
        If relationship.name = "<<" & stereotype & ">>" Then
            ' either context module or supplier module
            If toMod.GetUniqueID = relationship.supplierModule.GetUniqueID Then
                ' we got one and can stop this loop
                hasit = true
                Exit For
            End If
        End If
    Next i

    HasVisibilityRelationship = hasit

End Function


Function GetModule( aClass As Class ) As Module
    Dim Mods As ModuleCollection
    Dim aMod As Module

    Set aMod = Nothing
    Set Mods = aClass.GetAssignedModules
    For i = 1 To Mods.count
        Set aMod = Mods.GetAt(i)
        If lcase(aMod.Stereotype) = "asp page" Or _
           lcase(aMod.Stereotype) = "html page" Or _
           lcase(aMod.Stereotype) = "script library" Then
            Exit For
        End If
    Next i
    Set GetModule = aMod

End Function
```

Index

X

e-Business
Roadmap for Success
Ravi Kalakota and Marcia Robinson
Addison-Wesley Information Technology Series

e-Business: Roadmap for Success illustrates how managers are rewiring the enterprise to confront the e-commerce onslaught—uprooting traditional business applications as we know them. The authors create an innovative application framework for structural migration from a legacy model to an e-business model. Drawing on their experience with and research of leading businesses, Kalakota and Robinson identify the fundamental design principles for building the e-business blueprint.

0-201-60480-9 • Paperback • 400 pages • ©1999

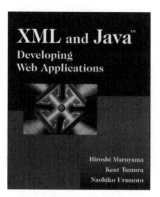

XML and Java™
Developing Web Applications
Hiroshi Maruyama, Kent Tamura, and Naohiko Uramoto

XML and Java™ is a tutorial that will teach Web developers, programmers, and system engineers how to create robust XML business applications for the Internet using the Java technology. The authors, a team of IBM XML experts, introduce the essentials of XML and Java development, from a review of basic concepts to thorough coverage of advanced techniques. Using a step-by-step approach, this book illustrates real-world implications of XML and Java technologies as they apply to Web applications. Readers should have a basic understanding of XML as well as experience in writing simple Java programs.

0-201-48543-55 • Paperback with CD-ROM • 400 pages • ©1999

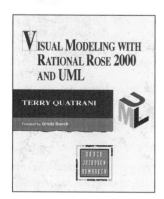

Visual Modeling with Rational Rose 2000 and UML
Terry Quatrani
Addison-Wesley Object Technology Series

Terry Quatrani, the Rose Evangelist from Rational Software Corporation, uses a simplified case study to teach readers how to the analyze and design an application using UML and how to implement the application using Rational Rose 2000. With the practical direction offered in this updated book, you will be able to specify, visualize, document, and create software solutions. Highlights include an examination of system behavior from a use case approach; a discussion of the concepts and notations used for finding objects and classes; an introduction to the notation needed to create and document a system's architecture; and a review of the iteration planning process.

0-201-69961-3 • Paperback • 288 pages • ©2000

Addison-Wesley Computer and Engineering Publishing Group

How to Interact with Us

1. Visit our Web site

http://www.awl.com/cseng

When you think you've read enough, there's always more content for you at Addison-Wesley's web site. Our web site contains a directory of complete product information including:

- Chapters
- Exclusive author interviews
- Links to authors' pages
- Tables of contents
- Source code

You can also discover what tradeshows and conferences Addison-Wesley will be attending, read what others are saying about our titles, and find out where and when you can meet our authors and have them sign your book.

2. Subscribe to Our Email Mailing Lists

Subscribe to our electronic mailing lists and be the first to know when new books are publishing. Here's how it works: Sign up for our electronic mailing at http://www.awl.com/cseng/mailinglists.html. Just select the subject areas that interest you and you will receive notification via email when we publish a book in that area.

3. Contact Us via Email

cepubprof@awl.com
Ask general questions about our books.
Sign up for our electronic mailing lists.
Submit corrections for our web site.

bexpress@awl.com
Request an Addison-Wesley catalog.
Get answers to questions regarding your order or our products.

innovations@awl.com
Request a current Innovations Newsletter.

webmaster@awl.com
Send comments about our web site.

jcs@awl.com
Submit a book proposal.
Send errata for an Addison-Wesley book.

cepubpublicity@awl.com
Request a review copy for a member of the media interested in reviewing new Addison-Wesley titles.

We encourage you to patronize the many fine retailers who stock Addison-Wesley titles. Visit our online directory to find stores near you or visit our online store: http://store.awl.com/ or call 800-824-7799.

Addison Wesley Longman
Computer and Engineering Publishing Group
One Jacob Way, Reading, Massachusetts 01867 USA
TEL 781-944-3700 • FAX 781-942-3076